ACTIVIST

A STORY OF THE MARJORY STONEMAN DOUGLAS SHOOTING

Written by **LAUREN ELIZABETH HOGG**

Art by **DONALD HUDSON**

Inked by **JOSE MARZAN JR**

Colors by **MONICA KUBINA**

Lettering by **JIMMY BETANCOURT** and **TYLER SMITH** for Comicraft

Zuiker Press

Los Angeles

ACTIVIST: A STORY OF THE MARJORY STONEMAN DOUGLAS SHOOTING

© 2019 Zuiker Press

Lauren Hogg Photographs © 2019 Lauren Elizabeth Hogg

Written by Anthony E. Zuiker
Art by Donald Hudson
Colors by Monica Kubina
Lettering by Jimmy Betancourt and Tyler Smith for Comicraft
Designed by Roberta Melzl
Edited by Rob Tokar

Founders: Michelle & Anthony E. Zuiker
Publisher: David Wilk

Published by Zuiker Press
16255 Ventura Blvd.
Suite #900
Encino, CA 91436
United States of America

Visit us online at www.zuikerpress.com

ISBN 978-1-947378-21-6 (hardcover)

PRINTED IN CANADA
November 2019
10 9 8 7 6 5 4 3 2 1

ZUIKER PRESS

... is a husband and wife publishing company that champions the voices of young authors. We are an **ISSUE-BASED** literary house. All of our authors have elected to tell their personal stories and be ambassadors of their cause. Their goal, as is ours, is that young people will learn from their pain and heroics and find **HOPE**, **CHANGE**, and **HAPPINESS** in their own lives.

DEDICATED TO ... every young person who needs to be reminded they are not alone.

HOPE lies within these pages.

TEACHER'S CORNER

SHANNON LIVELY

is a National Board Certified educator with a bachelor's degree in elementary education from the University of Nevada, Las Vegas, a master's degree from Southern Utah University, as well as advanced degrees in differentiated instruction and technology. In 2013, she was awarded the Barrick Gold One Classroom at a Time grant, and then chosen as Teacher of the Year. She is currently teaching fifth grade at John C. Vanderburg Elementary School in Henderson, Nevada.

WHY WE HONOR TEACHERS

We understand the amount of hard work, time and preparation it takes to be a teacher! At Zuiker Press, we have done the preparation for you. With each book we publish, we have created printable resources for you and your students. Our differentiated reading guides, vocabulary activities, writing prompts, extension activities, assessments, and answer keys are all available in one convenient location. Visit Zuikerpress.com, click on the For Educators tab, and access the **DOWNLOADABLE GUIDES** for teachers. These PDFs include everything you need to print and go! Each lesson is designed to cover Common Core standards for many subjects across the curriculum. We hope these resources help teachers utilize each story to the fullest extent!

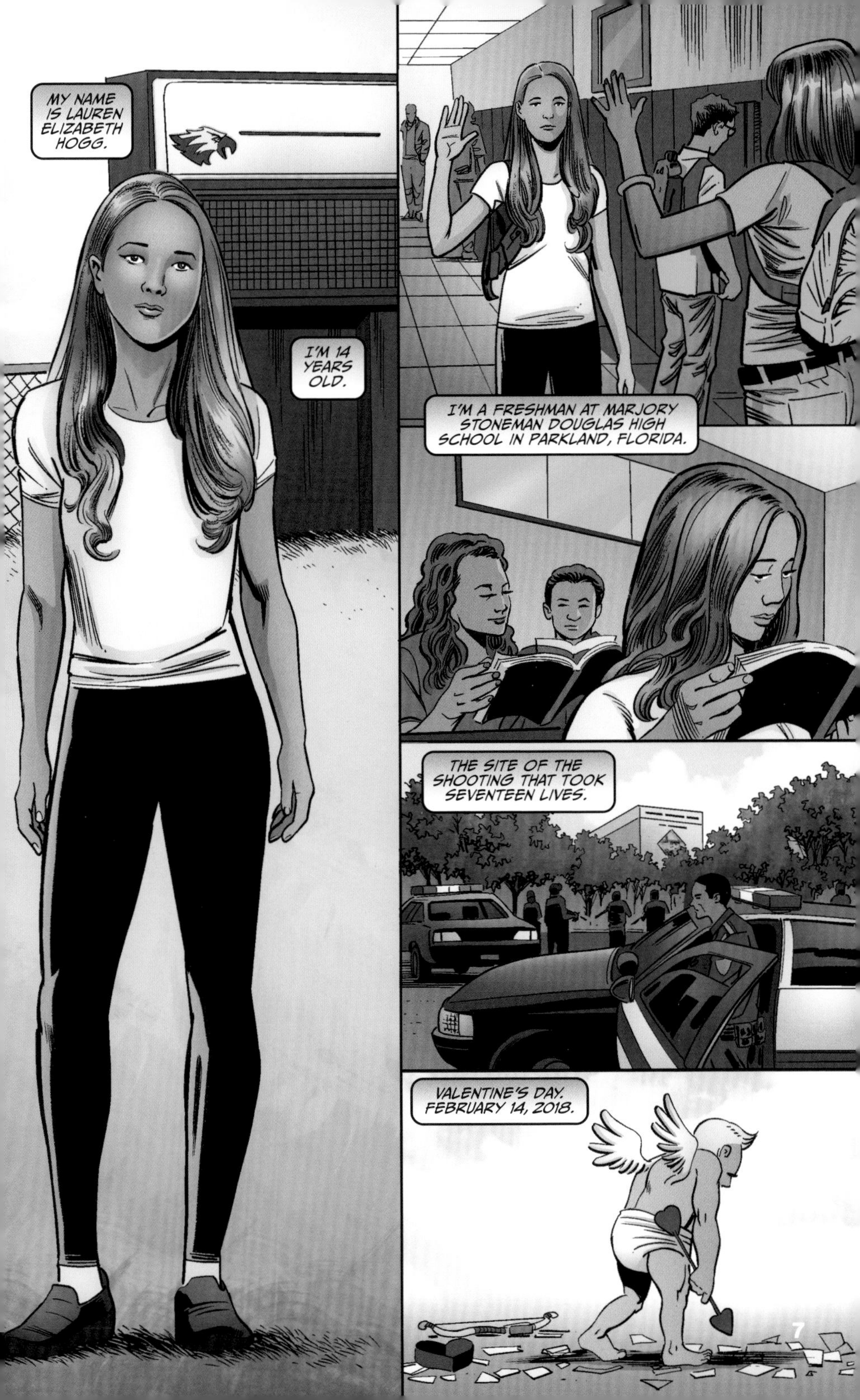
MY NAME IS LAUREN ELIZABETH HOGG.
I'M 14 YEARS OLD.
I'M A FRESHMAN AT MARJORY STONEMAN DOUGLAS HIGH SCHOOL IN PARKLAND, FLORIDA.
THE SITE OF THE SHOOTING THAT TOOK SEVENTEEN LIVES.
VALENTINE'S DAY. FEBRUARY 14, 2018.

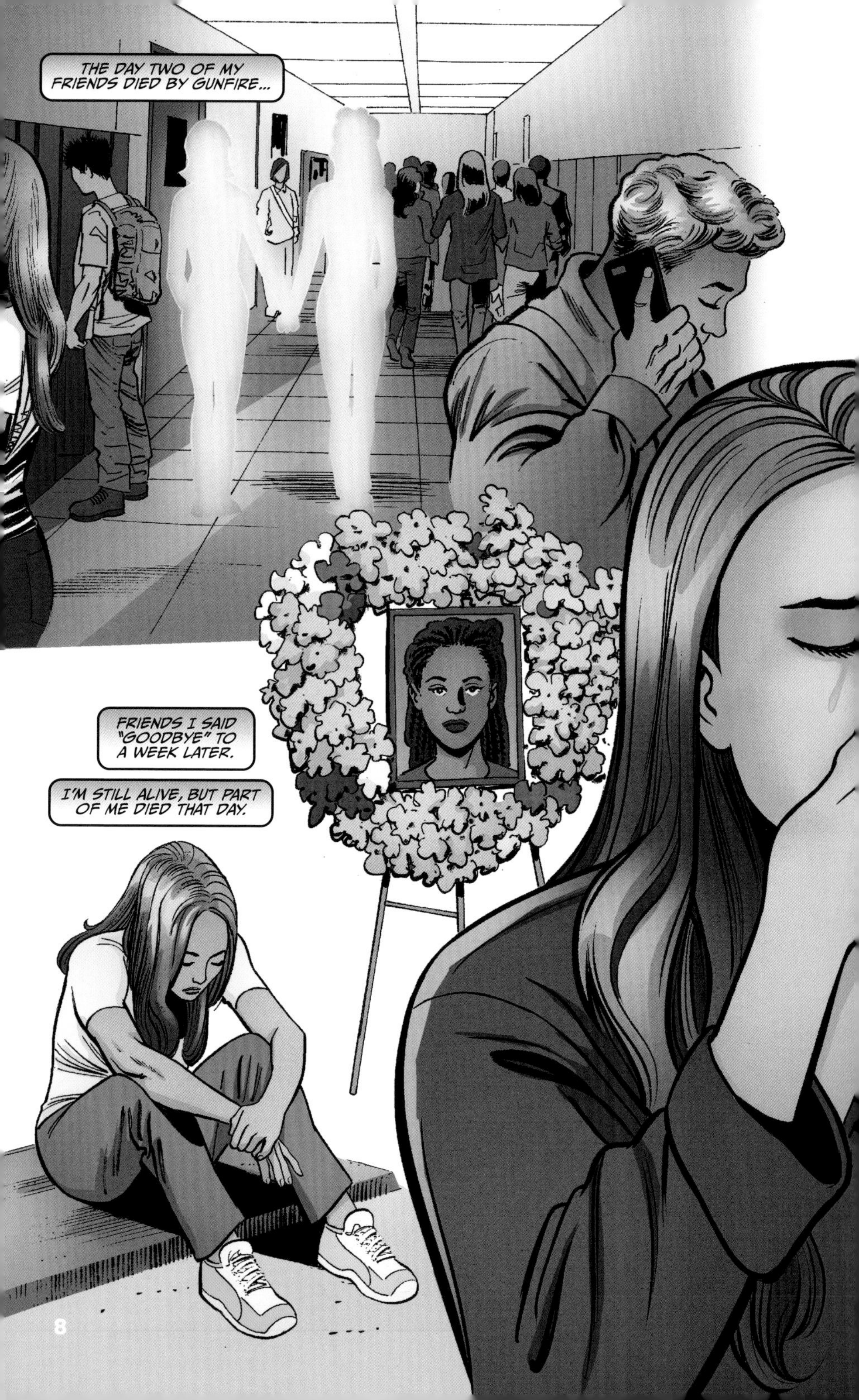
THE DAY TWO OF MY FRIENDS DIED BY GUNFIRE...
FRIENDS I SAID "GOODBYE" TO A WEEK LATER.
I'M STILL ALIVE, BUT PART OF ME DIED THAT DAY.

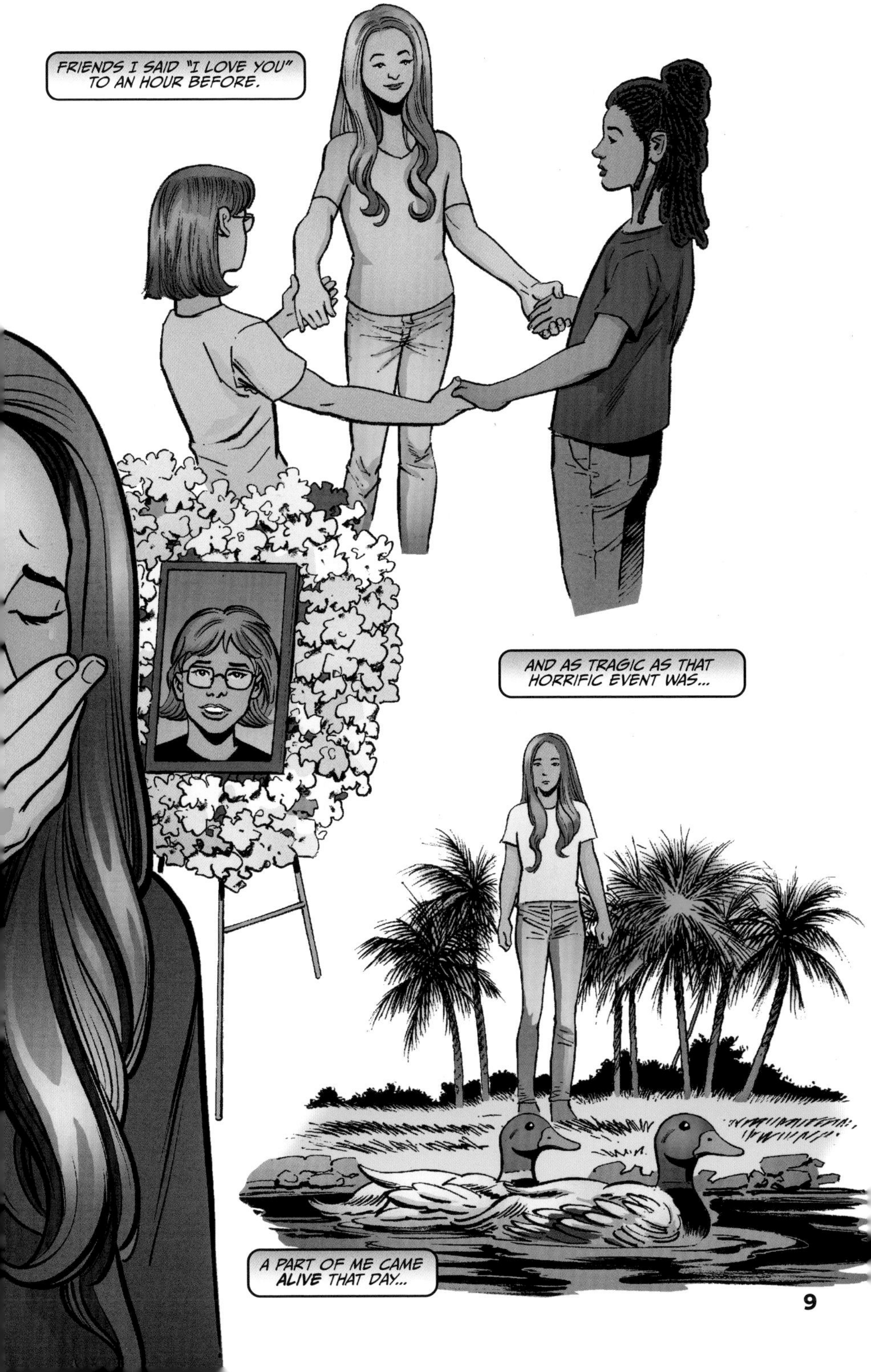
FRIENDS I SAID "I LOVE YOU" TO AN HOUR BEFORE.
AND AS TRAGIC AS THAT HORRIFIC EVENT WAS...
A PART OF ME CAME ALIVE THAT DAY...

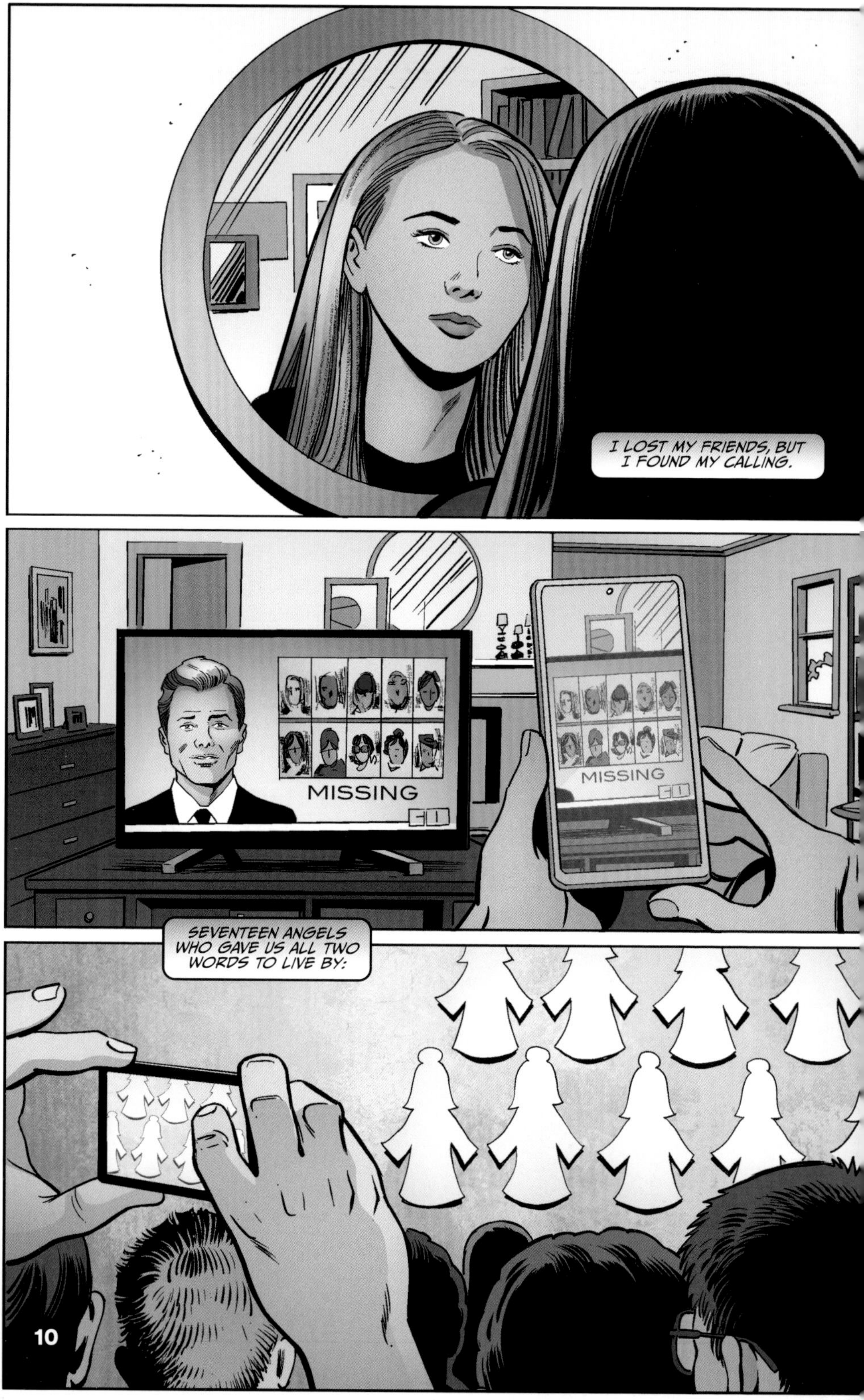
I LOST MY FRIENDS, BUT I FOUND MY CALLING.
MISSING
MISSING
SEVENTEEN ANGELS WHO GAVE US ALL TWO WORDS TO LIVE BY:

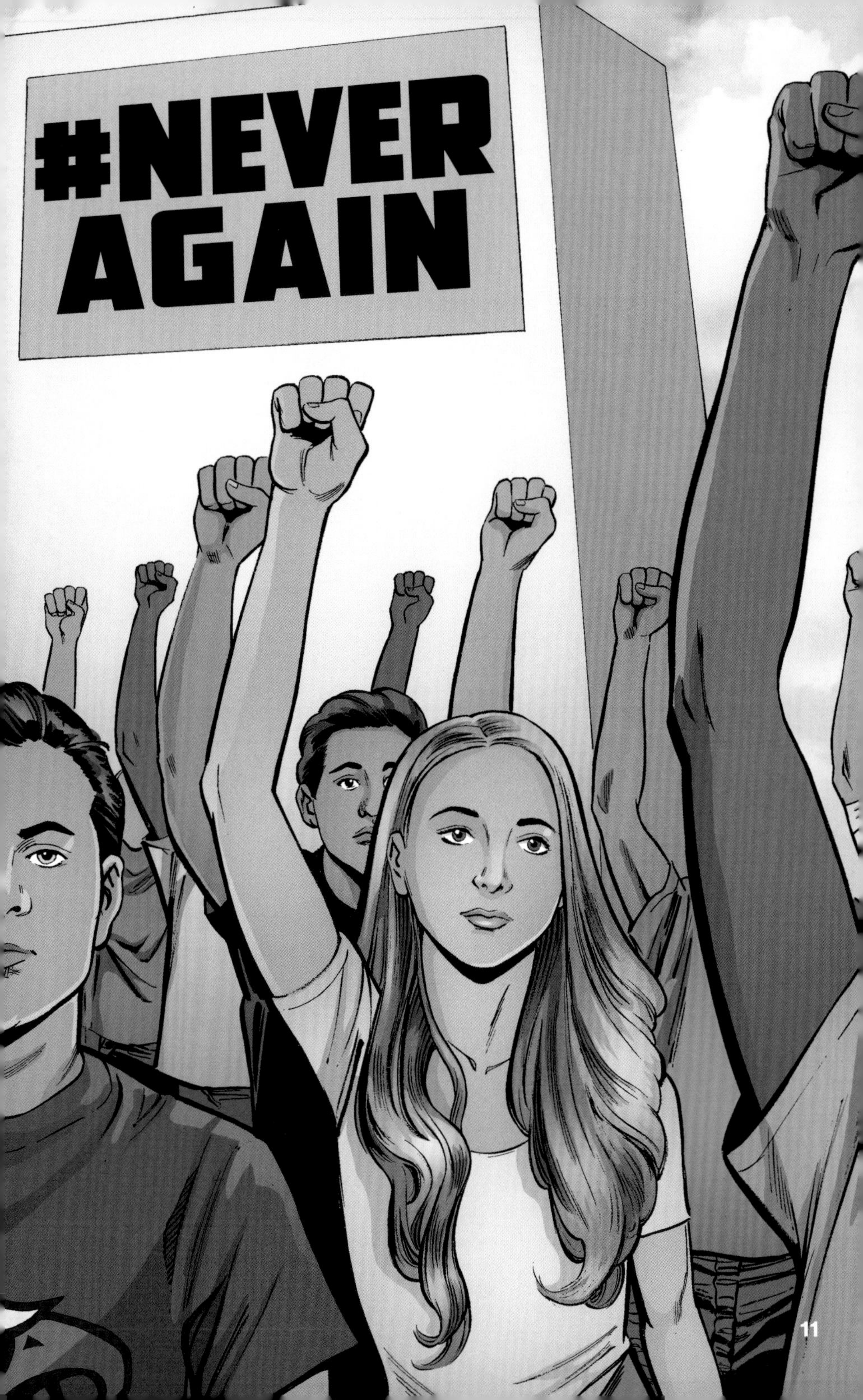
#NEVER
AGAIN

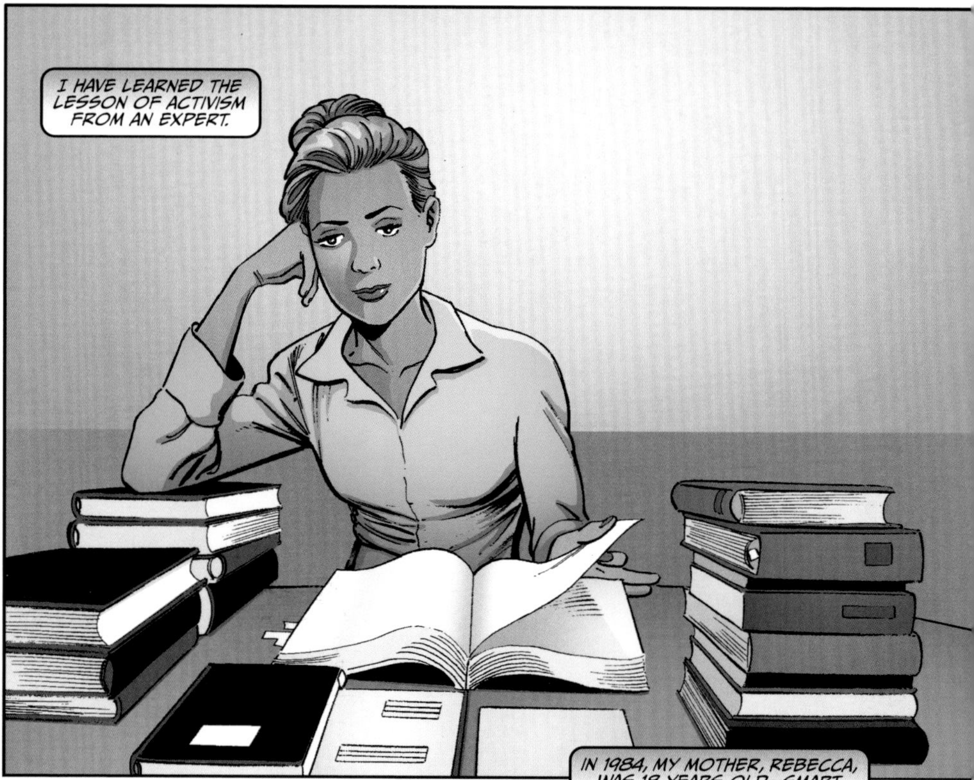
I HAVE LEARNED THE LESSON OF ACTIVISM FROM AN EXPERT.

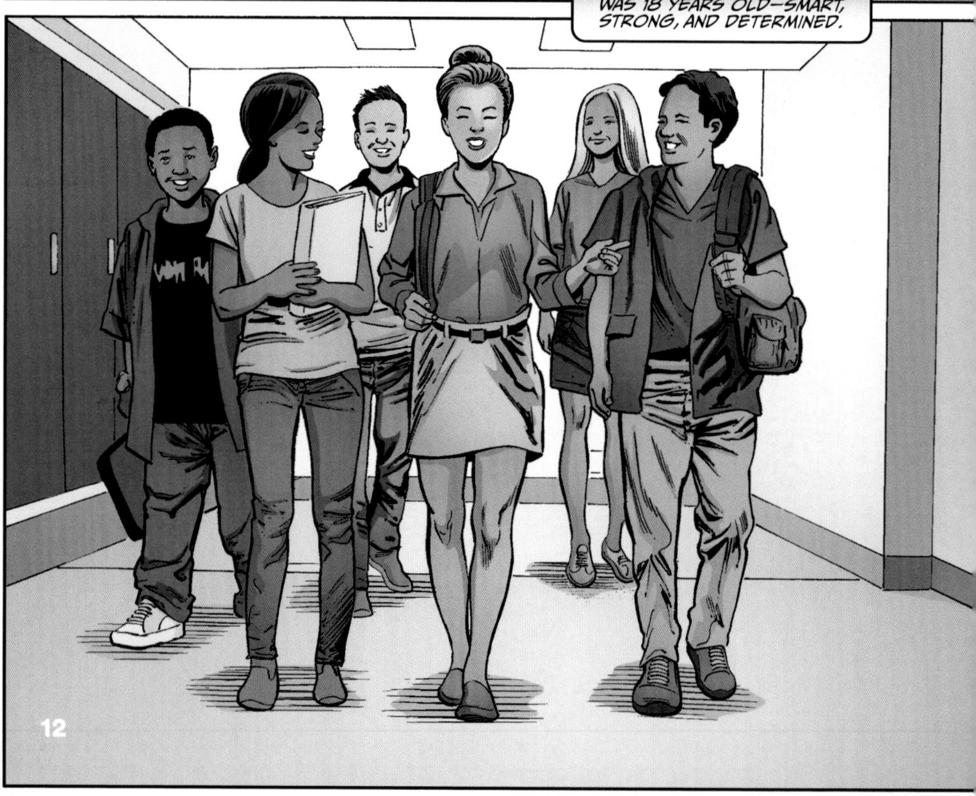
IN 1984, MY MOTHER, REBECCA, WAS 18 YEARS OLD—SMART, STRONG, AND DETERMINED.

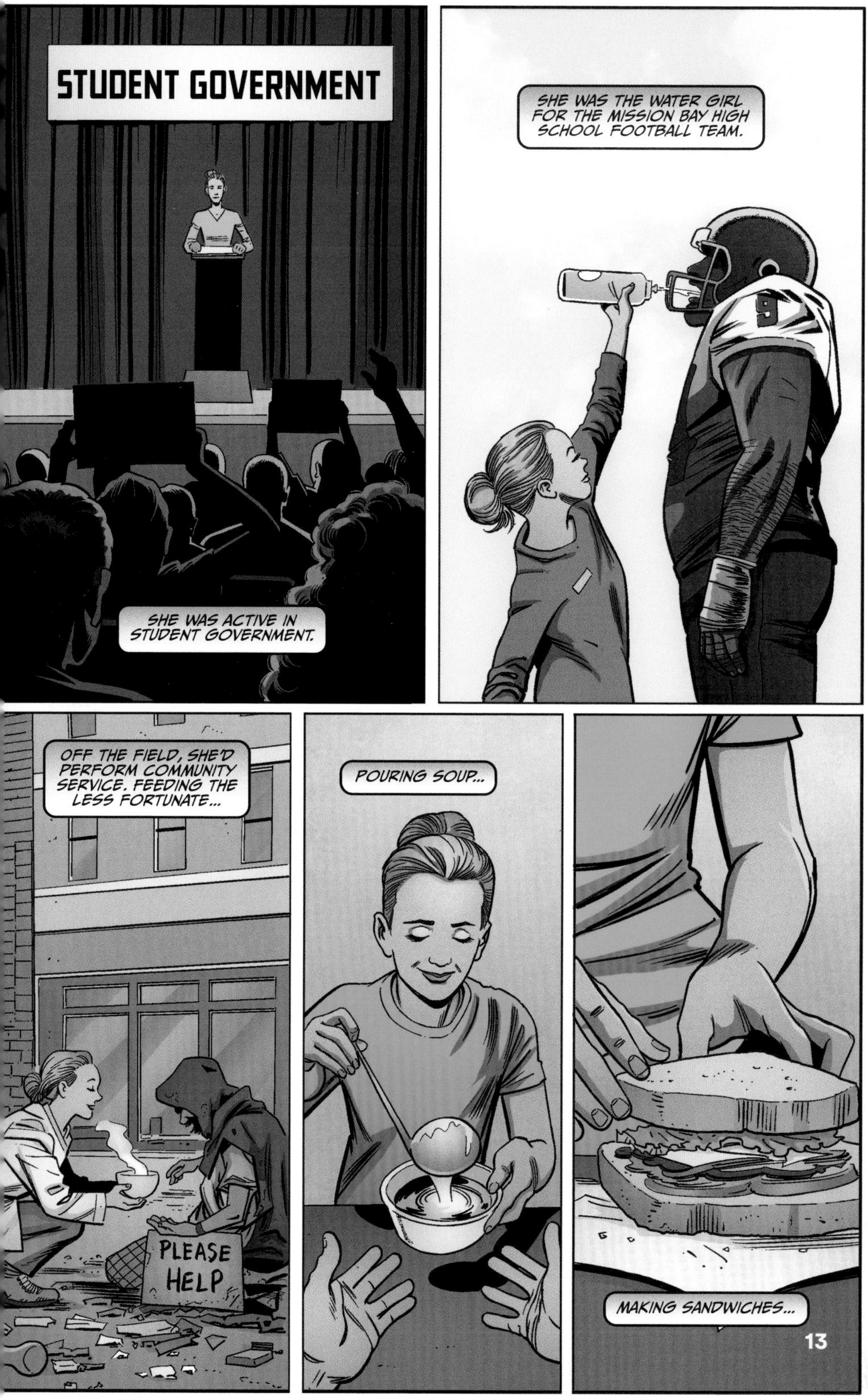
STUDENT GOVERNMENT
SHE WAS ACTIVE IN STUDENT GOVERNMENT.
SHE WAS THE WATER GIRL FOR THE MISSION BAY HIGH SCHOOL FOOTBALL TEAM.
OFF THE FIELD, SHE'D PERFORM COMMUNITY SERVICE. FEEDING THE LESS FORTUNATE...
PLEASE HELP
POURING SOUP...
MAKING SANDWICHES...

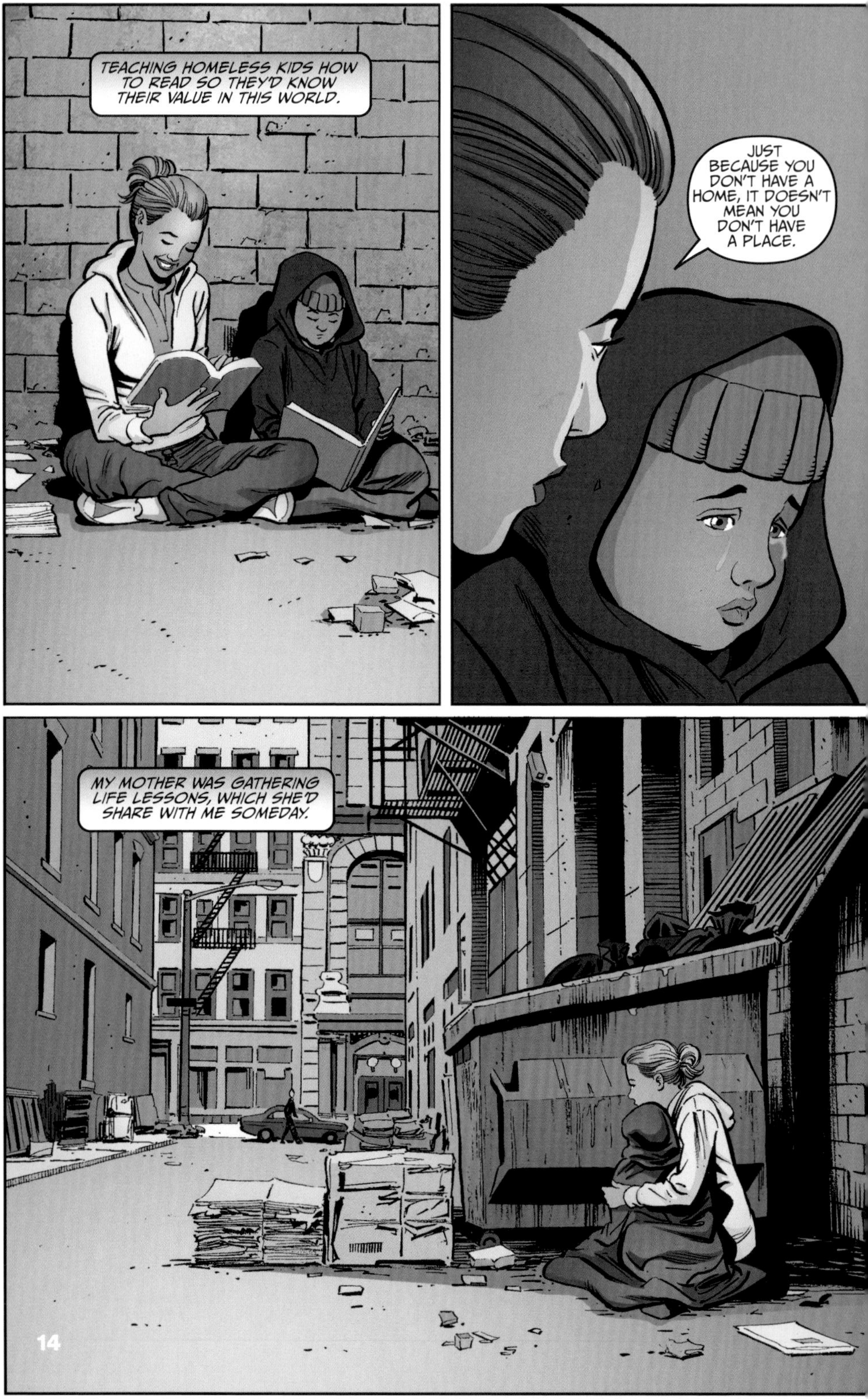
TEACHING HOMELESS KIDS HOW TO READ SO THEY'D KNOW THEIR VALUE IN THIS WORLD.
JUST BECAUSE YOU DON'T HAVE A HOME, IT DOESN'T MEAN YOU DON'T HAVE A PLACE.
MY MOTHER WAS GATHERING LIFE LESSONS, WHICH SHE'D SHARE WITH ME SOMEDAY.

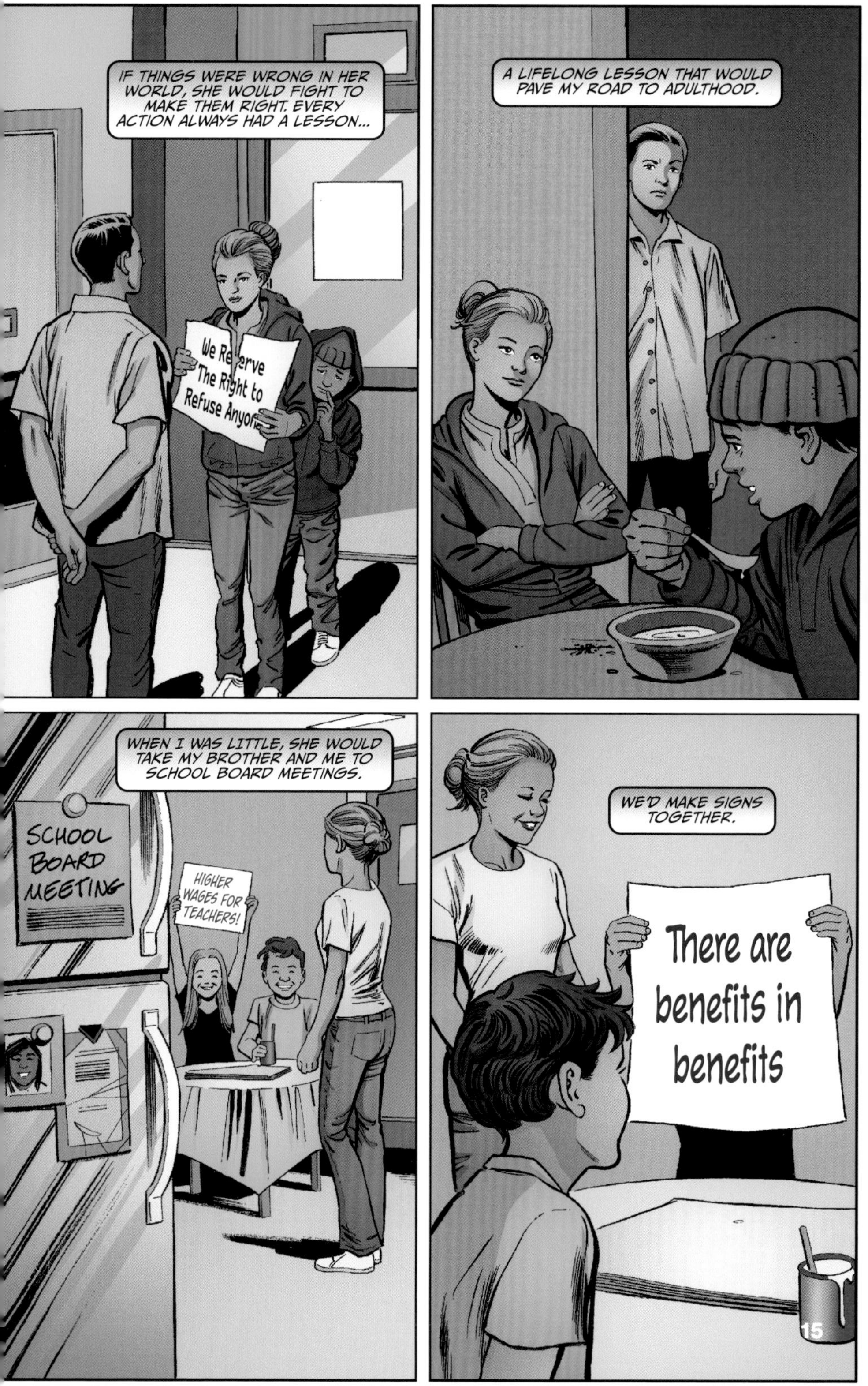
IF THINGS WERE WRONG IN HER WORLD, SHE WOULD FIGHT TO MAKE THEM RIGHT. EVERY ACTION ALWAYS HAD A LESSON...
A LIFELONG LESSON THAT WOULD PAVE MY ROAD TO ADULTHOOD.
WHEN I WAS LITTLE, SHE WOULD TAKE MY BROTHER AND ME TO SCHOOL BOARD MEETINGS.
SCHOOL BOARD MEETING
HIGHER WAGES FOR TEACHERS!
WE'D MAKE SIGNS TOGETHER.
There are benefits in benefits

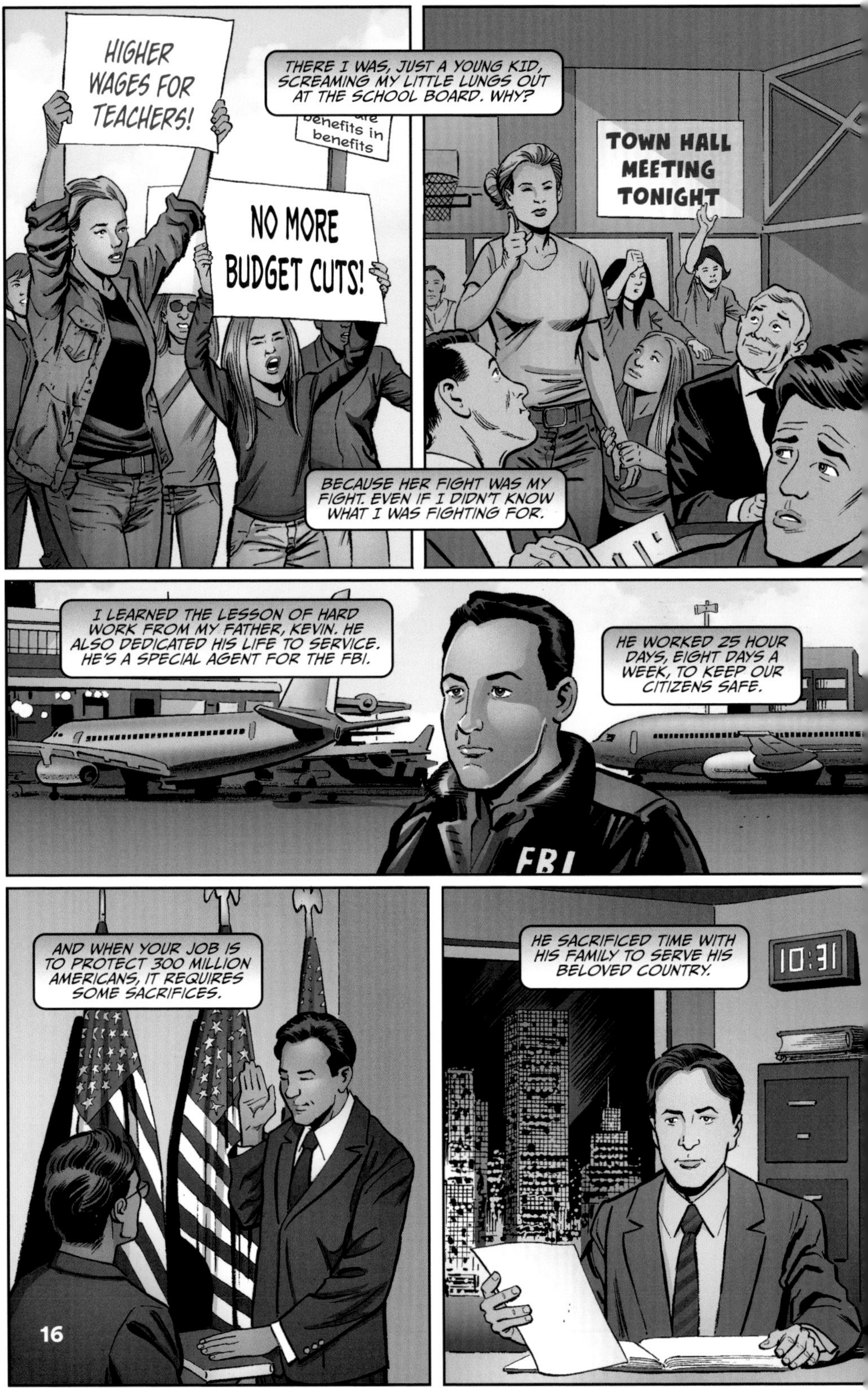
HIGHER WAGES FOR TEACHERS!
THERE I WAS, JUST A YOUNG KID, SCREAMING MY LITTLE LUNGS OUT AT THE SCHOOL BOARD. WHY?
benefits in benefits
NO MORE BUDGET CUTS!
TOWN HALL MEETING TONIGHT
BECAUSE HER FIGHT WAS MY FIGHT. EVEN IF I DIDN'T KNOW WHAT I WAS FIGHTING FOR.
I LEARNED THE LESSON OF HARD WORK FROM MY FATHER, KEVIN. HE ALSO DEDICATED HIS LIFE TO SERVICE. HE'S A SPECIAL AGENT FOR THE FBI.
HE WORKED 25 HOUR DAYS, EIGHT DAYS A WEEK, TO KEEP OUR CITIZENS SAFE.
FBI
AND WHEN YOUR JOB IS TO PROTECT 300 MILLION AMERICANS, IT REQUIRES SOME SACRIFICES.
HE SACRIFICED TIME WITH HIS FAMILY TO SERVE HIS BELOVED COUNTRY.
10:31

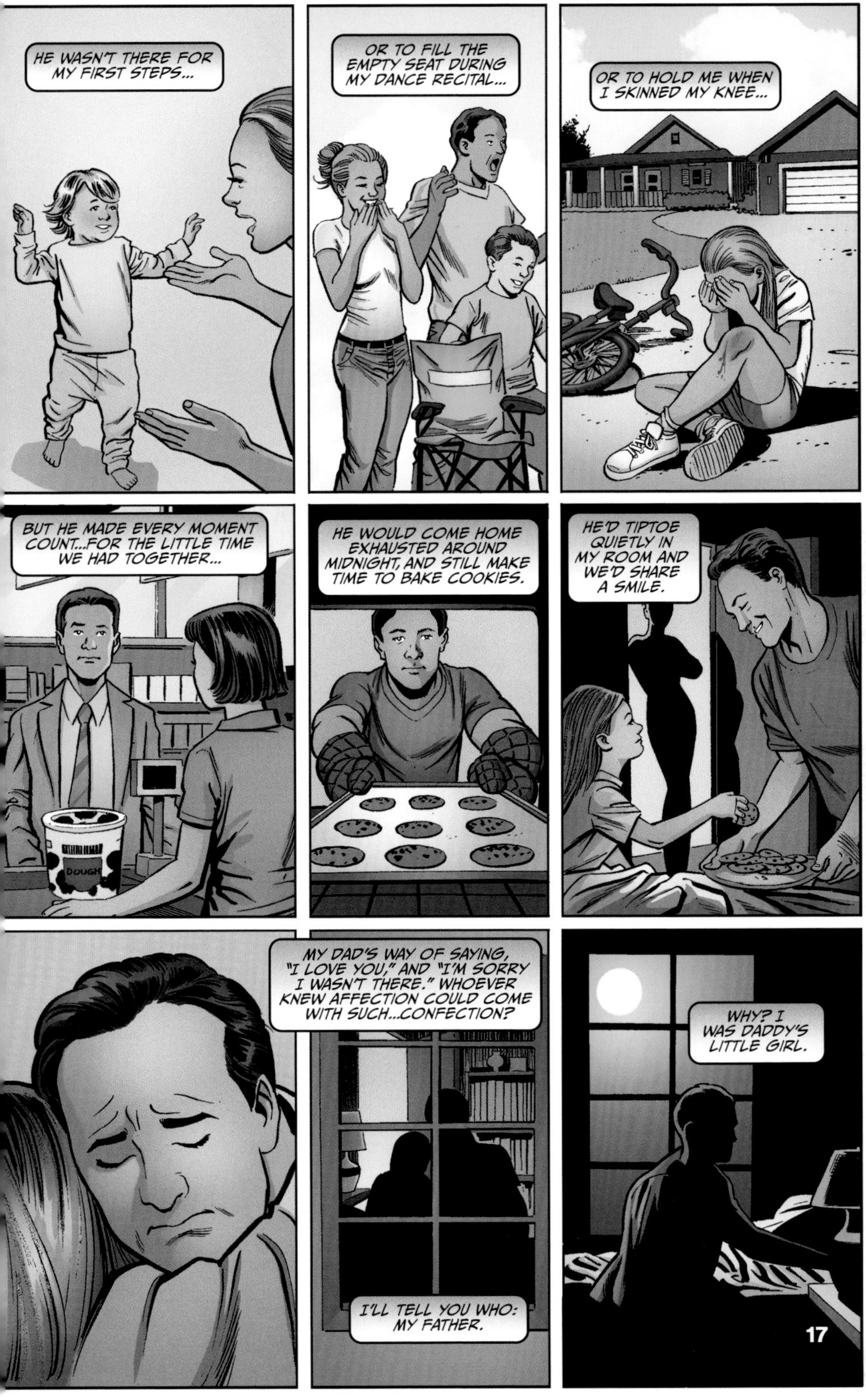
HE WASN'T THERE FOR MY FIRST STEPS...
OR TO FILL THE EMPTY SEAT DURING MY DANCE RECITAL...
OR TO HOLD ME WHEN I SKINNED MY KNEE...
BUT HE MADE EVERY MOMENT COUNT...FOR THE LITTLE TIME WE HAD TOGETHER...
DOUGH
HE WOULD COME HOME EXHAUSTED AROUND MIDNIGHT, AND STILL MAKE TIME TO BAKE COOKIES.
HE'D TIPTOE QUIETLY IN MY ROOM AND WE'D SHARE A SMILE.
MY DAD'S WAY OF SAYING, "I LOVE YOU," AND "I'M SORRY I WASN'T THERE." WHOEVER KNEW AFFECTION COULD COME WITH SUCH...CONFECTION?
I'LL TELL YOU WHO: MY FATHER.
WHY? I WAS DADDY'S LITTLE GIRL.

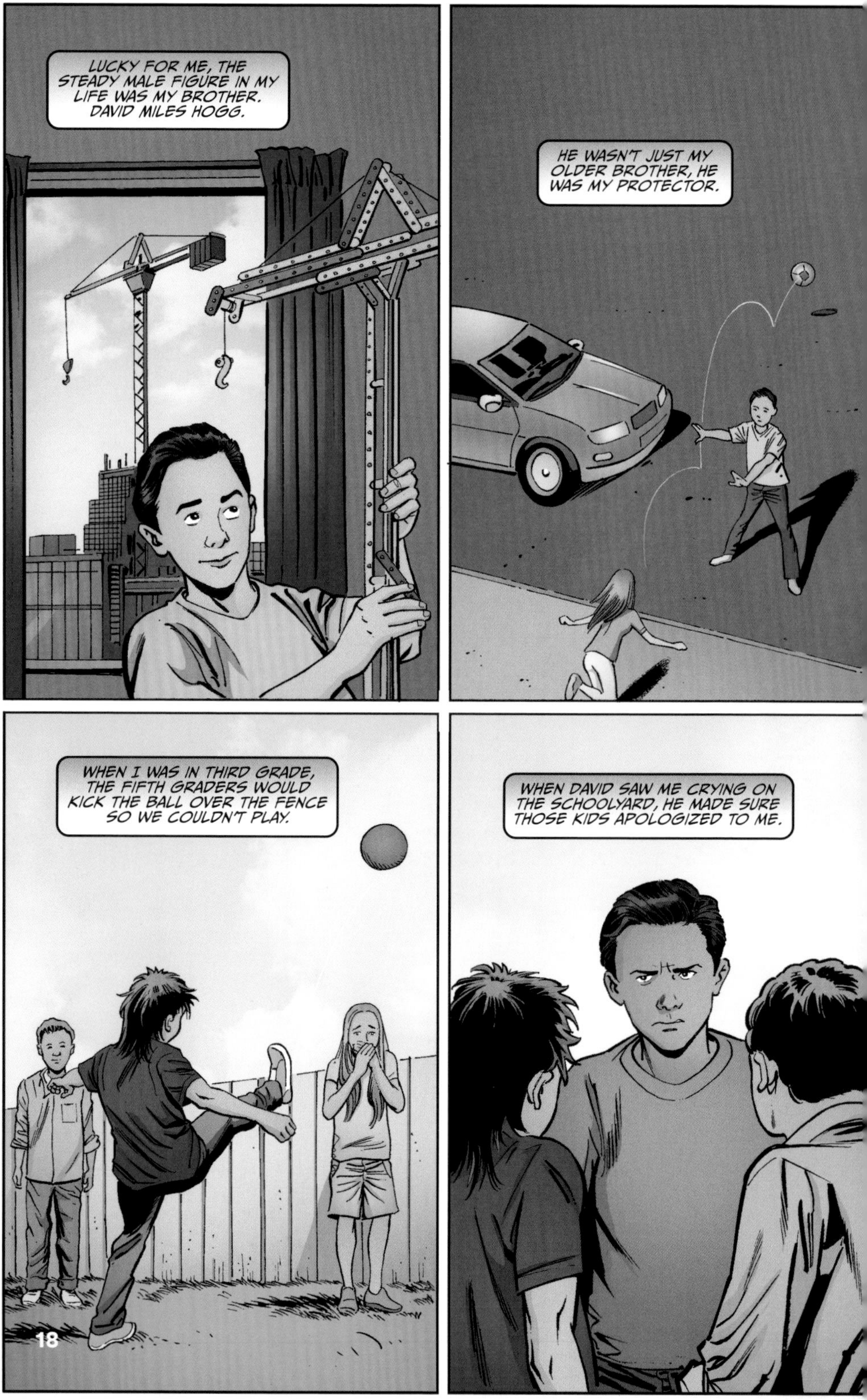
LUCKY FOR ME, THE STEADY MALE FIGURE IN MY LIFE WAS MY BROTHER. DAVID MILES HOGG.
HE WASN'T JUST MY OLDER BROTHER, HE WAS MY PROTECTOR.
WHEN I WAS IN THIRD GRADE, THE FIFTH GRADERS WOULD KICK THE BALL OVER THE FENCE SO WE COULDN'T PLAY.
WHEN DAVID SAW ME CRYING ON THE SCHOOLYARD, HE MADE SURE THOSE KIDS APOLOGIZED TO ME.

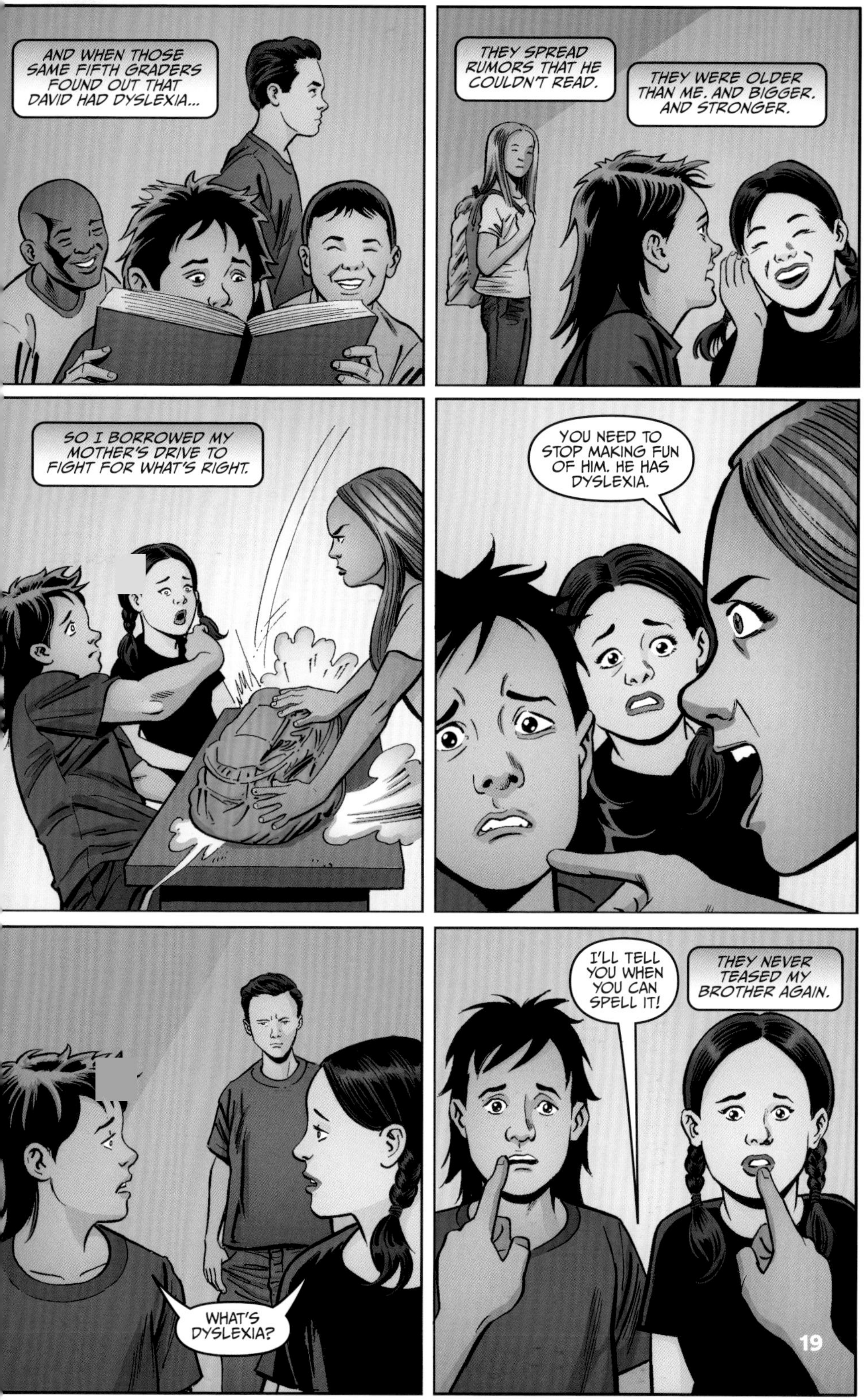
AND WHEN THOSE SAME FIFTH GRADERS FOUND OUT THAT DAVID HAD DYSLEXIA...
THEY SPREAD RUMORS THAT HE COULDN'T READ.
THEY WERE OLDER THAN ME. AND BIGGER. AND STRONGER.
SO I BORROWED MY MOTHER'S DRIVE TO FIGHT FOR WHAT'S RIGHT.
YOU NEED TO STOP MAKING FUN OF HIM. HE HAS DYSLEXIA.
WHAT'S DYSLEXIA?
I'LL TELL YOU WHEN YOU CAN SPELL IT!
THEY NEVER TEASED MY BROTHER AGAIN.

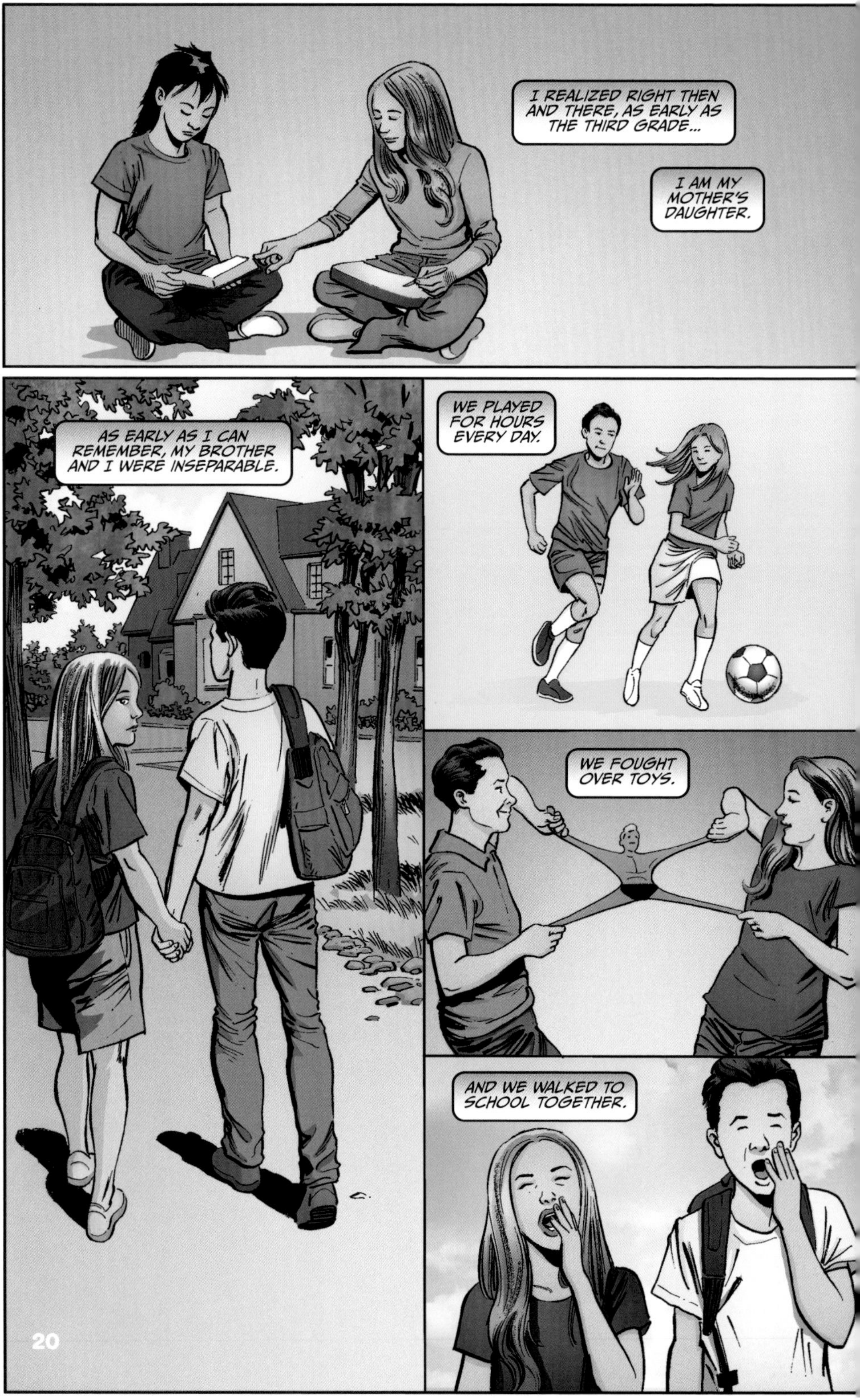
I REALIZED RIGHT THEN AND THERE, AS EARLY AS THE THIRD GRADE...
I AM MY MOTHER'S DAUGHTER.
AS EARLY AS I CAN REMEMBER, MY BROTHER AND I WERE INSEPARABLE.
WE PLAYED FOR HOURS EVERY DAY.
WE FOUGHT OVER TOYS.
AND WE WALKED TO SCHOOL TOGETHER.

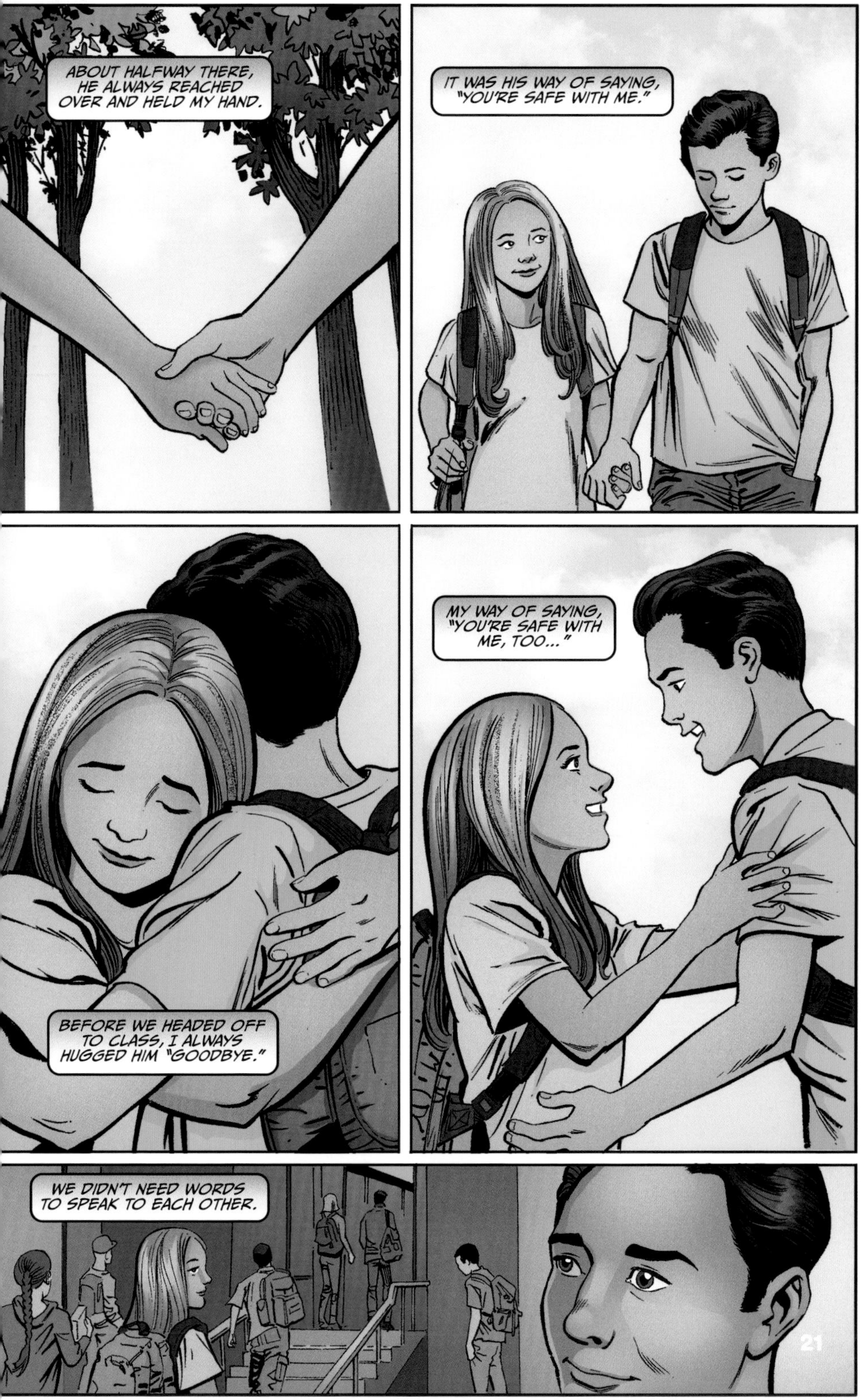
ABOUT HALFWAY THERE, HE ALWAYS REACHED OVER AND HELD MY HAND.
IT WAS HIS WAY OF SAYING, "YOU'RE SAFE WITH ME."
BEFORE WE HEADED OFF TO CLASS, I ALWAYS HUGGED HIM "GOODBYE."
MY WAY OF SAYING, "YOU'RE SAFE WITH ME, TOO..."
WE DIDN'T NEED WORDS TO SPEAK TO EACH OTHER.

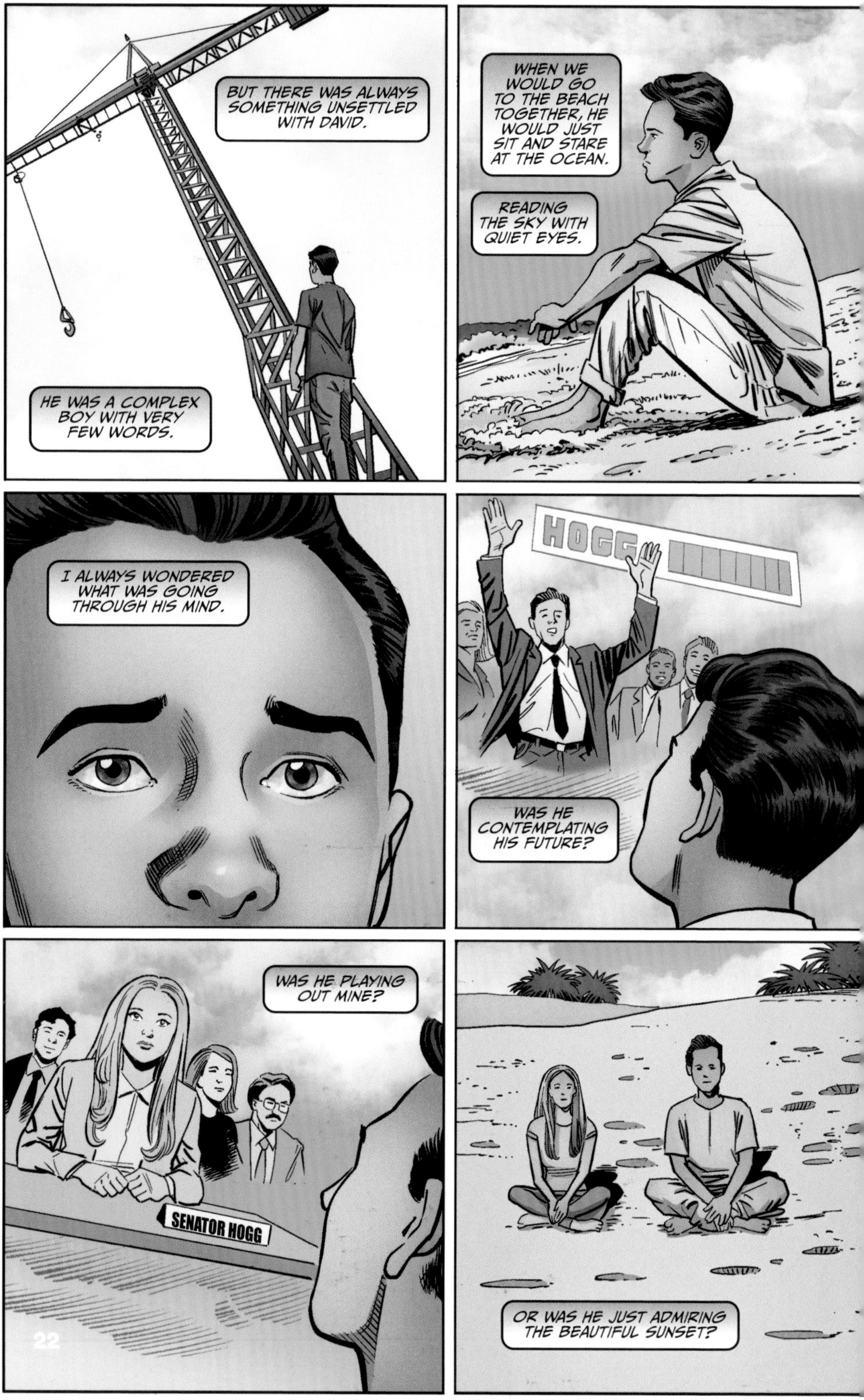
BUT THERE WAS ALWAYS SOMETHING UNSETTLED WITH DAVID.
HE WAS A COMPLEX BOY WITH VERY FEW WORDS.
WHEN WE WOULD GO TO THE BEACH TOGETHER, HE WOULD JUST SIT AND STARE AT THE OCEAN.
READING THE SKY WITH QUIET EYES.
I ALWAYS WONDERED WHAT WAS GOING THROUGH HIS MIND.
HOGG
WAS HE CONTEMPLATING HIS FUTURE?
WAS HE PLAYING OUT MINE?
SENATOR HOGG
OR WAS HE JUST ADMIRING THE BEAUTIFUL SUNSET?

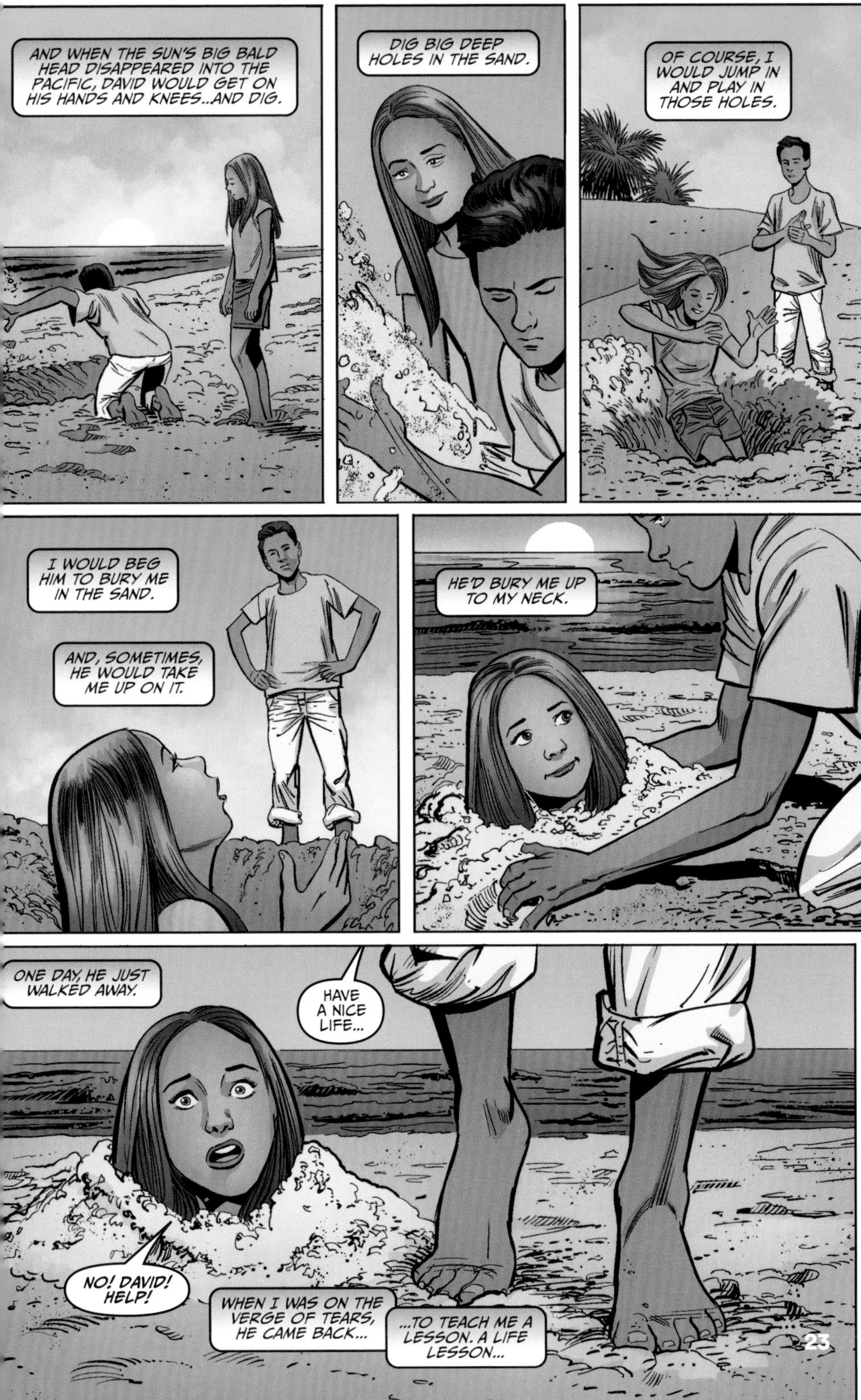

AND WHEN THE SUN'S BIG BALD HEAD DISAPPEARED INTO THE PACIFIC, DAVID WOULD GET ON HIS HANDS AND KNEES...AND DIG.
DIG BIG DEEP HOLES IN THE SAND.
OF COURSE, I WOULD JUMP IN AND PLAY IN THOSE HOLES.
I WOULD BEG HIM TO BURY ME IN THE SAND.
AND, SOMETIMES, HE WOULD TAKE ME UP ON IT.
HE'D BURY ME UP TO MY NECK.
ONE DAY, HE JUST WALKED AWAY.
HAVE A NICE LIFE...
NO! DAVID! HELP!
WHEN I WAS ON THE VERGE OF TEARS, HE CAME BACK...
...TO TEACH ME A LESSON. A LIFE LESSON...

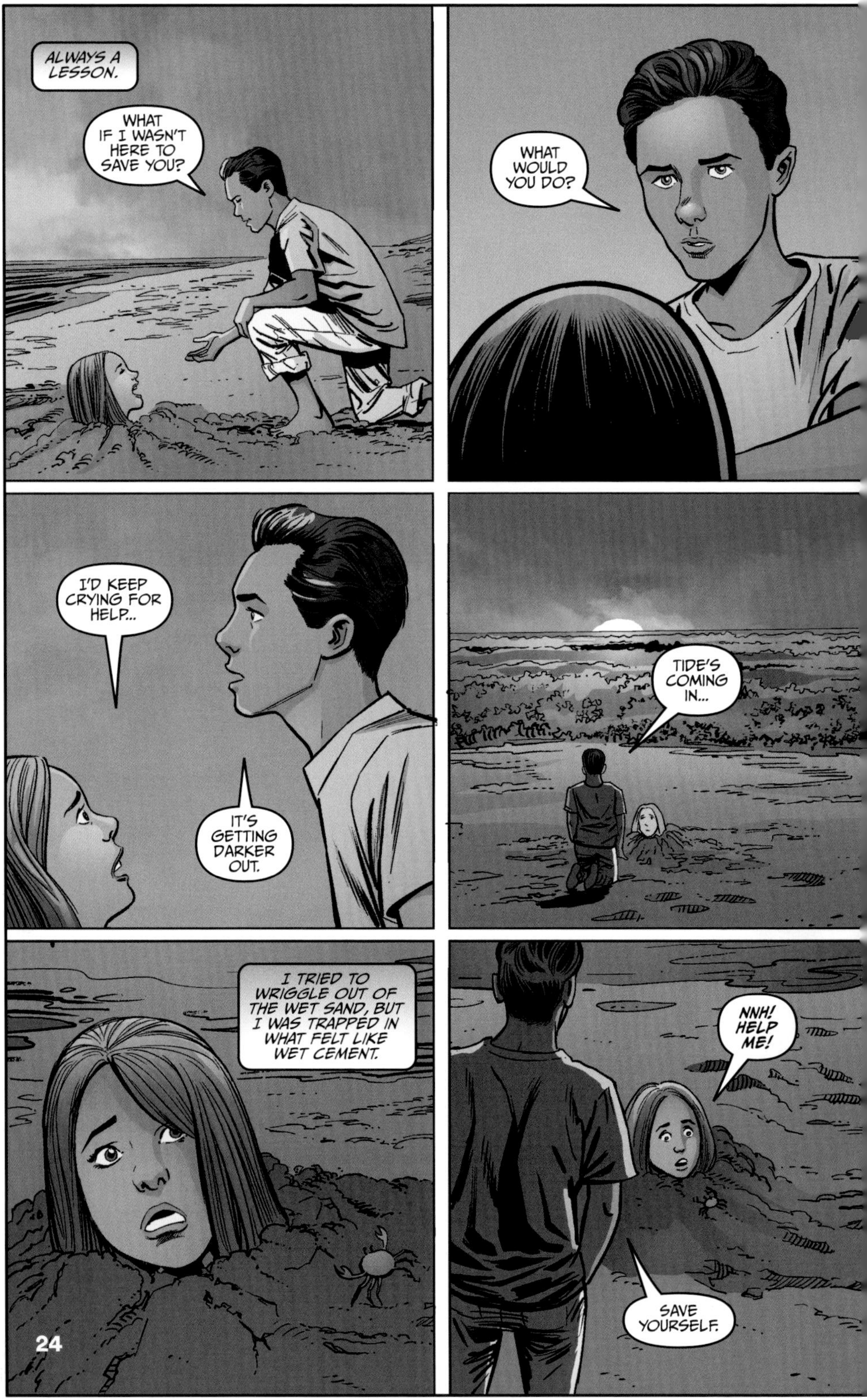
ALWAYS A LESSON.
WHAT IF I WASN'T HERE TO SAVE YOU?
WHAT WOULD YOU DO?
I'D KEEP CRYING FOR HELP...
IT'S GETTING DARKER OUT.
TIDE'S COMING IN...
I TRIED TO WRIGGLE OUT OF THE WET SAND, BUT I WAS TRAPPED IN WHAT FELT LIKE WET CEMENT.
NNH! HELP ME!
SAVE YOURSELF.

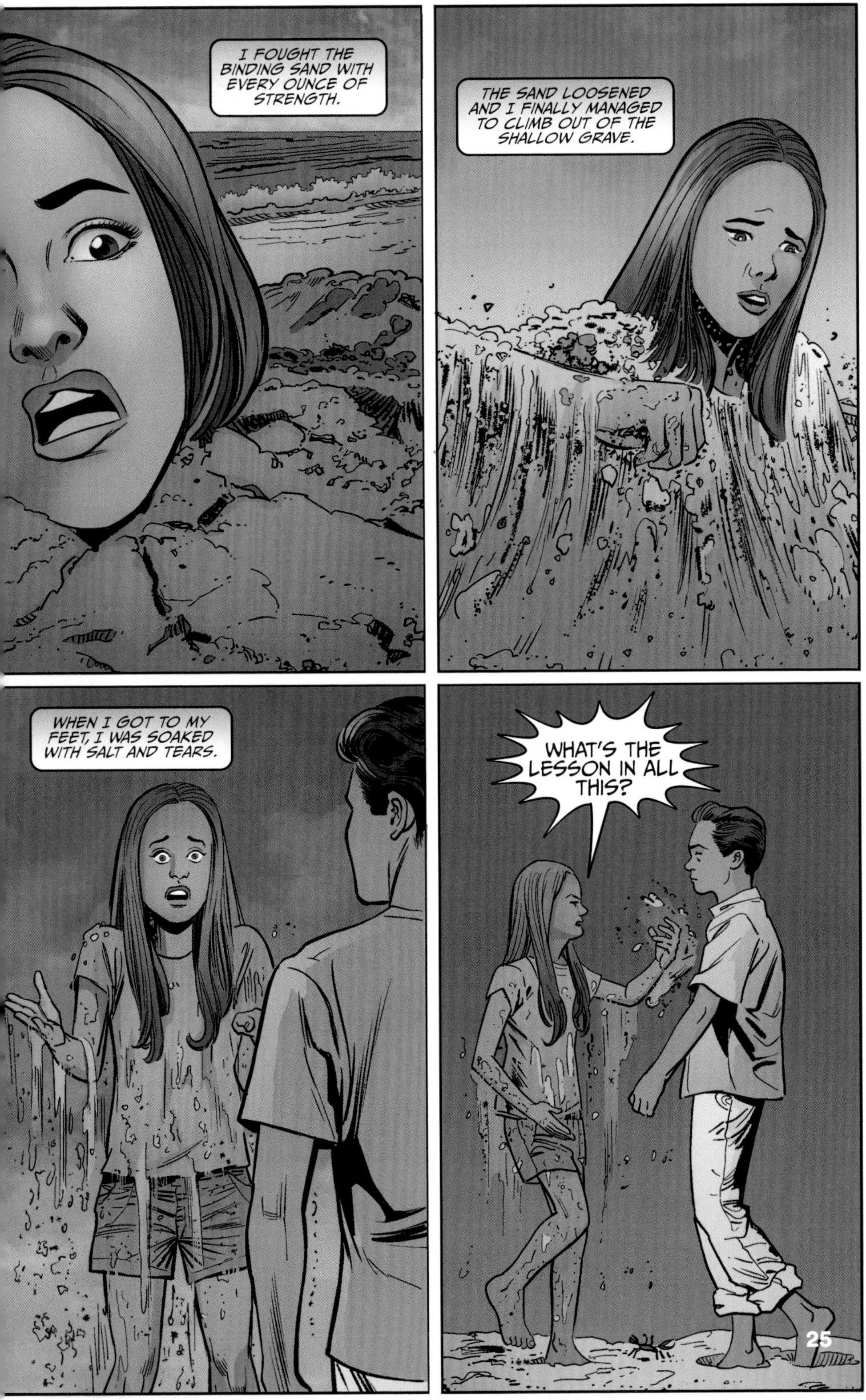
I FOUGHT THE BINDING SAND WITH EVERY OUNCE OF STRENGTH.
THE SAND LOOSENED AND I FINALLY MANAGED TO CLIMB OUT OF THE SHALLOW GRAVE.
WHEN I GOT TO MY FEET, I WAS SOAKED WITH SALT AND TEARS.
WHAT'S THE LESSON IN ALL THIS?

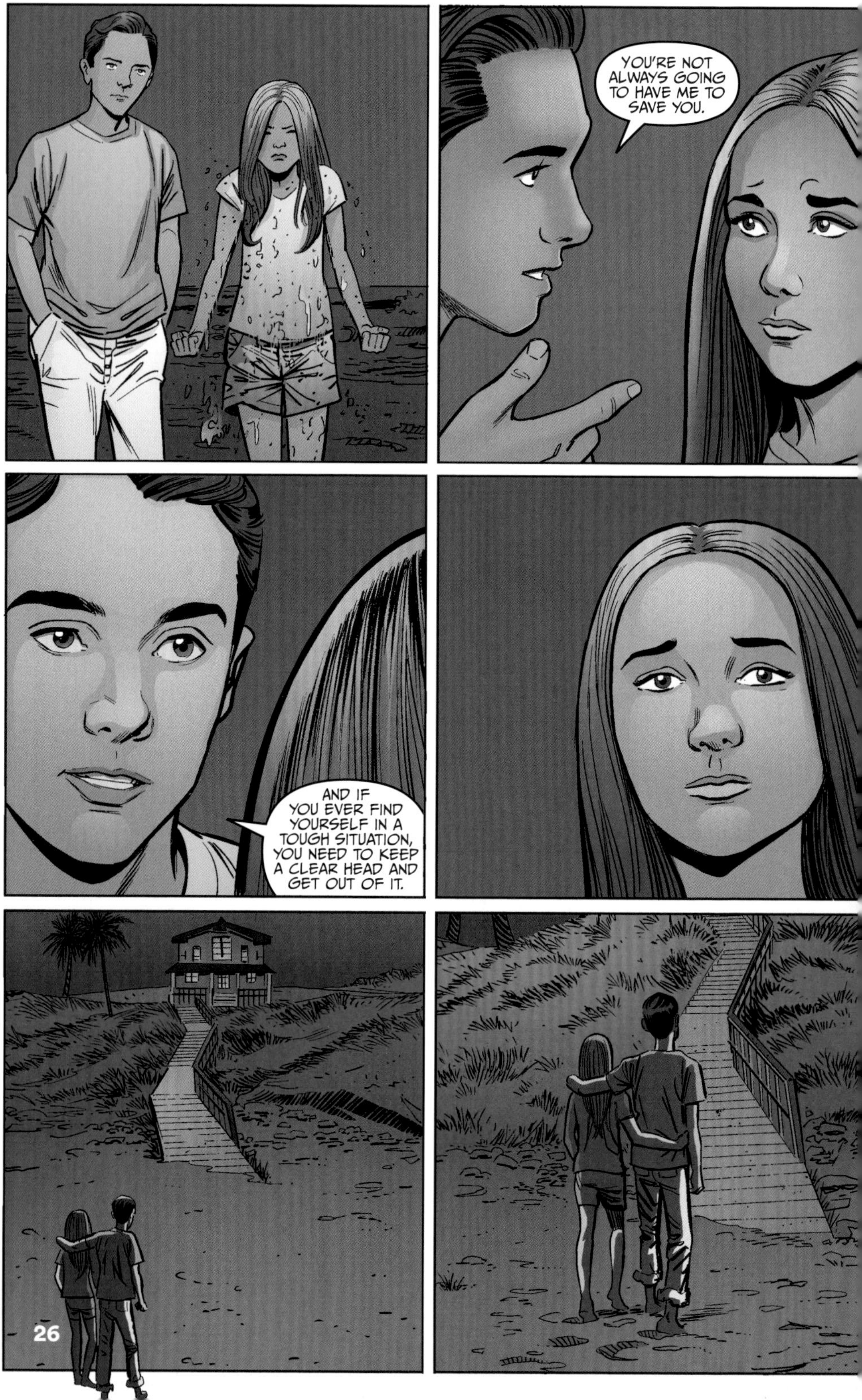
YOU'RE NOT ALWAYS GOING TO HAVE ME TO SAVE YOU.
AND IF YOU EVER FIND YOURSELF IN A TOUGH SITUATION, YOU NEED TO KEEP A CLEAR HEAD AND GET OUT OF IT.

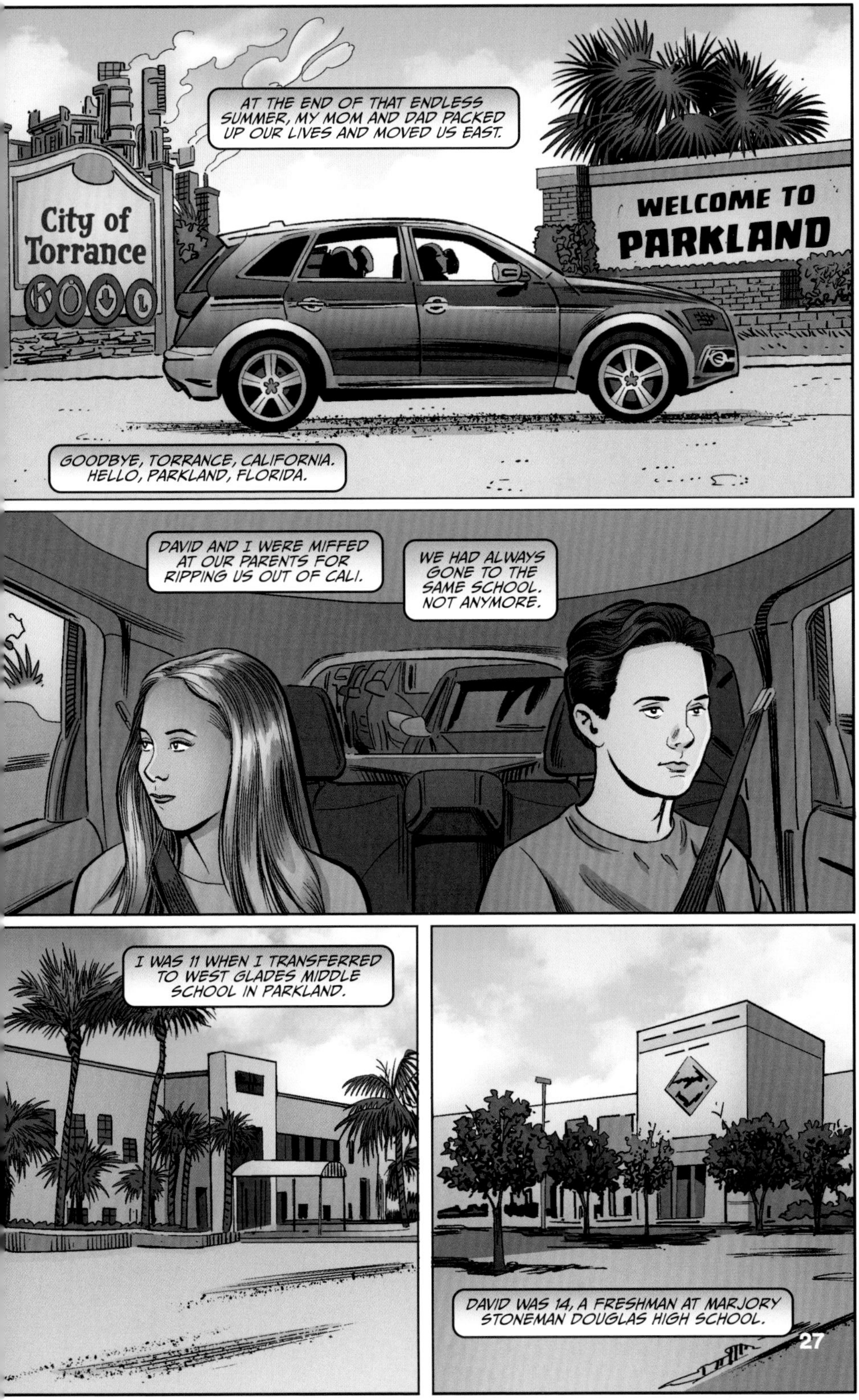
City of Torrance
AT THE END OF THAT ENDLESS SUMMER, MY MOM AND DAD PACKED UP OUR LIVES AND MOVED US EAST.
WELCOME TO PARKLAND
GOODBYE, TORRANCE, CALIFORNIA. HELLO, PARKLAND, FLORIDA.
DAVID AND I WERE MIFFED AT OUR PARENTS FOR RIPPING US OUT OF CALI.
WE HAD ALWAYS GONE TO THE SAME SCHOOL. NOT ANYMORE.
I WAS 11 WHEN I TRANSFERRED TO WEST GLADES MIDDLE SCHOOL IN PARKLAND.
DAVID WAS 14, A FRESHMAN AT MARJORY STONEMAN DOUGLAS HIGH SCHOOL.

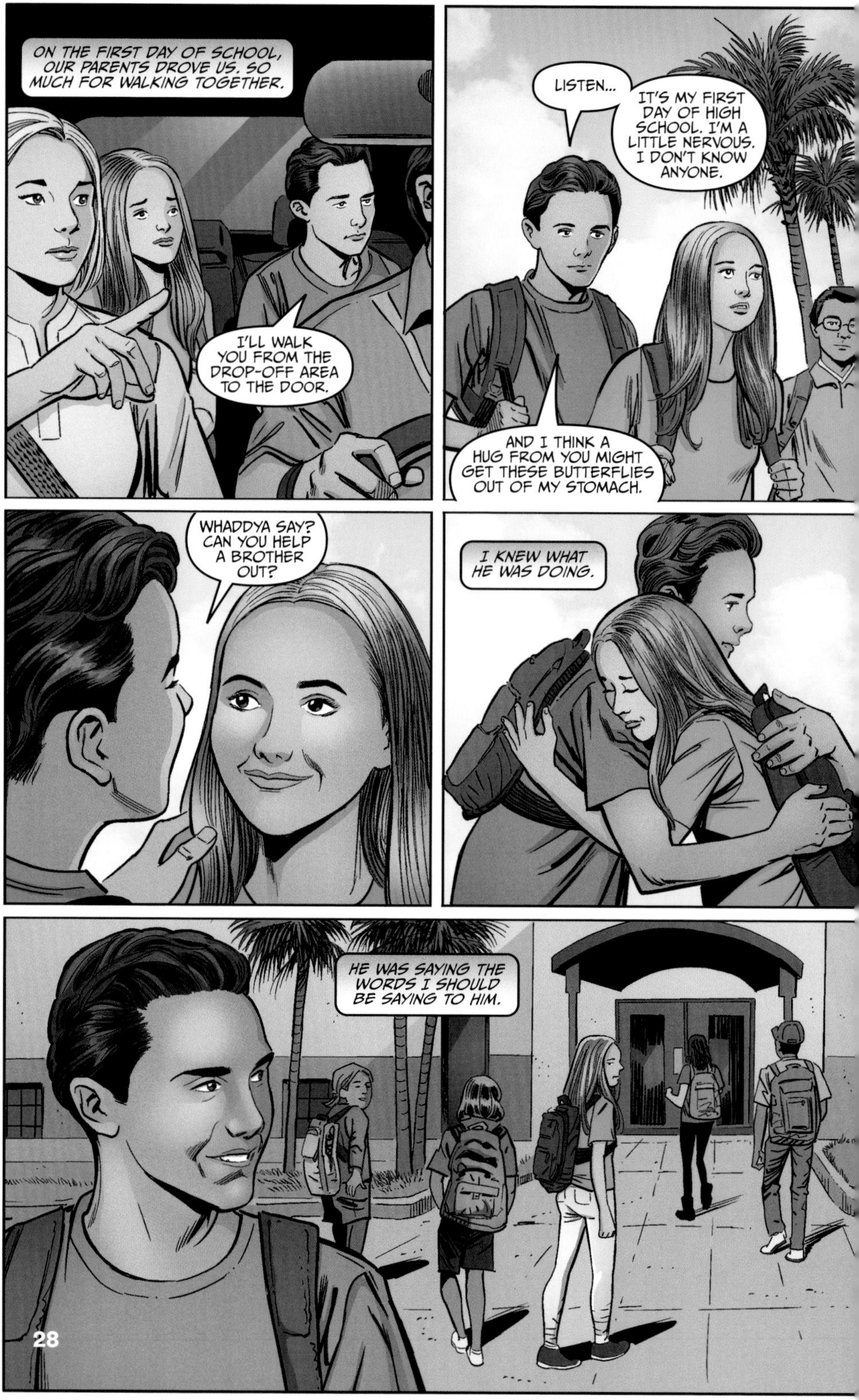
ON THE FIRST DAY OF SCHOOL, OUR PARENTS DROVE US. SO MUCH FOR WALKING TOGETHER.
I'LL WALK YOU FROM THE DROP-OFF AREA TO THE DOOR.
LISTEN...
IT'S MY FIRST DAY OF HIGH SCHOOL. I'M A LITTLE NERVOUS. I DON'T KNOW ANYONE.
AND I THINK A HUG FROM YOU MIGHT GET THESE BUTTERFLIES OUT OF MY STOMACH.
WHADDYA SAY? CAN YOU HELP A BROTHER OUT?
I KNEW WHAT HE WAS DOING.
HE WAS SAYING THE WORDS I SHOULD BE SAYING TO HIM.

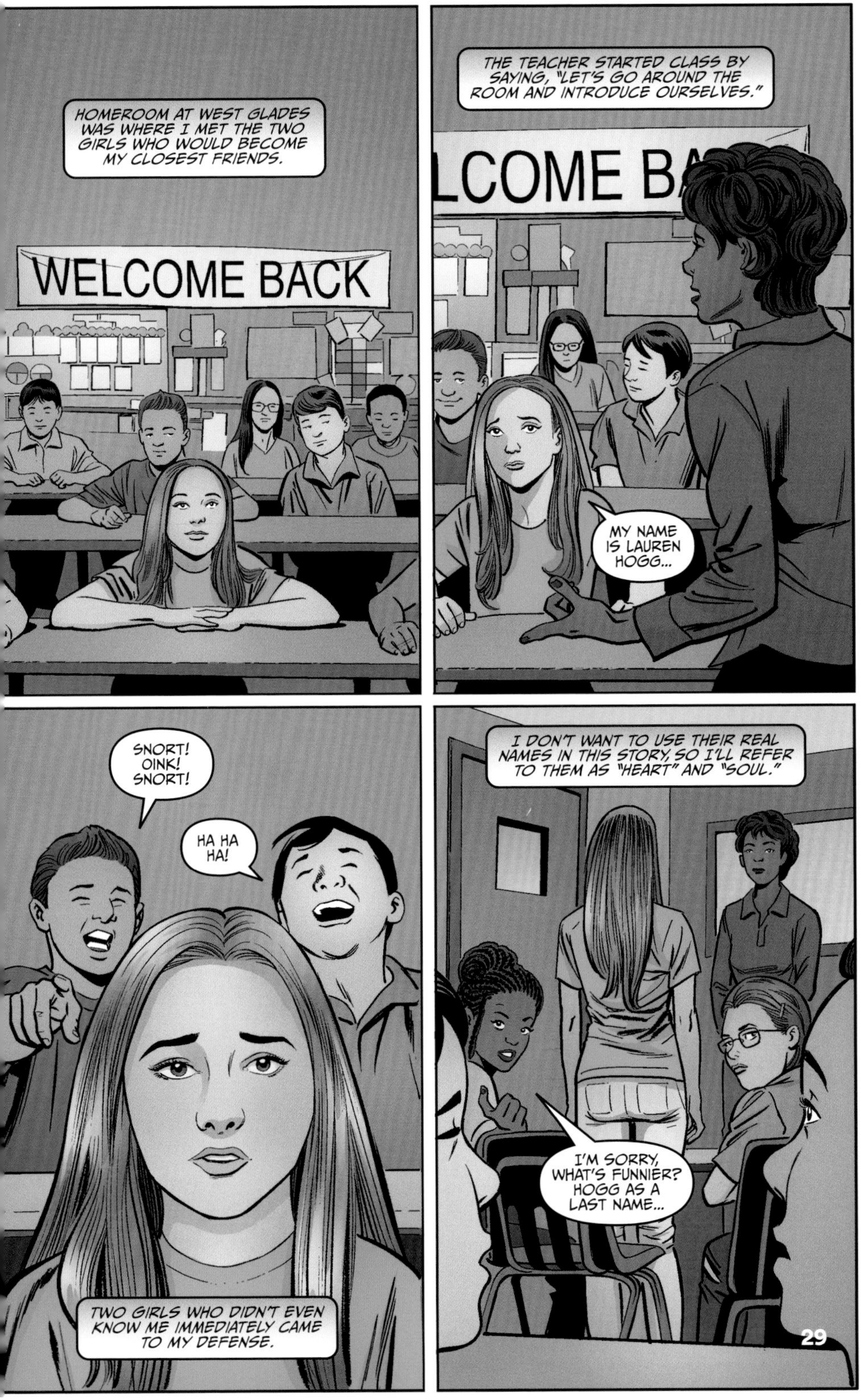
HOMEROOM AT WEST GLADES WAS WHERE I MET THE TWO GIRLS WHO WOULD BECOME MY CLOSEST FRIENDS.
WELCOME BACK
THE TEACHER STARTED CLASS BY SAYING, "LET'S GO AROUND THE ROOM AND INTRODUCE OURSELVES."
LCOME BA
MY NAME IS LAUREN HOGG...
SNORT! OINK! SNORT!
HA HA HA!
TWO GIRLS WHO DIDN'T EVEN KNOW ME IMMEDIATELY CAME TO MY DEFENSE.
I DON'T WANT TO USE THEIR REAL NAMES IN THIS STORY, SO I'LL REFER TO THEM AS "HEART" AND "SOUL."
I'M SORRY, WHAT'S FUNNIER? HOGG AS A LAST NAME...

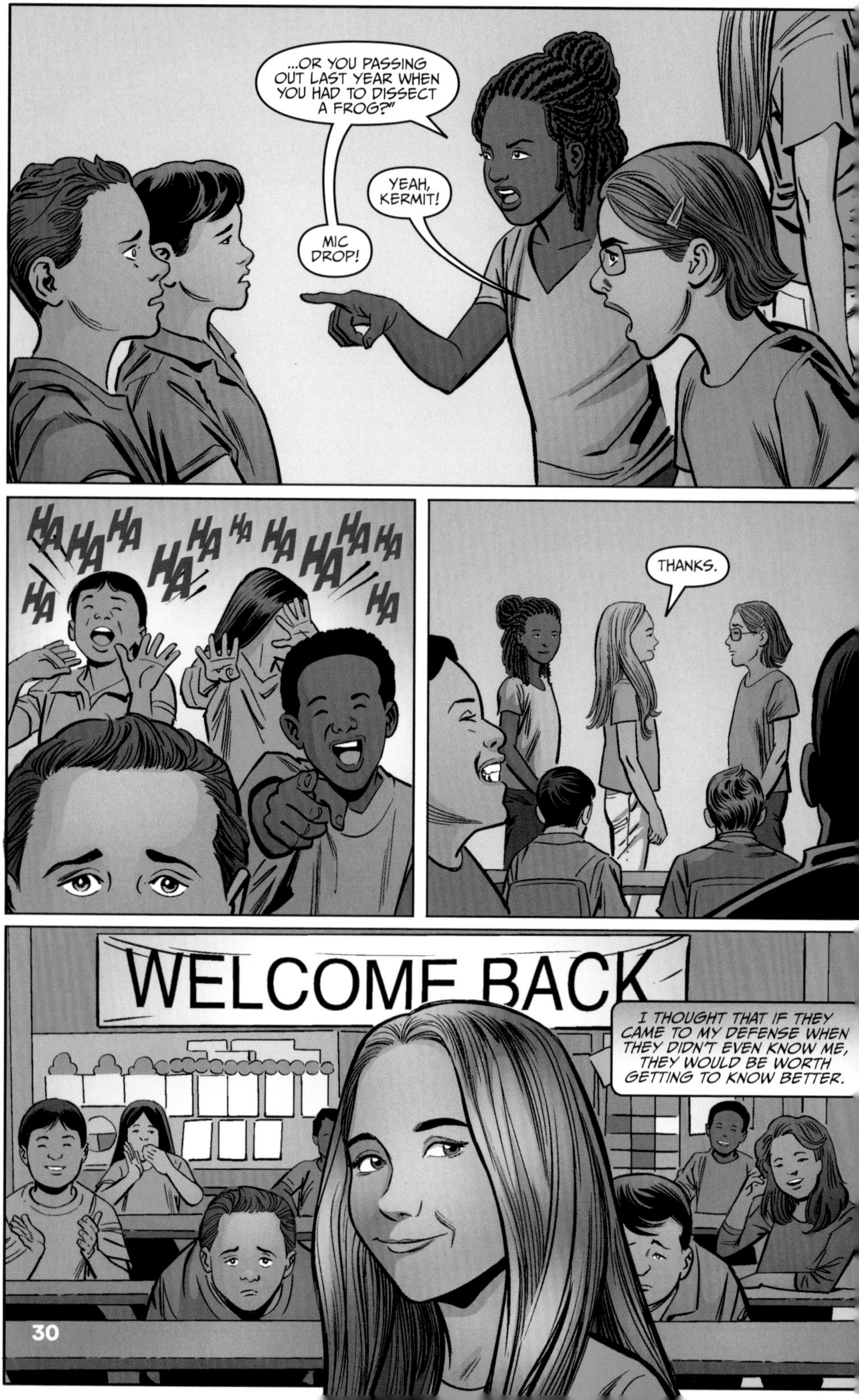
...OR YOU PASSING OUT LAST YEAR WHEN YOU HAD TO DISSECT A FROG?"
MIC DROP!
YEAH, KERMIT!
HA HA HA HA HA HA HA HA HA HA HA HA HA HA
THANKS.
WELCOME BACK
I THOUGHT THAT IF THEY CAME TO MY DEFENSE WHEN THEY DIDN'T EVEN KNOW ME, THEY WOULD BE WORTH GETTING TO KNOW BETTER.

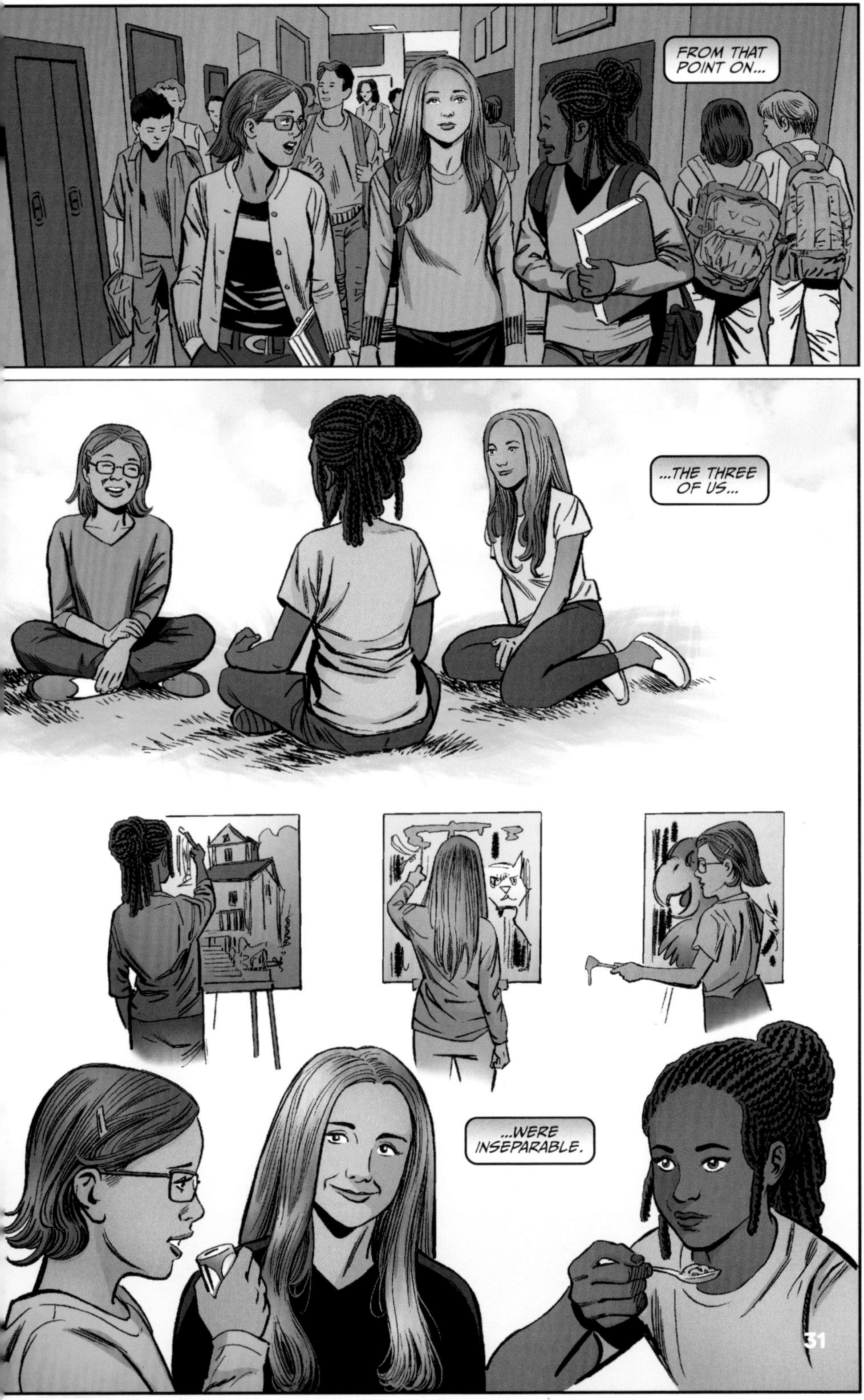
FROM THAT POINT ON...
...THE THREE OF US...
...WERE INSEPARABLE.

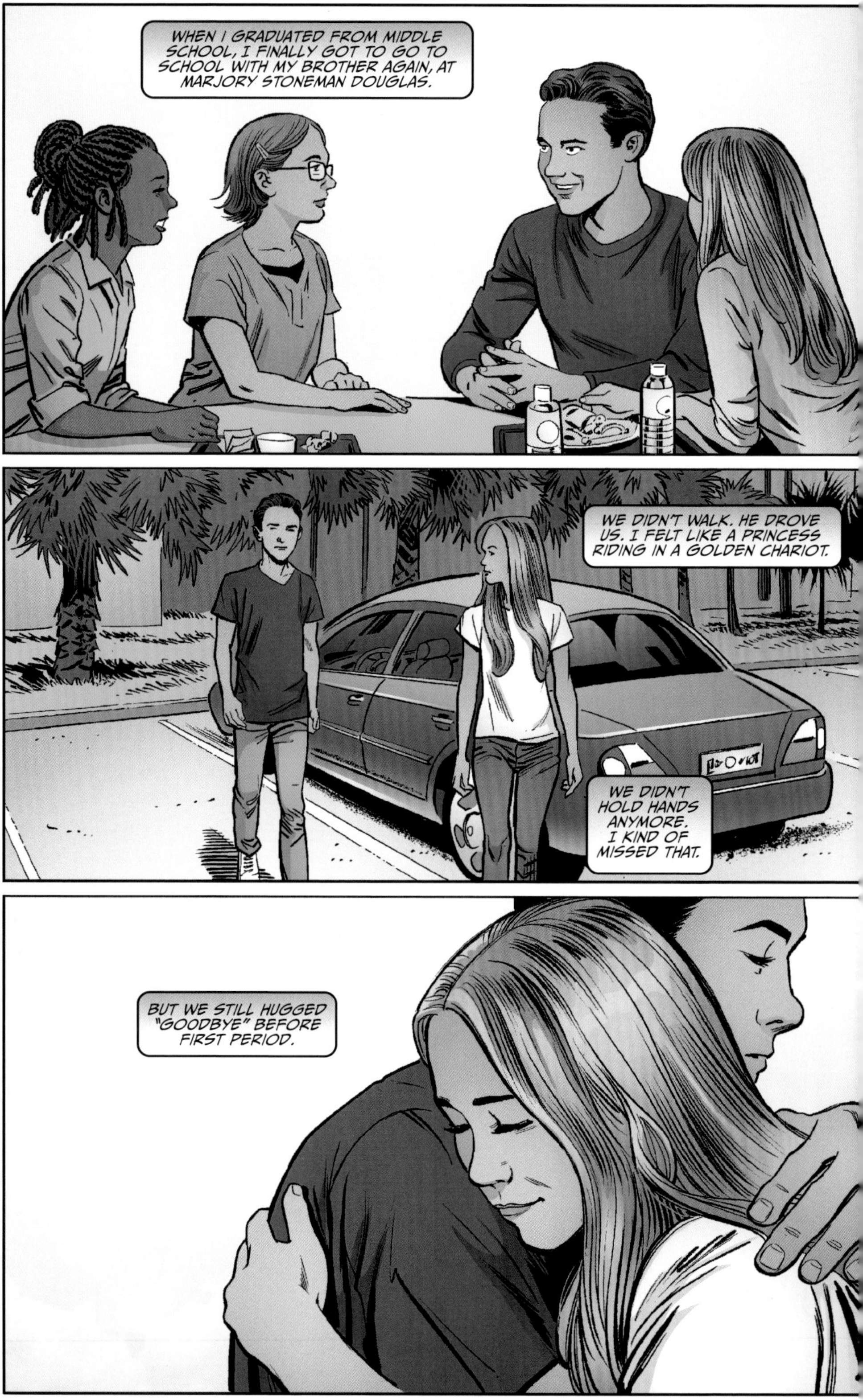
WHEN I GRADUATED FROM MIDDLE SCHOOL, I FINALLY GOT TO GO TO SCHOOL WITH MY BROTHER AGAIN, AT MARJORY STONEMAN DOUGLAS.
WE DIDN'T WALK. HE DROVE US. I FELT LIKE A PRINCESS RIDING IN A GOLDEN CHARIOT.
WE DIDN'T HOLD HANDS ANYMORE. I KIND OF MISSED THAT.
BUT WE STILL HUGGED "GOODBYE" BEFORE FIRST PERIOD.

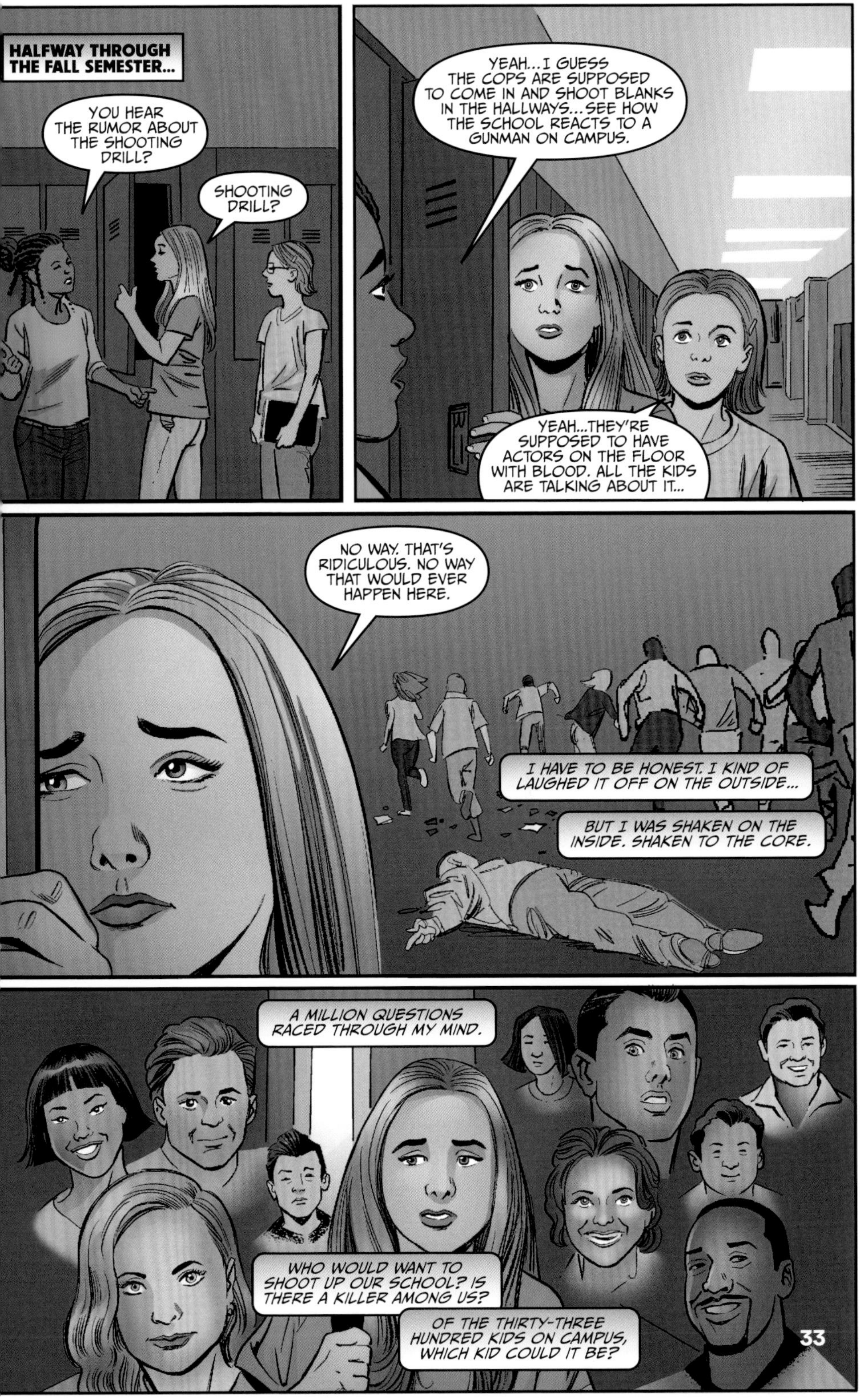
HALFWAY THROUGH THE FALL SEMESTER...
YOU HEAR THE RUMOR ABOUT THE SHOOTING DRILL?
SHOOTING DRILL?
YEAH... I GUESS THE COPS ARE SUPPOSED TO COME IN AND SHOOT BLANKS IN THE HALLWAYS... SEE HOW THE SCHOOL REACTS TO A GUNMAN ON CAMPUS.
YEAH...THEY'RE SUPPOSED TO HAVE ACTORS ON THE FLOOR WITH BLOOD. ALL THE KIDS ARE TALKING ABOUT IT...
NO WAY. THAT'S RIDICULOUS. NO WAY THAT WOULD EVER HAPPEN HERE.
I HAVE TO BE HONEST. I KIND OF LAUGHED IT OFF ON THE OUTSIDE...
BUT I WAS SHAKEN ON THE INSIDE. SHAKEN TO THE CORE.
A MILLION QUESTIONS RACED THROUGH MY MIND.
WHO WOULD WANT TO SHOOT UP OUR SCHOOL? IS THERE A KILLER AMONG US?
OF THE THIRTY-THREE HUNDRED KIDS ON CAMPUS, WHICH KID COULD IT BE?

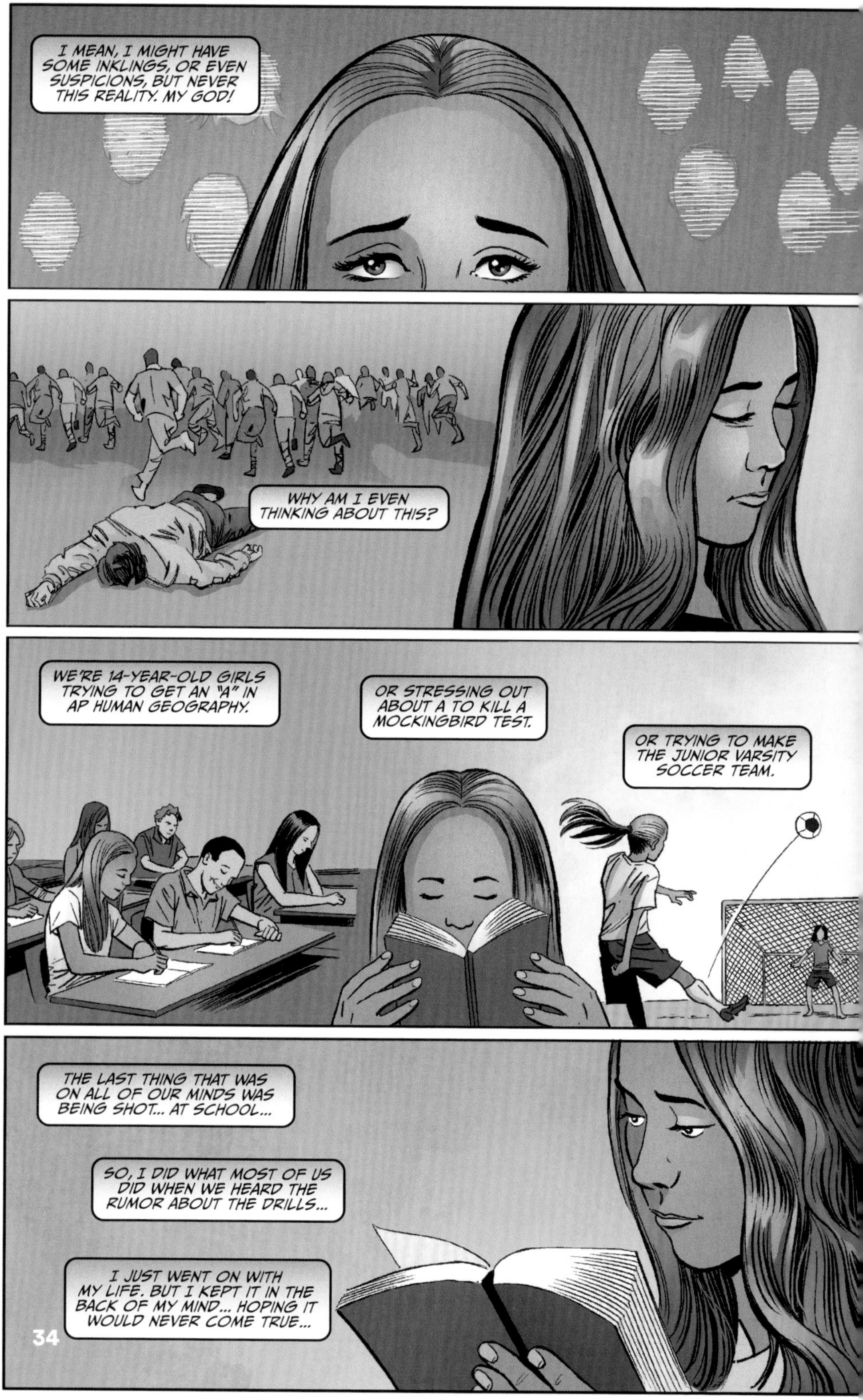
I MEAN, I MIGHT HAVE SOME INKLINGS, OR EVEN SUSPICIONS, BUT NEVER THIS REALITY. MY GOD!
WHY AM I EVEN THINKING ABOUT THIS?
WE'RE 14-YEAR-OLD GIRLS TRYING TO GET AN "A" IN AP HUMAN GEOGRAPHY.
OR STRESSING OUT ABOUT A TO KILL A MOCKINGBIRD TEST.
OR TRYING TO MAKE THE JUNIOR VARSITY SOCCER TEAM.
THE LAST THING THAT WAS ON ALL OF OUR MINDS WAS BEING SHOT... AT SCHOOL...
SO, I DID WHAT MOST OF US DID WHEN WE HEARD THE RUMOR ABOUT THE DRILLS...
I JUST WENT ON WITH MY LIFE. BUT I KEPT IT IN THE BACK OF MY MIND... HOPING IT WOULD NEVER COME TRUE...

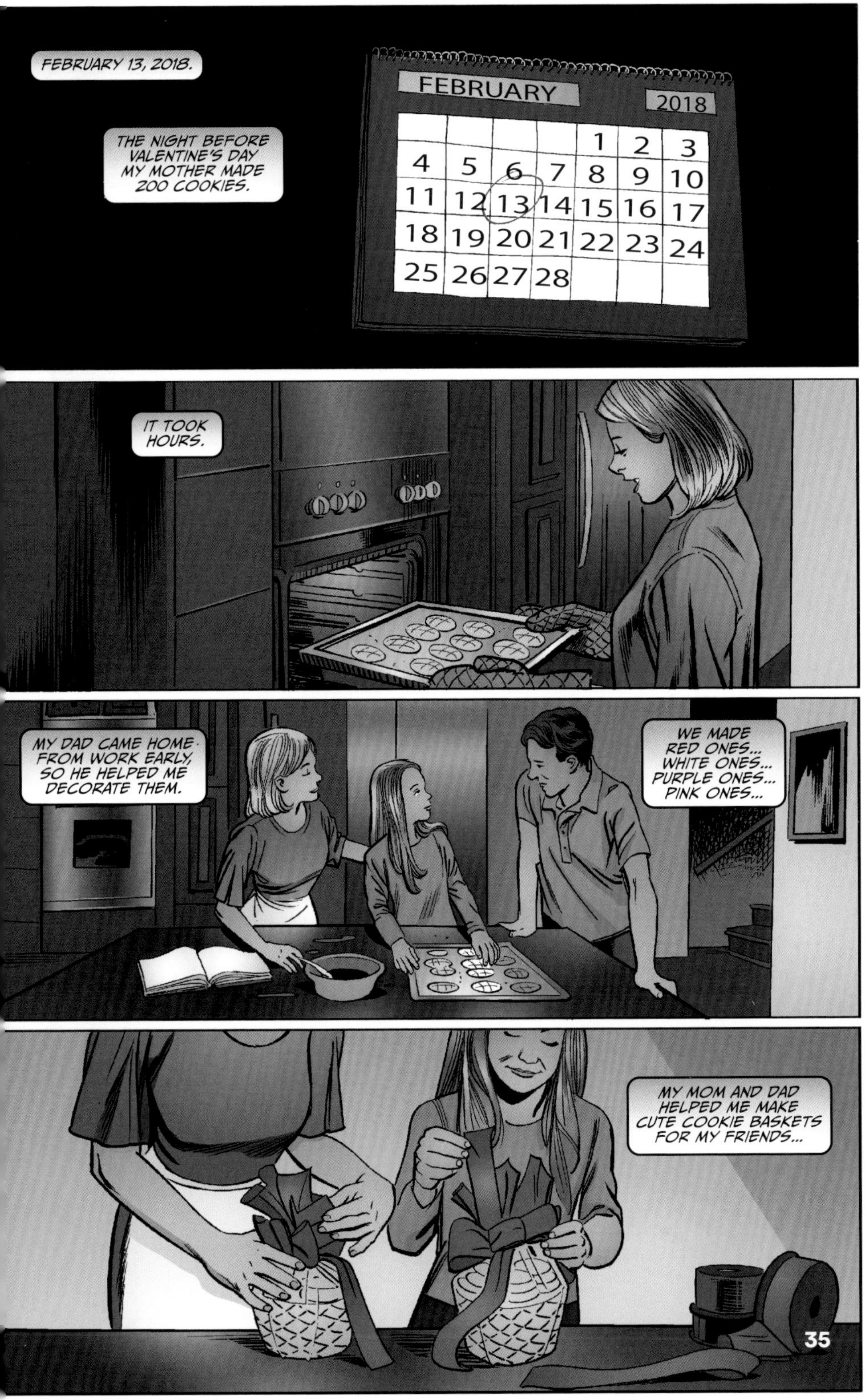
FEBRUARY 13, 2018.
FEBRUARY
2018
1 2 3
4 5 6 7 8 9 10
11 12 13 14 15 16 17
18 19 20 21 22 23 24
25 26 27 28
THE NIGHT BEFORE VALENTINE'S DAY MY MOTHER MADE 200 COOKIES.
IT TOOK HOURS.
MY DAD CAME HOME FROM WORK EARLY, SO HE HELPED ME DECORATE THEM.
WE MADE RED ONES... WHITE ONES... PURPLE ONES... PINK ONES...
MY MOM AND DAD HELPED ME MAKE CUTE COOKIE BASKETS FOR MY FRIENDS...

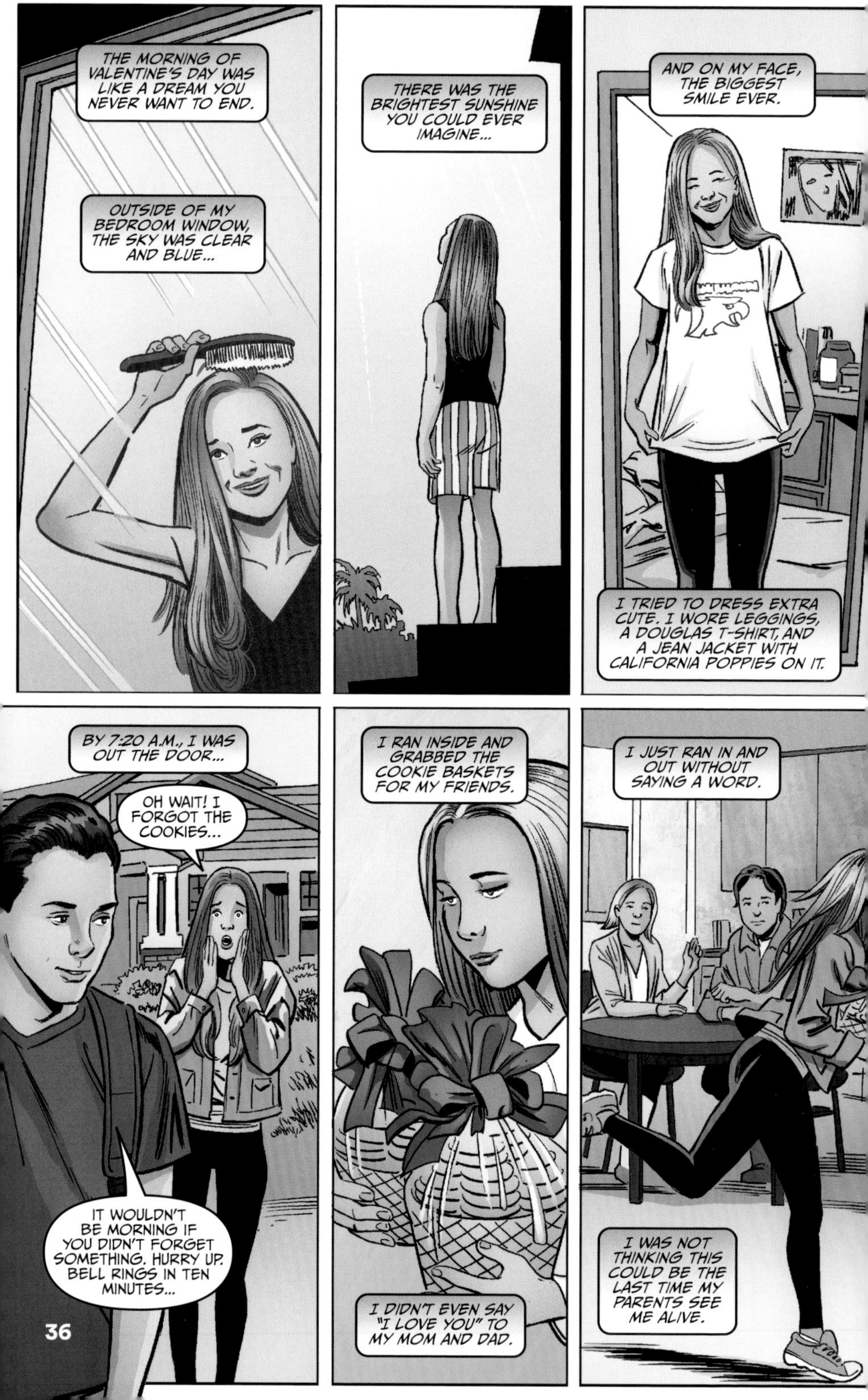
THE MORNING OF VALENTINE'S DAY WAS LIKE A DREAM YOU NEVER WANT TO END.
OUTSIDE OF MY BEDROOM WINDOW, THE SKY WAS CLEAR AND BLUE...
THERE WAS THE BRIGHTEST SUNSHINE YOU COULD EVER IMAGINE...
AND ON MY FACE, THE BIGGEST SMILE EVER.
I TRIED TO DRESS EXTRA CUTE. I WORE LEGGINGS, A DOUGLAS T-SHIRT, AND A JEAN JACKET WITH CALIFORNIA POPPIES ON IT.
BY 7:20 A.M., I WAS OUT THE DOOR...
OH WAIT! I FORGOT THE COOKIES...
IT WOULDN'T BE MORNING IF YOU DIDN'T FORGET SOMETHING. HURRY UP. BELL RINGS IN TEN MINUTES...
I RAN INSIDE AND GRABBED THE COOKIE BASKETS FOR MY FRIENDS.
I DIDN'T EVEN SAY "I LOVE YOU" TO MY MOM AND DAD.
I JUST RAN IN AND OUT WITHOUT SAYING A WORD.
I WAS NOT THINKING THIS COULD BE THE LAST TIME MY PARENTS SEE ME ALIVE.

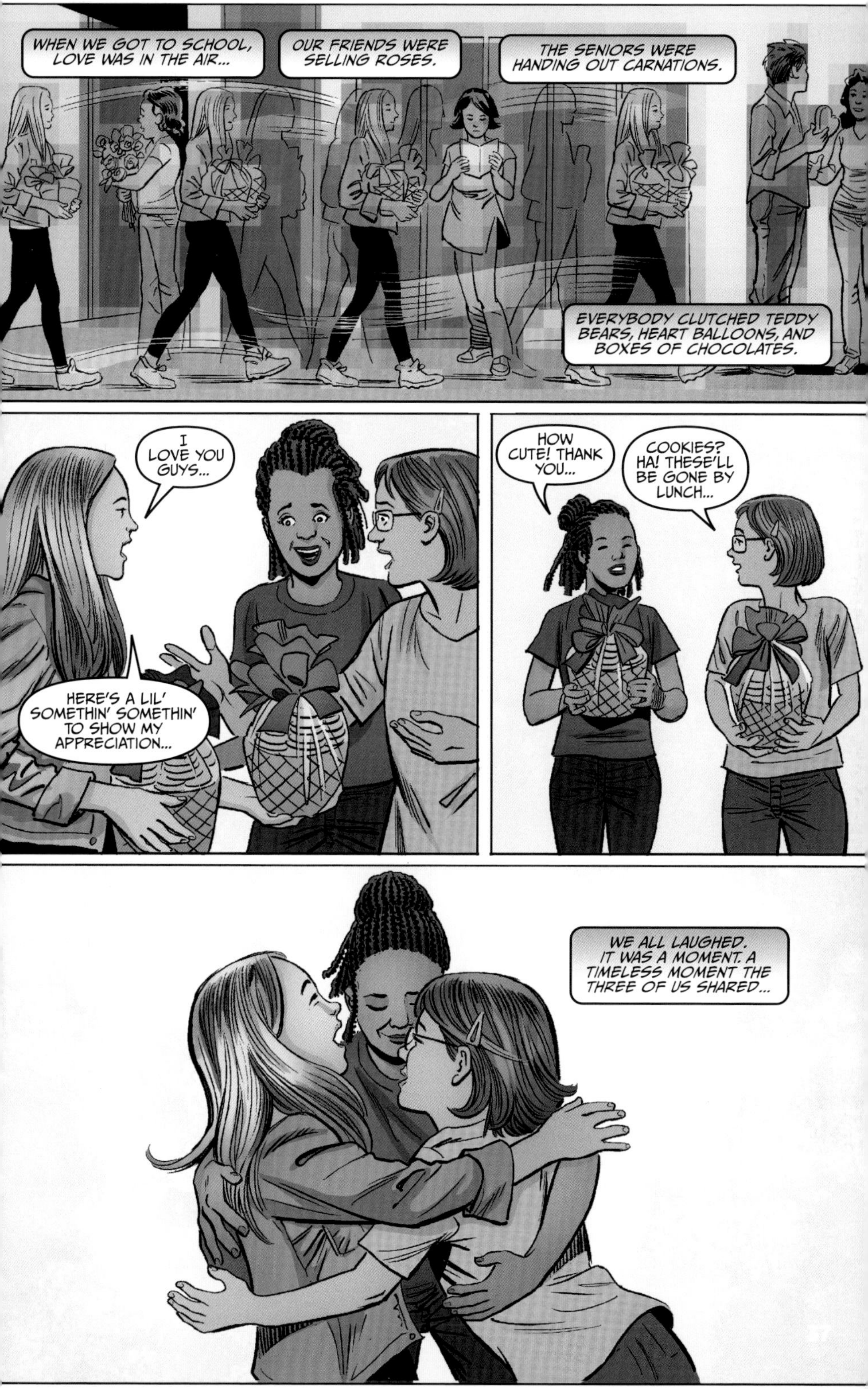

WHEN WE GOT TO SCHOOL, LOVE WAS IN THE AIR...
OUR FRIENDS WERE SELLING ROSES.
THE SENIORS WERE HANDING OUT CARNATIONS.
EVERYBODY CLUTCHED TEDDY BEARS, HEART BALLOONS, AND BOXES OF CHOCOLATES.
I LOVE YOU GUYS...
HERE'S A LIL' SOMETHIN' SOMETHIN' TO SHOW MY APPRECIATION...
HOW CUTE! THANK YOU...
COOKIES? HA! THESE'LL BE GONE BY LUNCH...
WE ALL LAUGHED. IT WAS A MOMENT. A TIMELESS MOMENT THE THREE OF US SHARED...

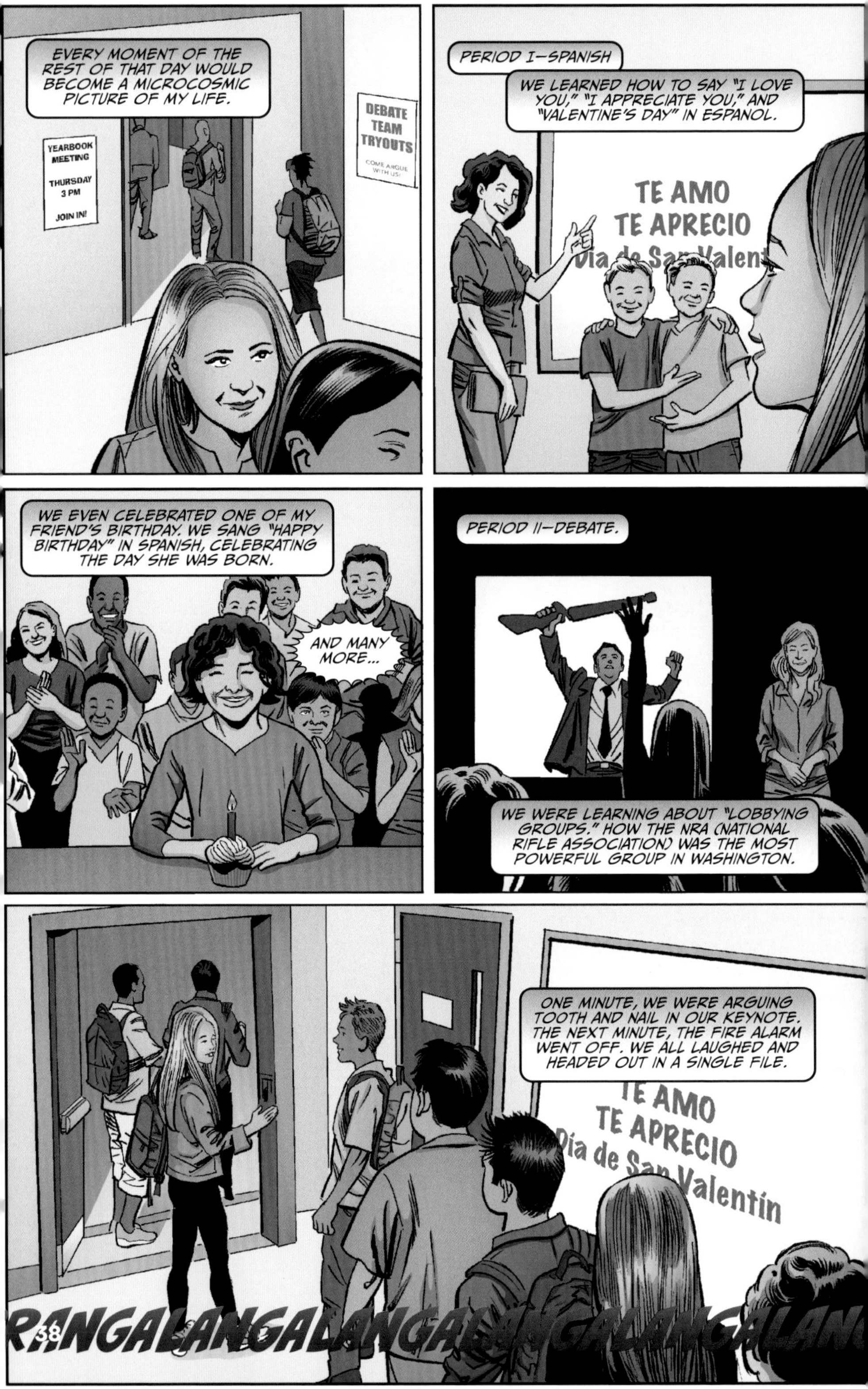
EVERY MOMENT OF THE REST OF THAT DAY WOULD BECOME A MICROCOSMIC PICTURE OF MY LIFE.
YEARBOOK MEETING THURSDAY 3 PM JOIN IN!
DEBATE TEAM TRYOUTS
COME ARGUE WITH US!
PERIOD I—SPANISH
WE LEARNED HOW TO SAY "I LOVE YOU," "I APPRECIATE YOU," AND "VALENTINE'S DAY" IN ESPANOL.
TE AMO
TE APRECIO
WE EVEN CELEBRATED ONE OF MY FRIEND'S BIRTHDAY. WE SANG "HAPPY BIRTHDAY" IN SPANISH, CELEBRATING THE DAY SHE WAS BORN.
AND MANY MORE...
PERIOD II—DEBATE.
WE WERE LEARNING ABOUT "LOBBYING GROUPS." HOW THE NRA (NATIONAL RIFLE ASSOCIATION) WAS THE MOST POWERFUL GROUP IN WASHINGTON.
ONE MINUTE, WE WERE ARGUING TOOTH AND NAIL IN OUR KEYNOTE. THE NEXT MINUTE, THE FIRE ALARM WENT OFF. WE ALL LAUGHED AND HEADED OUT IN A SINGLE FILE.
TE AMO
TE APRECIO
Día de San Valentín
RANGALANGALANGALANGALANGALANGALANG

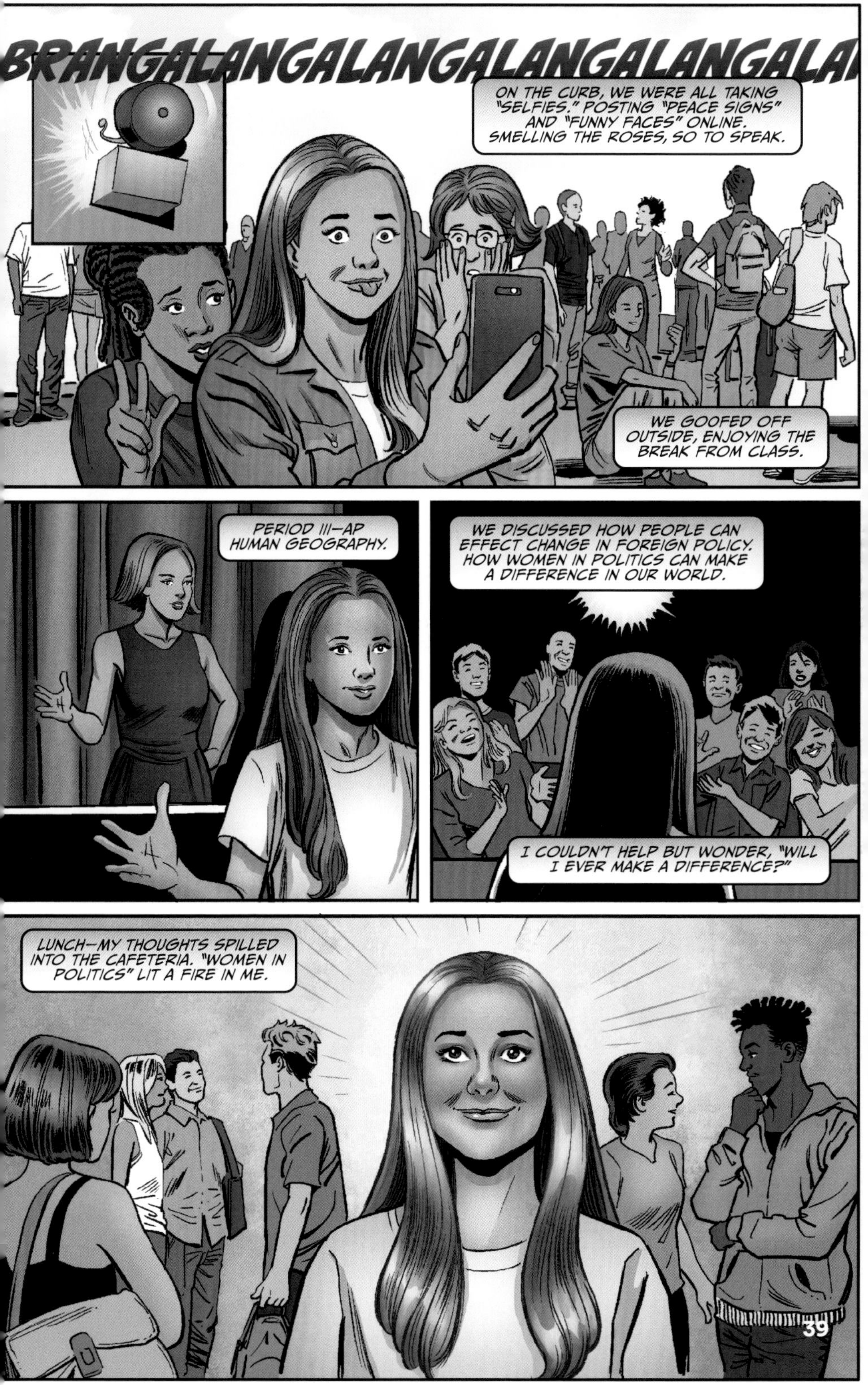
BRANGALANGALANGALANGALANGALA
ON THE CURB, WE WERE ALL TAKING "SELFIES." POSTING "PEACE SIGNS" AND "FUNNY FACES" ONLINE. SMELLING THE ROSES, SO TO SPEAK.
WE GOOFED OFF OUTSIDE, ENJOYING THE BREAK FROM CLASS.
PERIOD III—AP HUMAN GEOGRAPHY.
WE DISCUSSED HOW PEOPLE CAN EFFECT CHANGE IN FOREIGN POLICY. HOW WOMEN IN POLITICS CAN MAKE A DIFFERENCE IN OUR WORLD.
I COULDN'T HELP BUT WONDER, "WILL I EVER MAKE A DIFFERENCE?"
LUNCH—MY THOUGHTS SPILLED INTO THE CAFETERIA. "WOMEN IN POLITICS" LIT A FIRE IN ME.

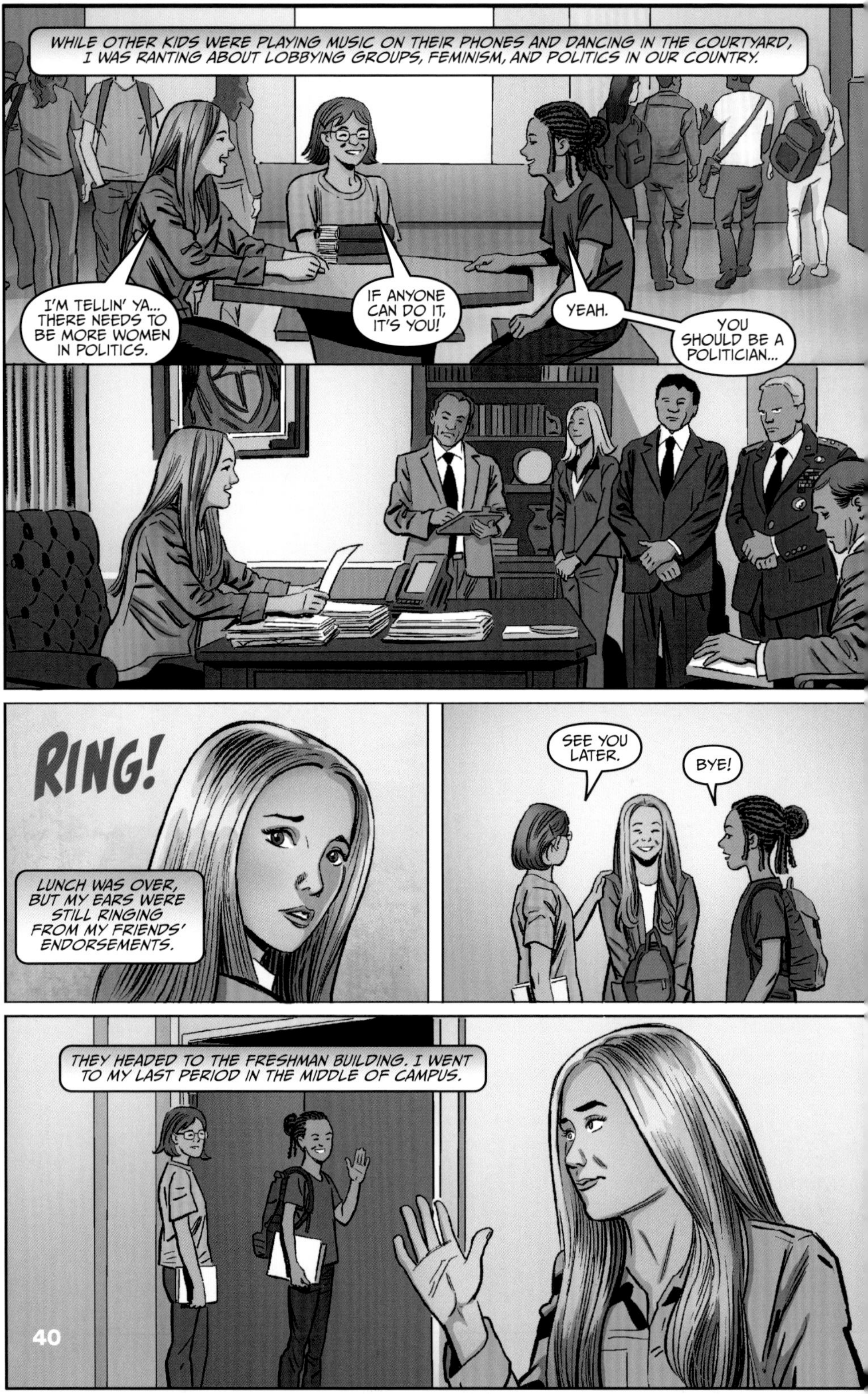
WHILE OTHER KIDS WERE PLAYING MUSIC ON THEIR PHONES AND DANCING IN THE COURTYARD, I WAS RANTING ABOUT LOBBYING GROUPS, FEMINISM, AND POLITICS IN OUR COUNTRY.
I'M TELLIN' YA... THERE NEEDS TO BE MORE WOMEN IN POLITICS.
IF ANYONE CAN DO IT, IT'S YOU!
YEAH.
YOU SHOULD BE A POLITICIAN...
RING!
LUNCH WAS OVER, BUT MY EARS WERE STILL RINGING FROM MY FRIENDS' ENDORSEMENTS.
SEE YOU LATER.
BYE!
THEY HEADED TO THE FRESHMAN BUILDING. I WENT TO MY LAST PERIOD IN THE MIDDLE OF CAMPUS.

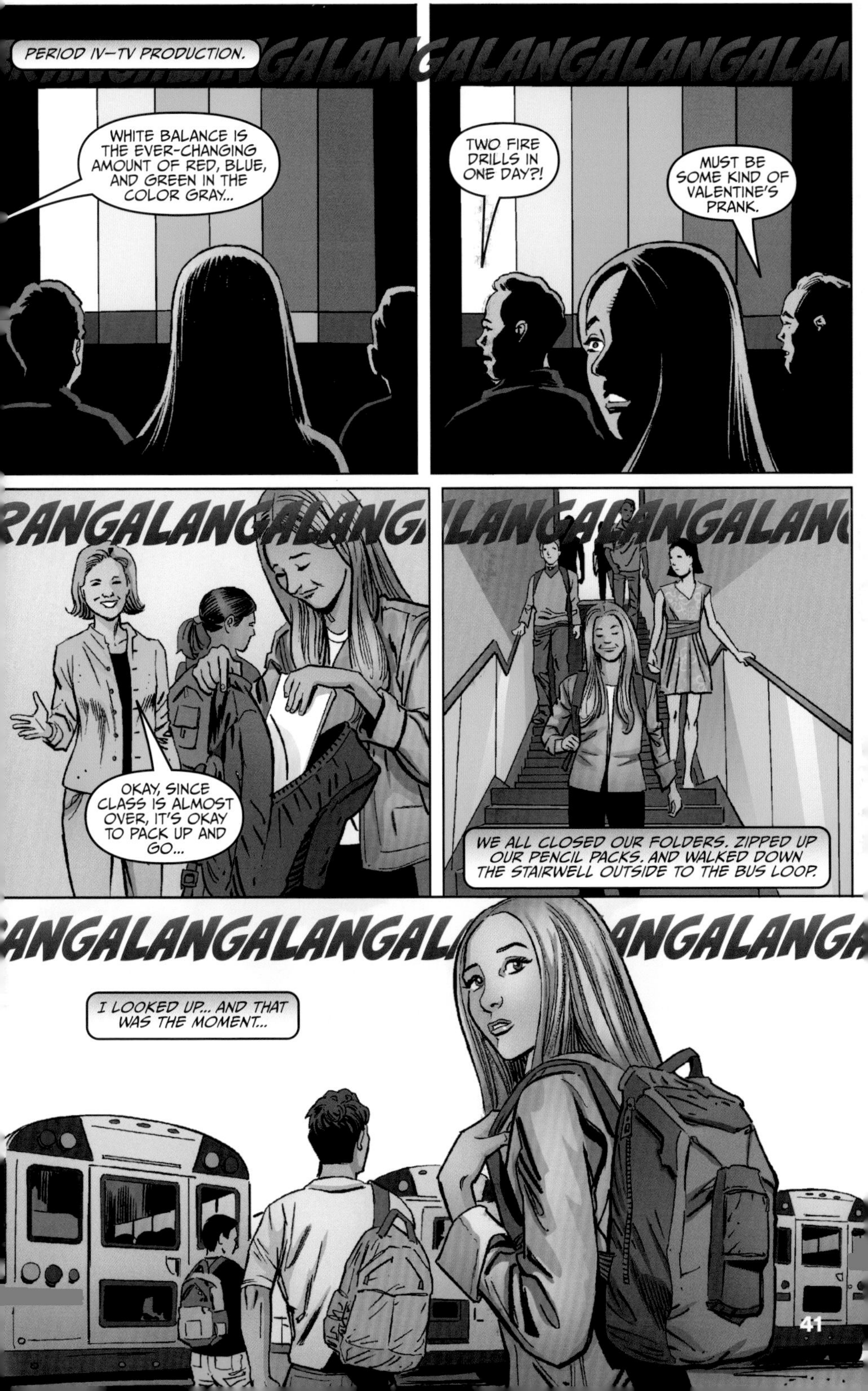
PERIOD IV—TV PRODUCTION.
GALANGALANGALANGALAN
WHITE BALANCE IS THE EVER-CHANGING AMOUNT OF RED, BLUE, AND GREEN IN THE COLOR GRAY...
TWO FIRE DRILLS IN ONE DAY?!
MUST BE SOME KIND OF VALENTINE'S PRANK.
RANGALANGALANG
OKAY, SINCE CLASS IS ALMOST OVER, IT'S OKAY TO PACK UP AND GO...
LANGALANGALANG
WE ALL CLOSED OUR FOLDERS. ZIPPED UP OUR PENCIL PACKS. AND WALKED DOWN THE STAIRWELL OUTSIDE TO THE BUS LOOP.
ANGALANGALANGALANGALANGA
I LOOKED UP... AND THAT WAS THE MOMENT...

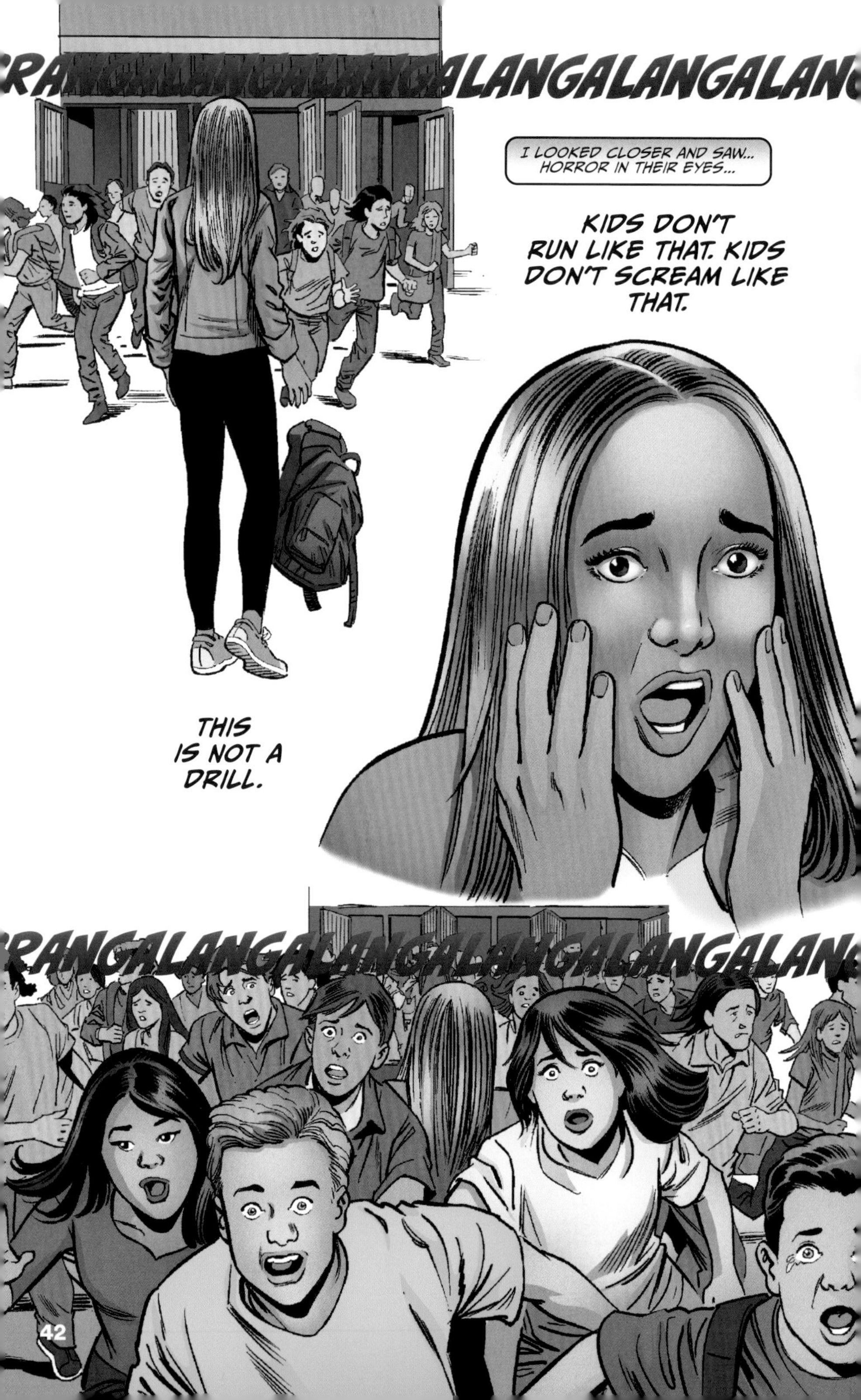
RANGALANGALANGALANGALANGALANG
I LOOKED CLOSER AND SAW... HORROR IN THEIR EYES...
KIDS DON'T RUN LIKE THAT. KIDS DON'T SCREAM LIKE THAT.
THIS IS NOT A DRILL.
RANGALANGALANGALANGALANGALANG

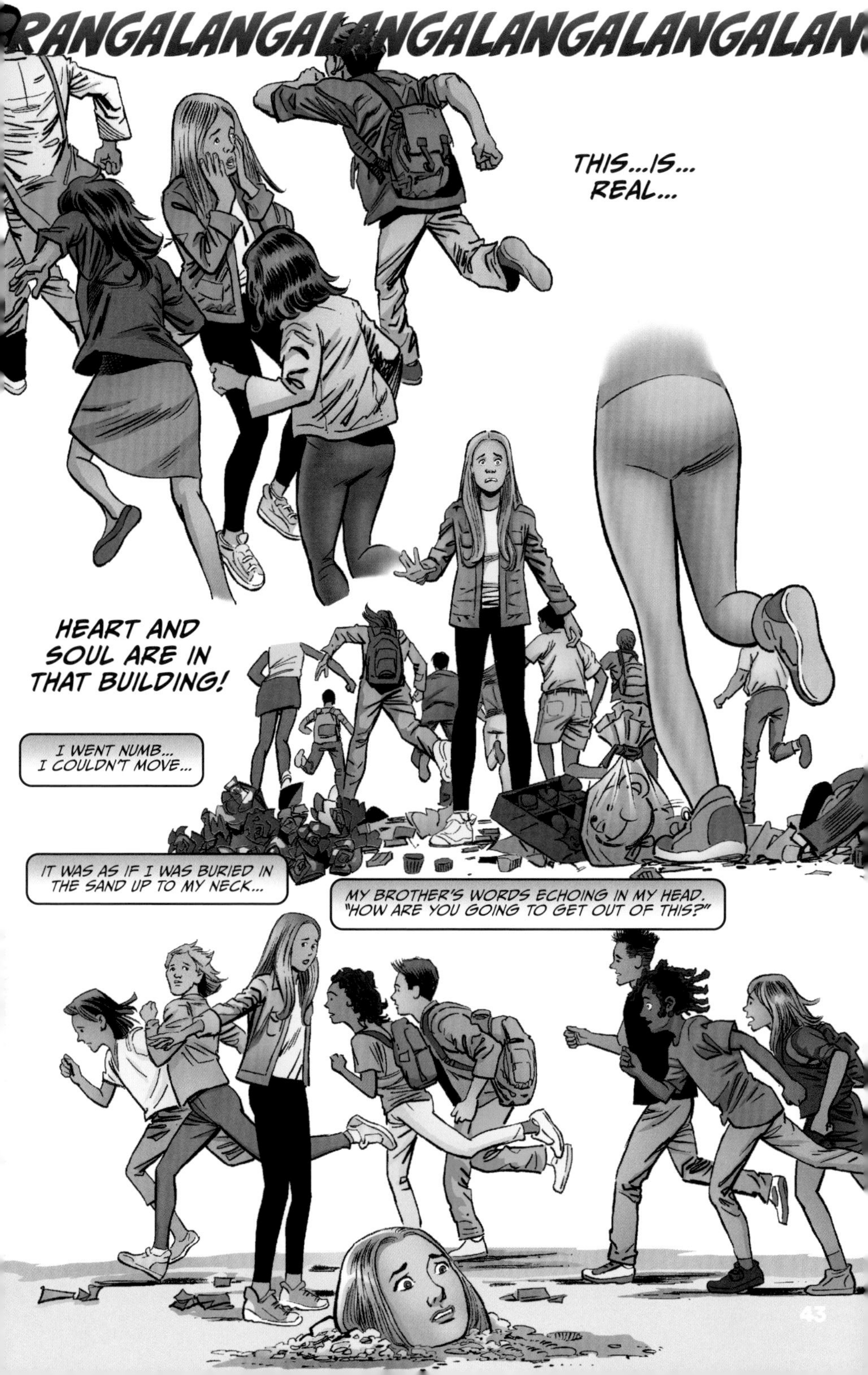
RANGALANGALANGALANGALANGALAN
THIS...IS... REAL...
HEART AND SOUL ARE IN THAT BUILDING!
I WENT NUMB... I COULDN'T MOVE...
IT WAS AS IF I WAS BURIED IN THE SAND UP TO MY NECK...
MY BROTHER'S WORDS ECHOING IN MY HEAD. "HOW ARE YOU GOING TO GET OUT OF THIS?"

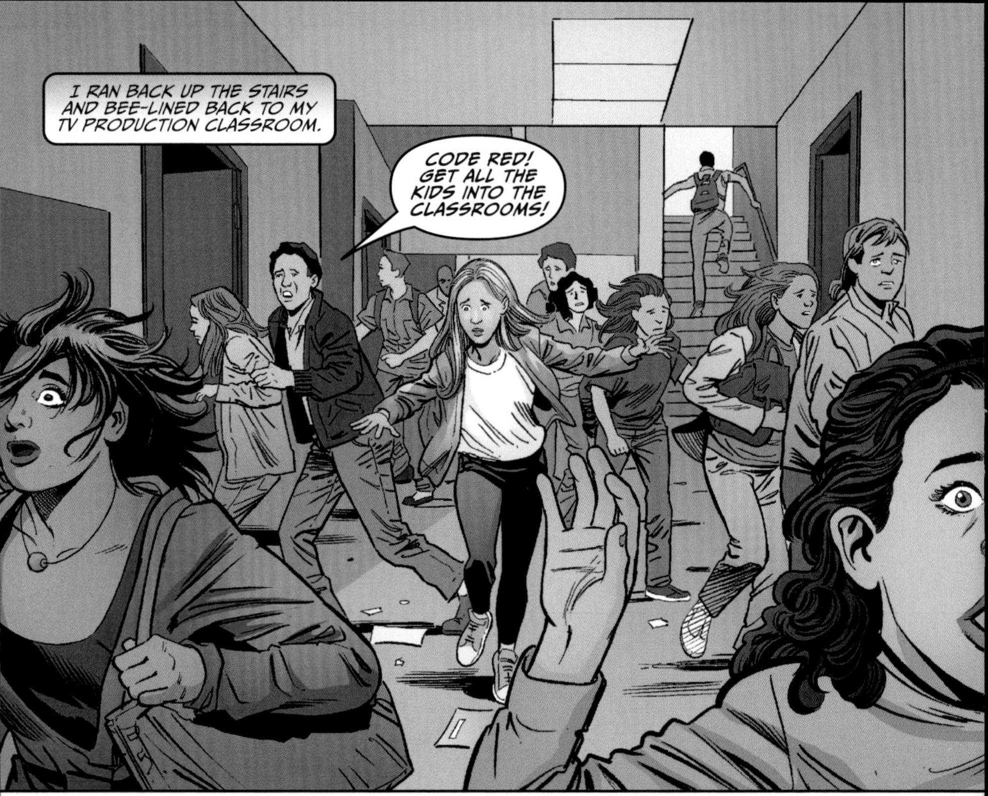
I RAN BACK UP THE STAIRS AND BEE-LINED BACK TO MY TV PRODUCTION CLASSROOM.
CODE RED! GET ALL THE KIDS INTO THE CLASSROOMS!

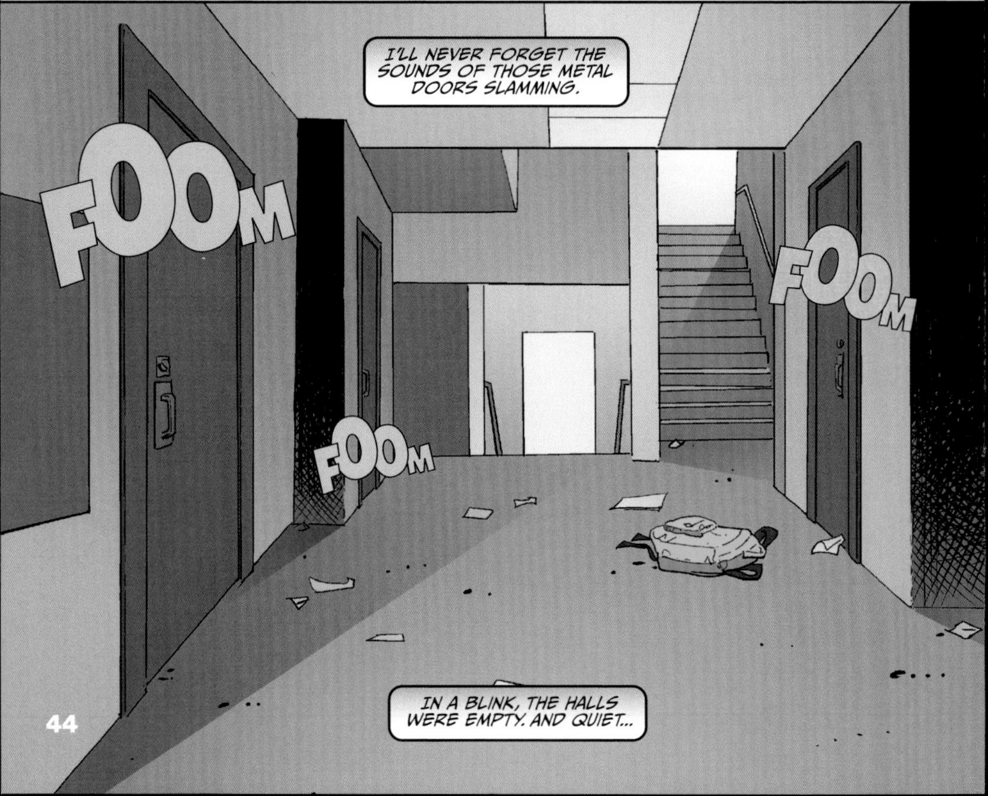
I'LL NEVER FORGET THE SOUNDS OF THOSE METAL DOORS SLAMMING.
FOOM
FOOM
FOOM
IN A BLINK, THE HALLS WERE EMPTY. AND QUIET...

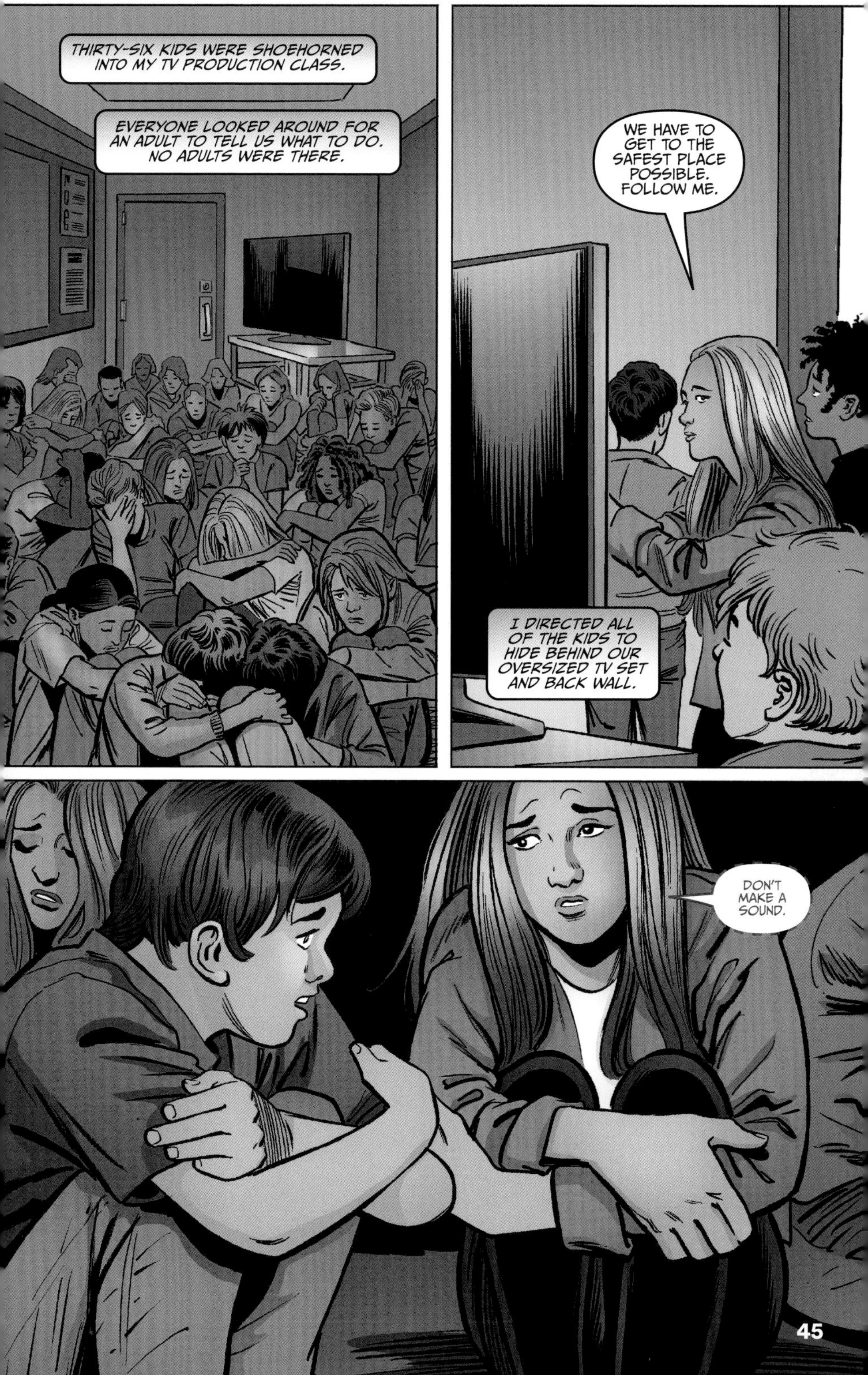
THIRTY-SIX KIDS WERE SHOEHORNED INTO MY TV PRODUCTION CLASS.
EVERYONE LOOKED AROUND FOR AN ADULT TO TELL US WHAT TO DO. NO ADULTS WERE THERE.
WE HAVE TO GET TO THE SAFEST PLACE POSSIBLE. FOLLOW ME.
I DIRECTED ALL OF THE KIDS TO HIDE BEHIND OUR OVERSIZED TV SET AND BACK WALL.
DON'T MAKE A SOUND.

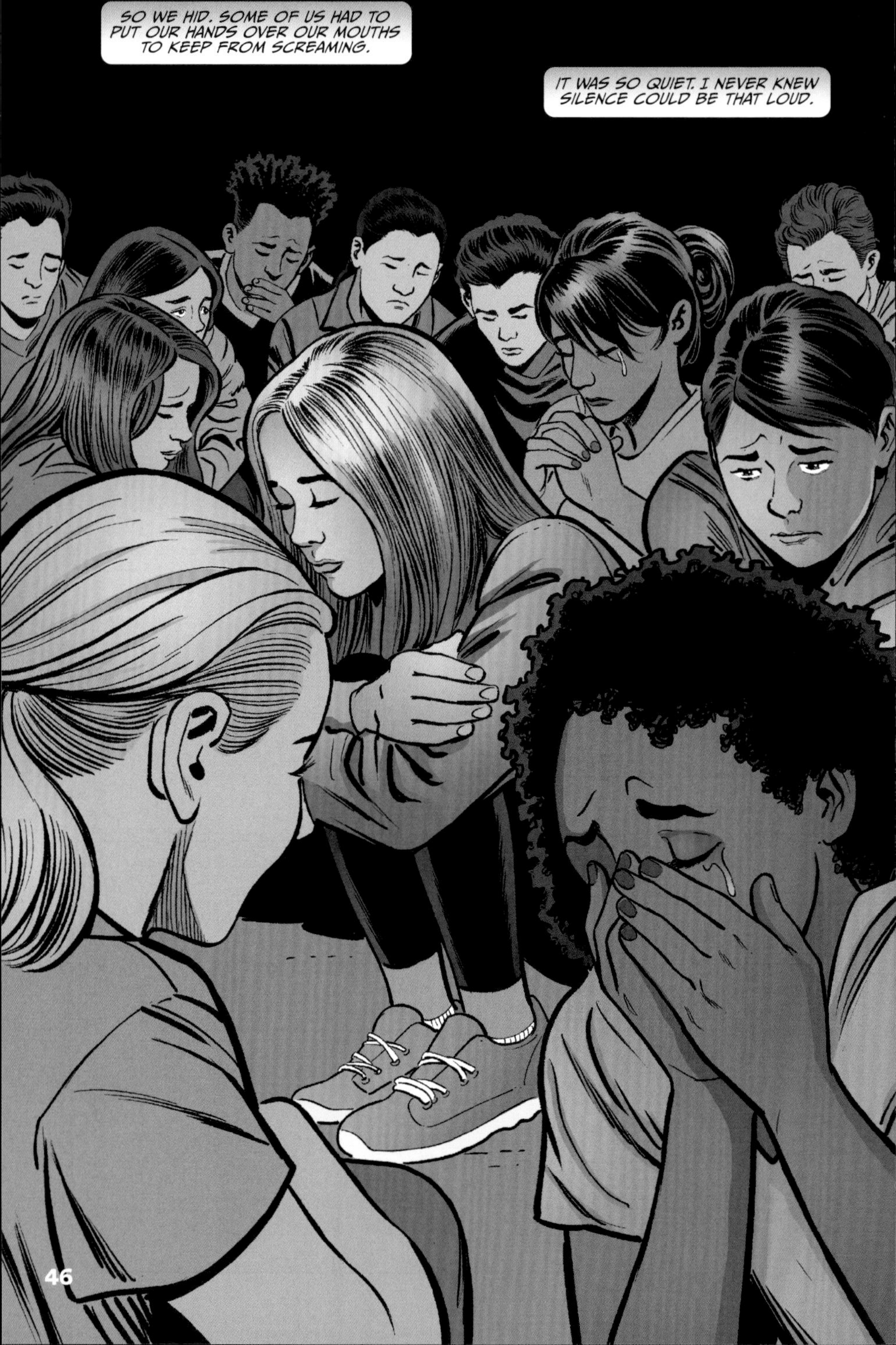
SO WE HID. SOME OF US HAD TO PUT OUR HANDS OVER OUR MOUTHS TO KEEP FROM SCREAMING.
IT WAS SO QUIET. I NEVER KNEW SILENCE COULD BE THAT LOUD.

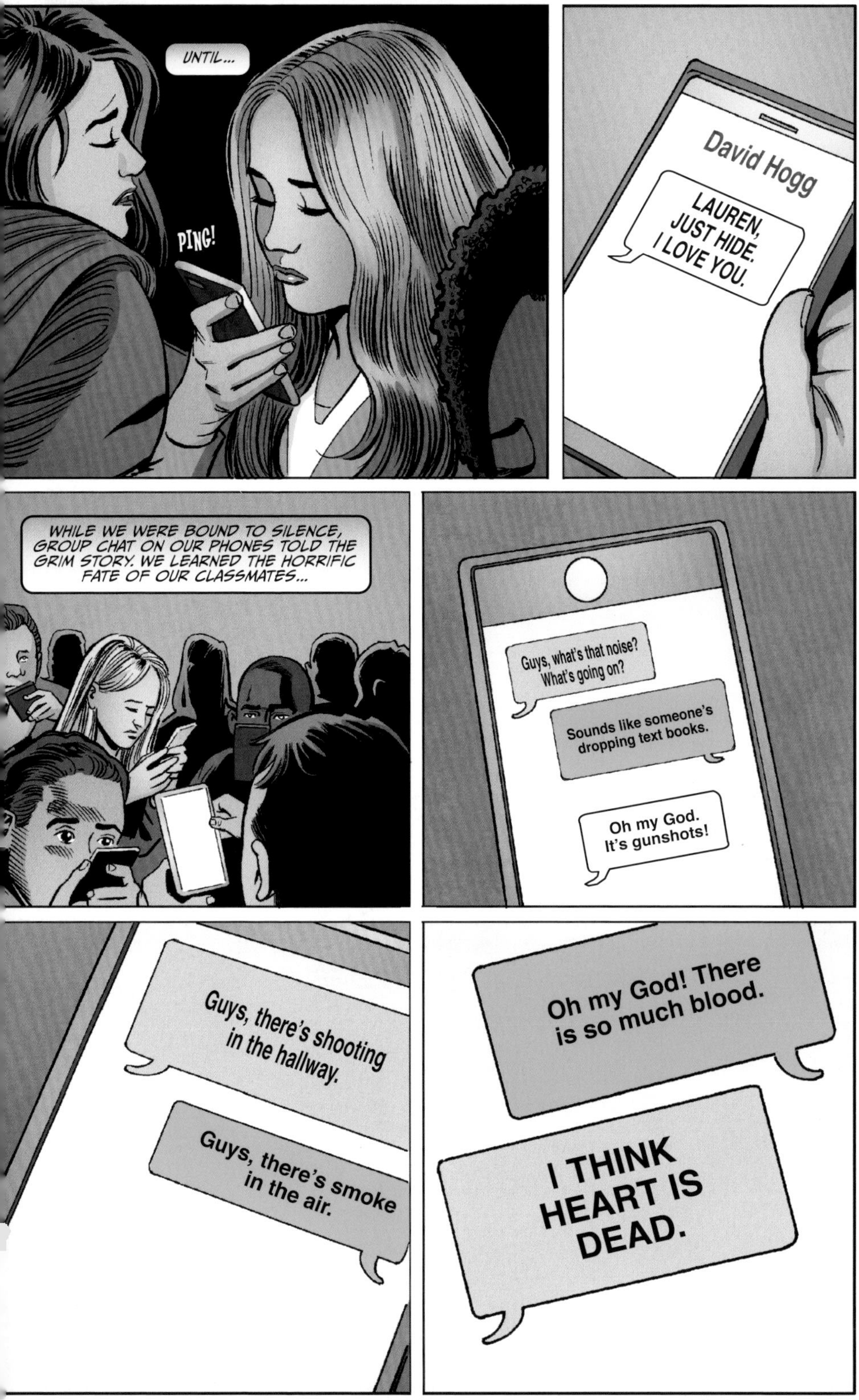

UNTIL...
PING!
David Hogg
LAUREN, JUST HIDE. I LOVE YOU.
WHILE WE WERE BOUND TO SILENCE, GROUP CHAT ON OUR PHONES TOLD THE GRIM STORY. WE LEARNED THE HORRIFIC FATE OF OUR CLASSMATES...
Guys, what's that noise? What's going on?
Sounds like someone's dropping text books.
Oh my God. It's gunshots!
Guys, there's shooting in the hallway.
Guys, there's smoke in the air.
Oh my God! There is so much blood.
I THINK HEART IS DEAD.

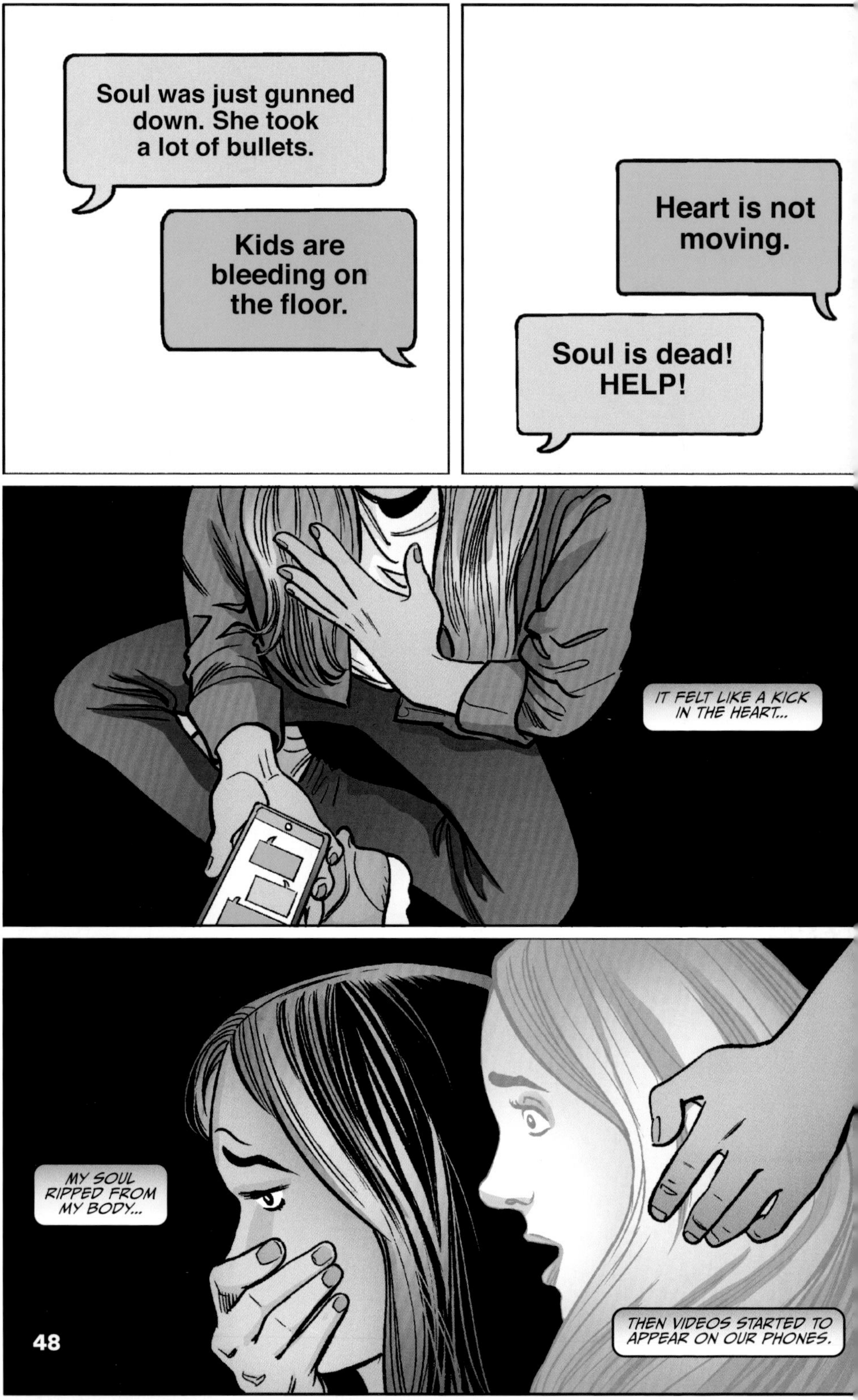
Soul was just gunned down. She took a lot of bullets.
Kids are bleeding on the floor.
Heart is not moving.
Soul is dead! HELP!
IT FELT LIKE A KICK IN THE HEART...
MY SOUL RIPPED FROM MY BODY...
THEN VIDEOS STARTED TO APPEAR ON OUR PHONES.

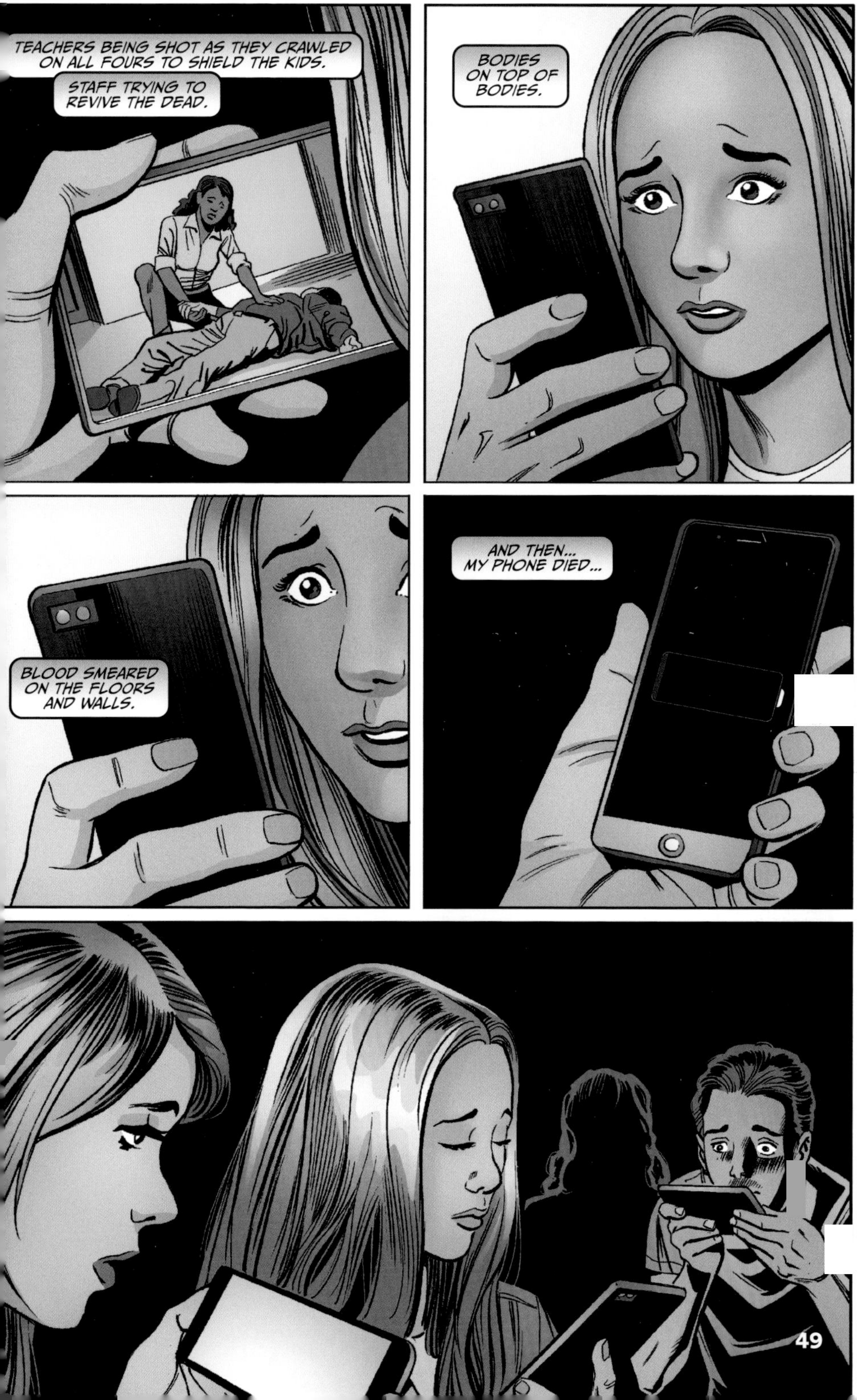
TEACHERS BEING SHOT AS THEY CRAWLED ON ALL FOURS TO SHIELD THE KIDS.
STAFF TRYING TO REVIVE THE DEAD.
BODIES ON TOP OF BODIES.
BLOOD SMEARED ON THE FLOORS AND WALLS.
AND THEN... MY PHONE DIED...

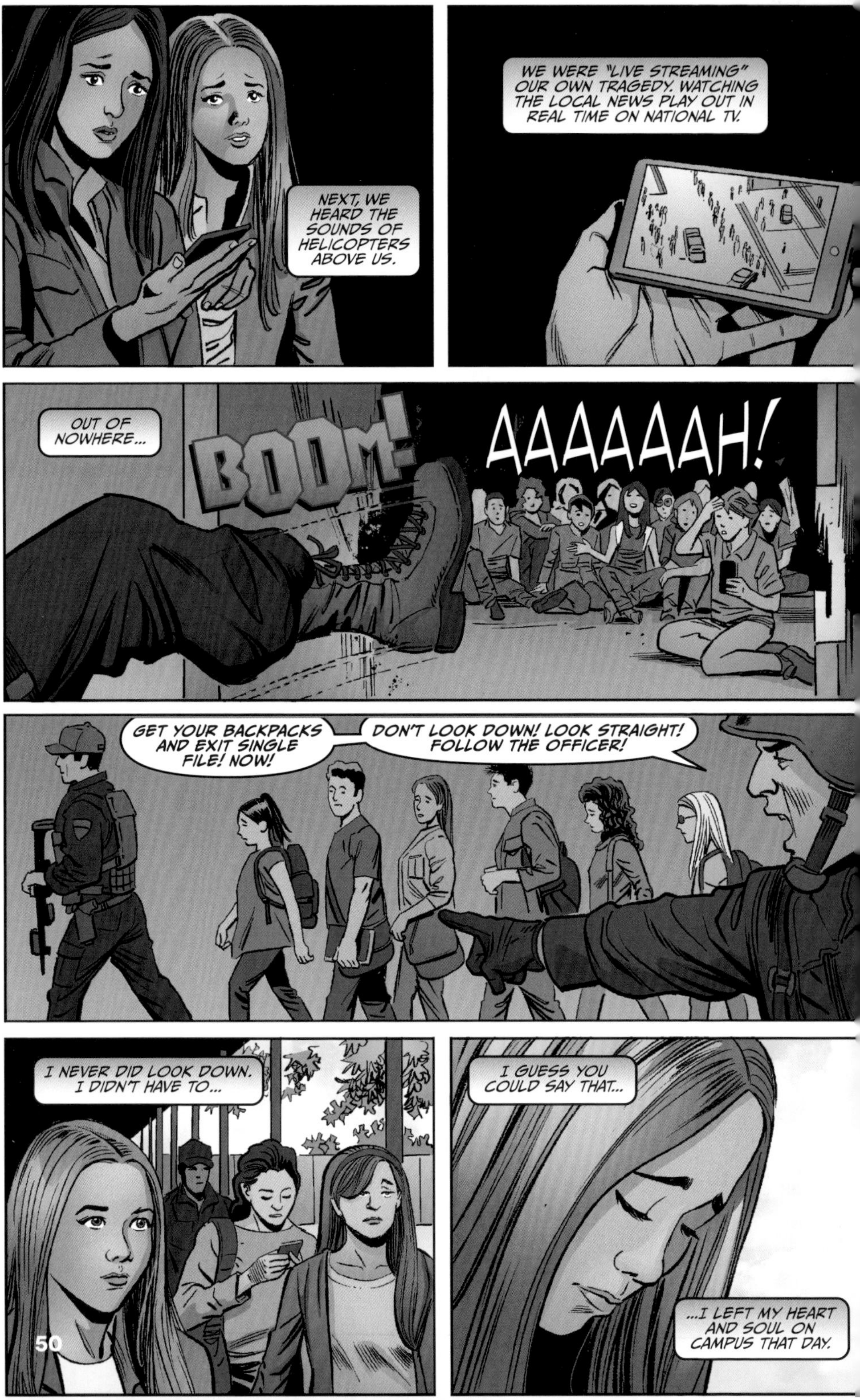
NEXT, WE HEARD THE SOUNDS OF HELICOPTERS ABOVE US.
WE WERE "LIVE STREAMING" OUR OWN TRAGEDY. WATCHING THE LOCAL NEWS PLAY OUT IN REAL TIME ON NATIONAL TV.
OUT OF NOWHERE...
BOOM!
AAAAAAH!
GET YOUR BACKPACKS AND EXIT SINGLE FILE! NOW!
DON'T LOOK DOWN! LOOK STRAIGHT! FOLLOW THE OFFICER!
I NEVER DID LOOK DOWN. I DIDN'T HAVE TO...
I GUESS YOU COULD SAY THAT...
...I LEFT MY HEART AND SOUL ON CAMPUS THAT DAY.

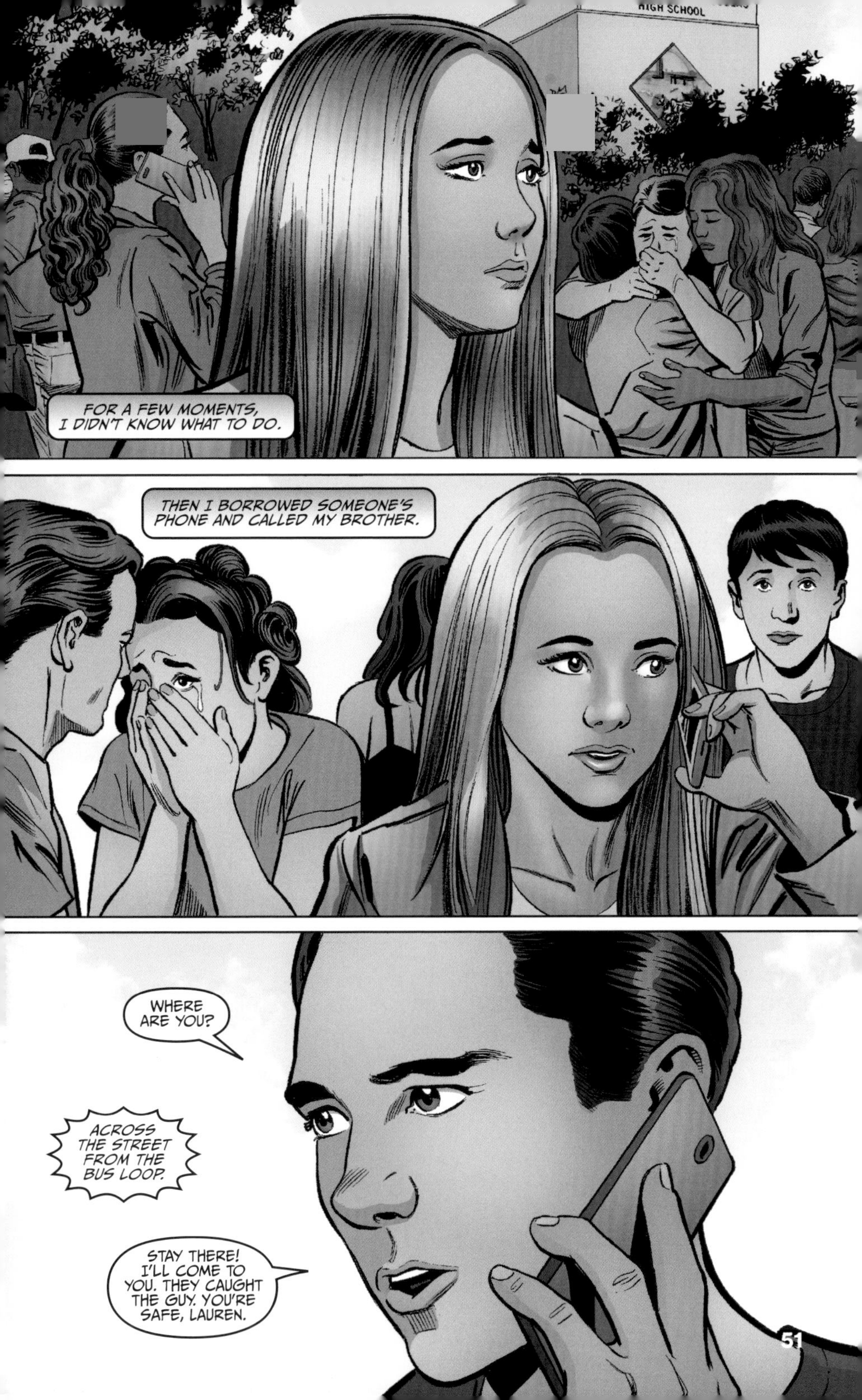
HIGH SCHOOL
FOR A FEW MOMENTS, I DIDN'T KNOW WHAT TO DO.
THEN I BORROWED SOMEONE'S PHONE AND CALLED MY BROTHER.
WHERE ARE YOU?
ACROSS THE STREET FROM THE BUS LOOP.
STAY THERE! I'LL COME TO YOU. THEY CAUGHT THE GUY. YOU'RE SAFE, LAUREN.

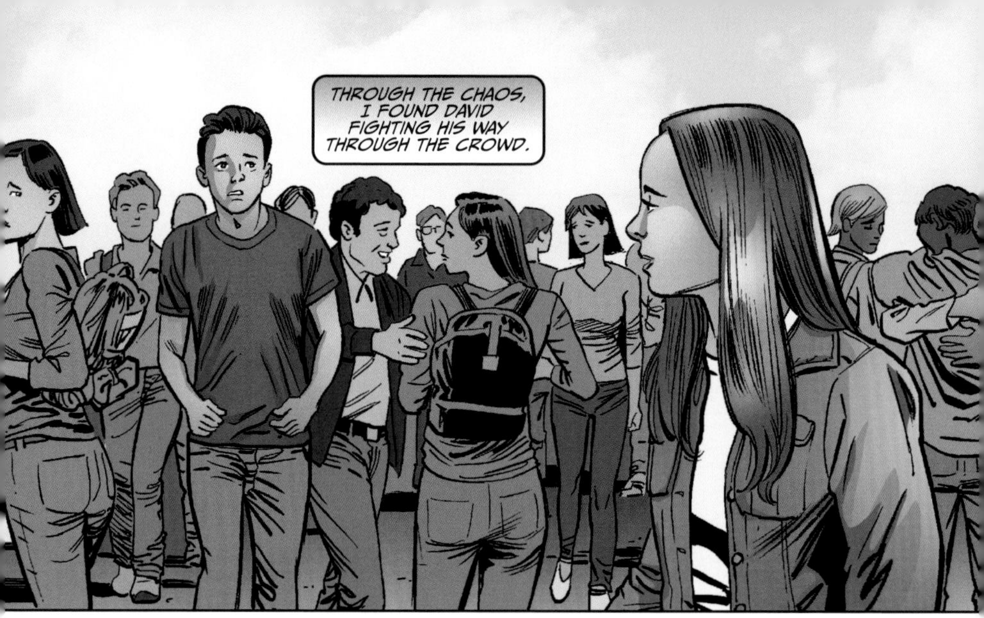
THROUGH THE CHAOS, I FOUND DAVID FIGHTING HIS WAY THROUGH THE CROWD.

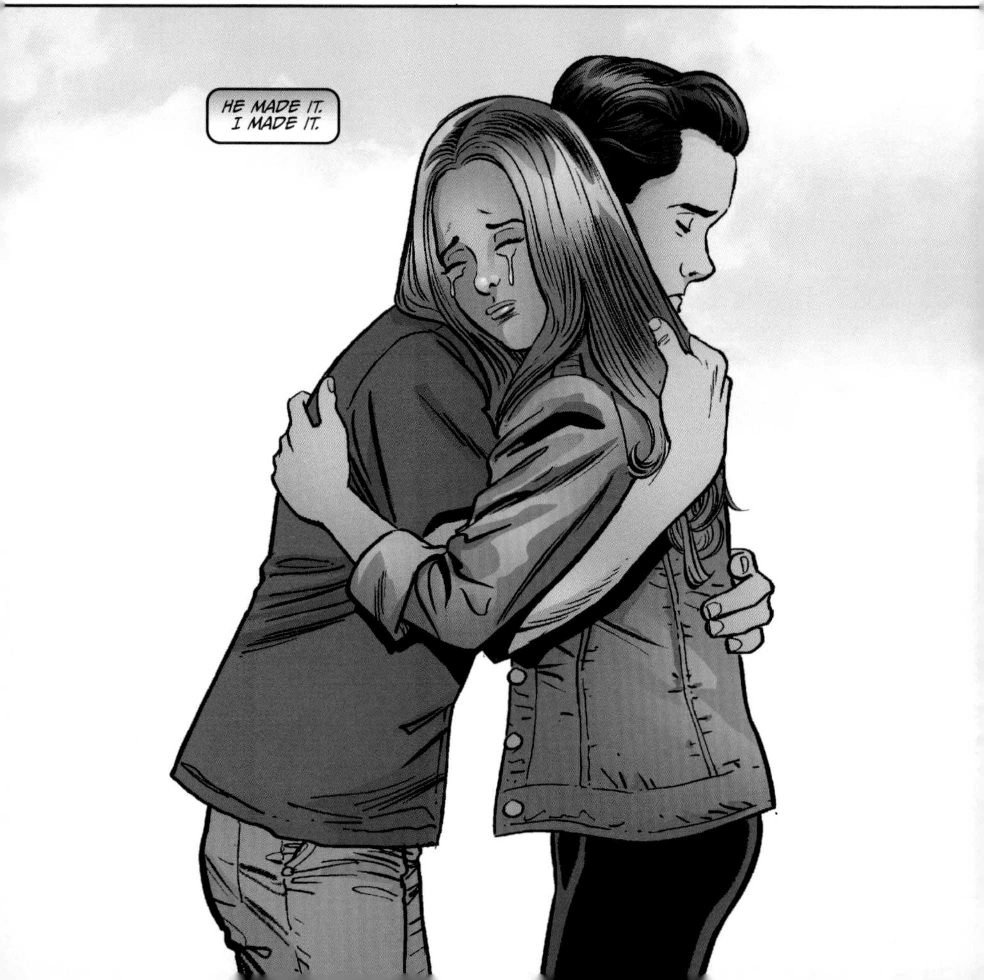
HE MADE IT. I MADE IT.

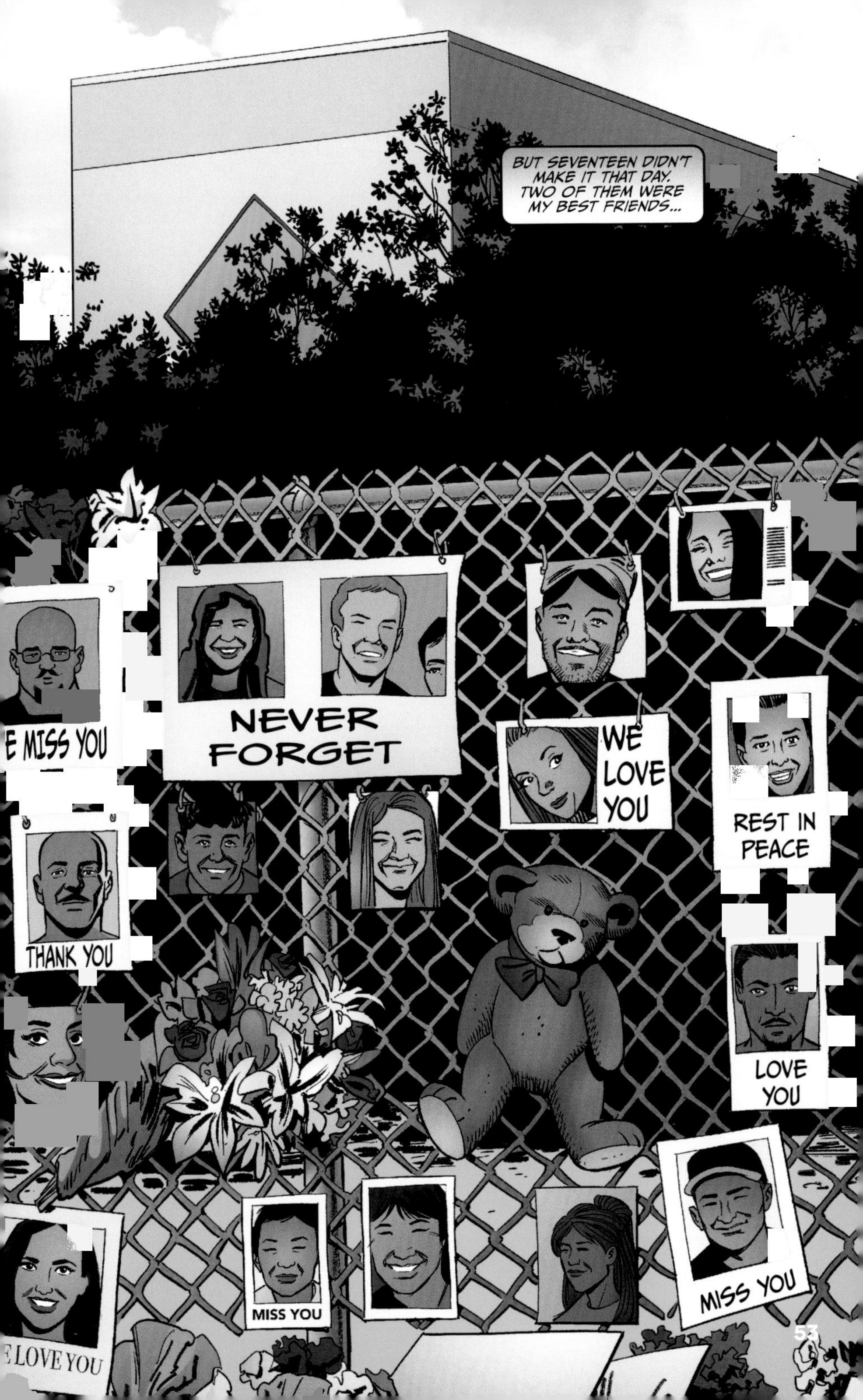
BUT SEVENTEEN DIDN'T MAKE IT THAT DAY. TWO OF THEM WERE MY BEST FRIENDS...
E MISS YOU
NEVER FORGET
WE LOVE YOU
REST IN PEACE
THANK YOU
LOVE YOU
MISS YOU
MISS YOU
E LOVE YOU

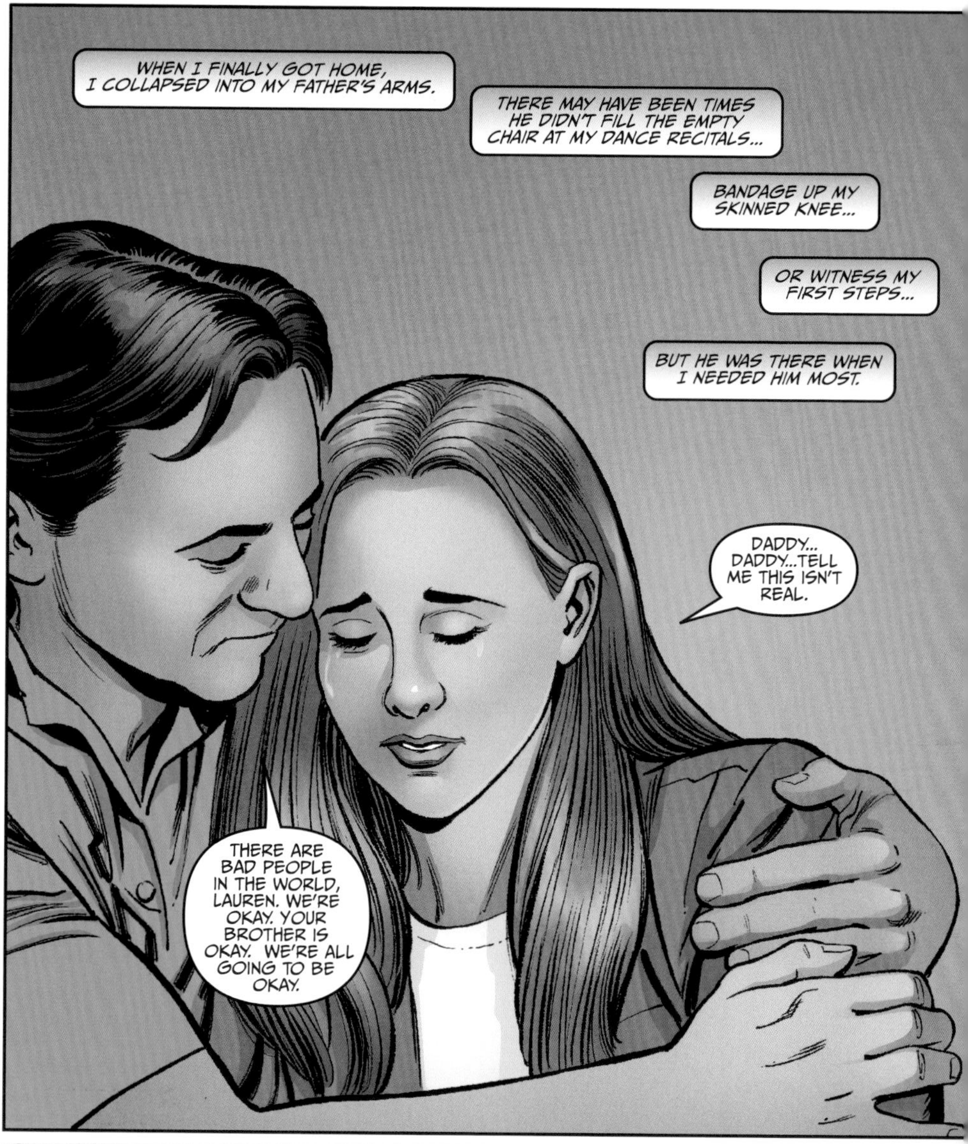
WHEN I FINALLY GOT HOME, I COLLAPSED INTO MY FATHER'S ARMS.
THERE MAY HAVE BEEN TIMES HE DIDN'T FILL THE EMPTY CHAIR AT MY DANCE RECITALS...
BANDAGE UP MY SKINNED KNEE...
OR WITNESS MY FIRST STEPS...
BUT HE WAS THERE WHEN I NEEDED HIM MOST.
DADDY... DADDY...TELL ME THIS ISN'T REAL.
THERE ARE BAD PEOPLE IN THE WORLD, LAUREN. WE'RE OKAY. YOUR BROTHER IS OKAY. WE'RE ALL GOING TO BE OKAY.
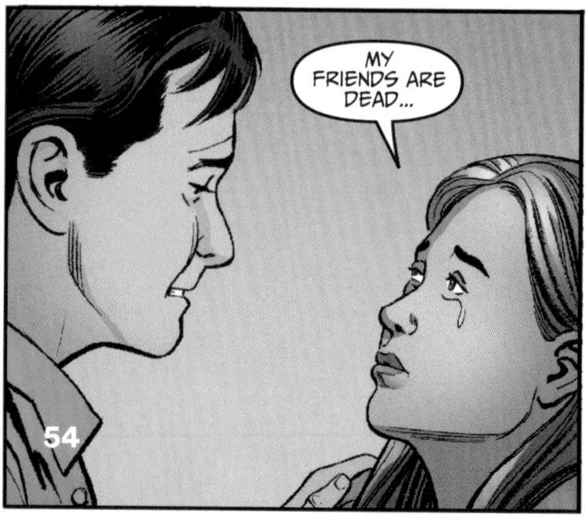
MY FRIENDS ARE DEAD...
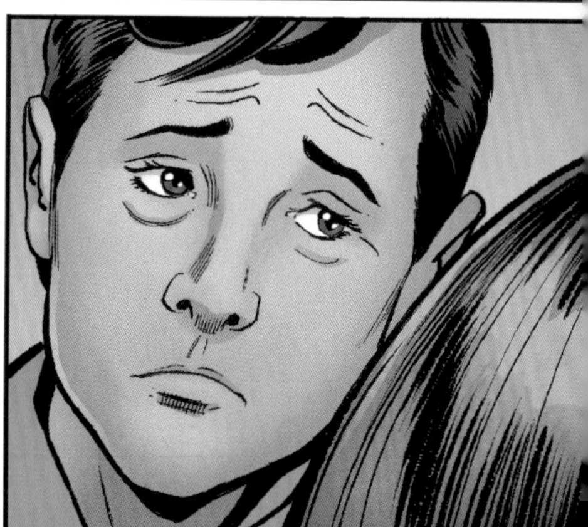

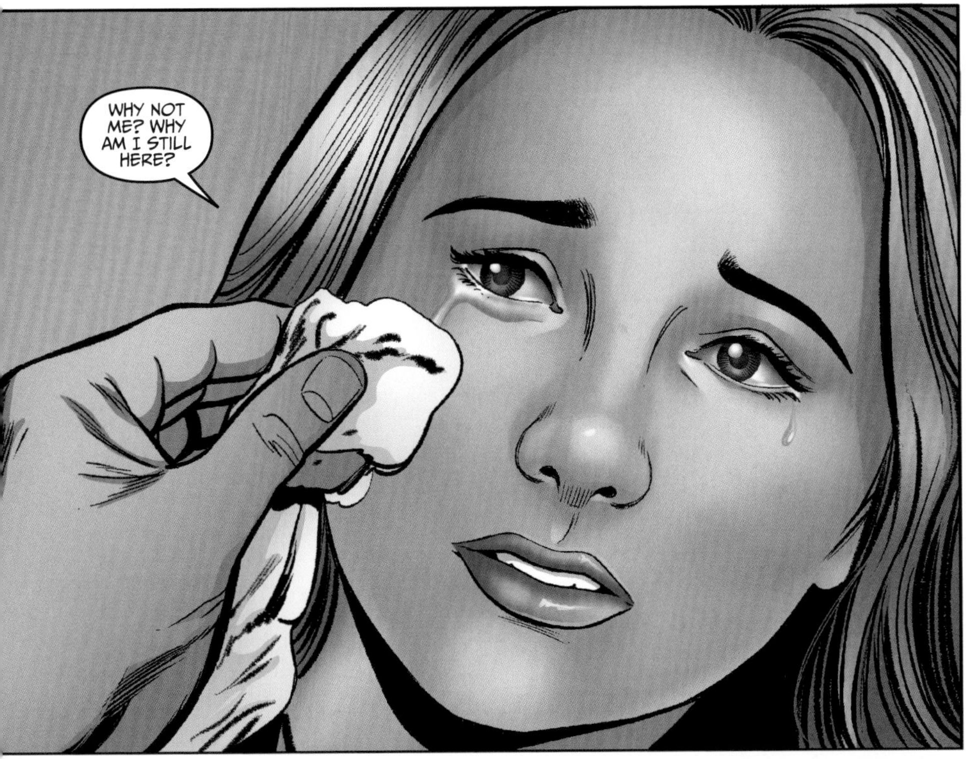
WHY NOT ME? WHY AM I STILL HERE?

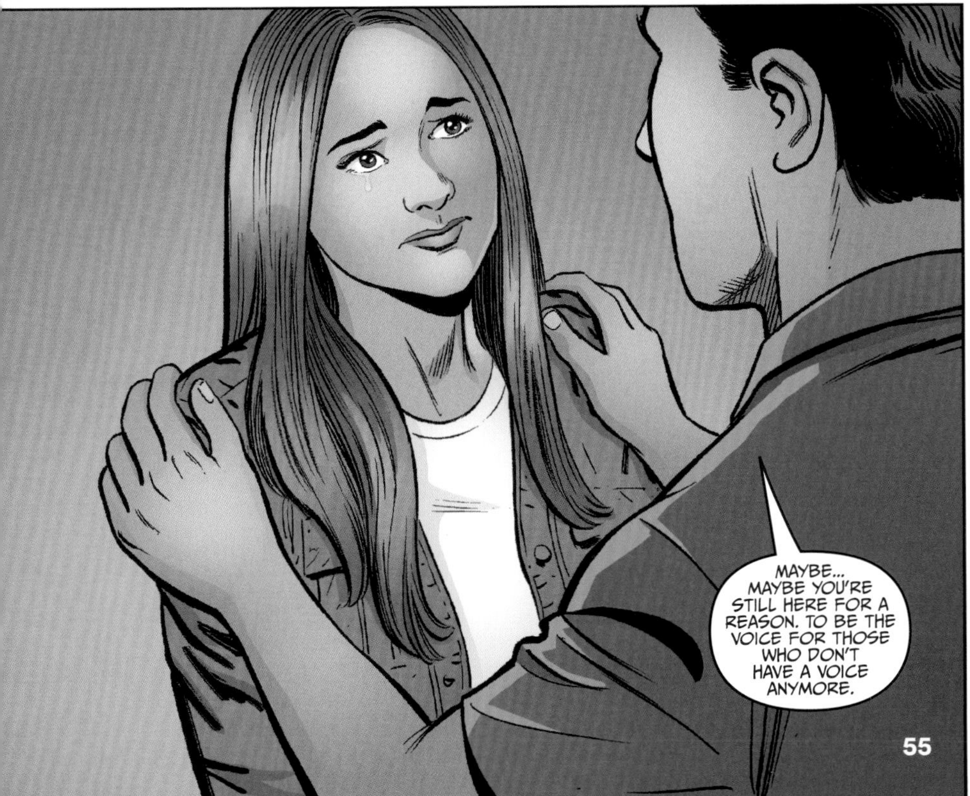
MAYBE... MAYBE YOU'RE STILL HERE FOR A REASON. TO BE THE VOICE FOR THOSE WHO DON'T HAVE A VOICE ANYMORE.

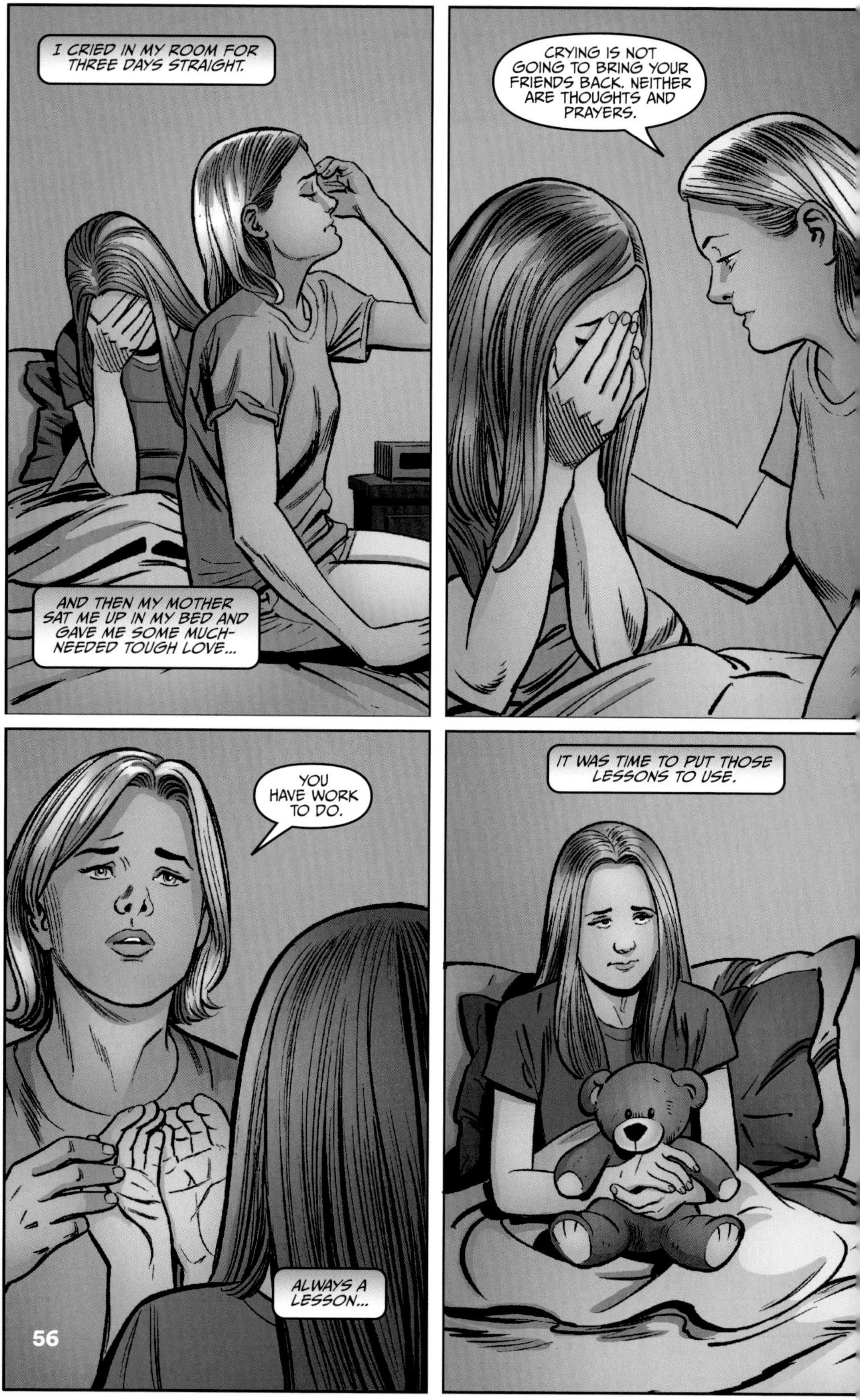
I CRIED IN MY ROOM FOR THREE DAYS STRAIGHT.
AND THEN MY MOTHER SAT ME UP IN MY BED AND GAVE ME SOME MUCH-NEEDED TOUGH LOVE...
CRYING IS NOT GOING TO BRING YOUR FRIENDS BACK. NEITHER ARE THOUGHTS AND PRAYERS.
YOU HAVE WORK TO DO.
ALWAYS A LESSON...
IT WAS TIME TO PUT THOSE LESSONS TO USE.

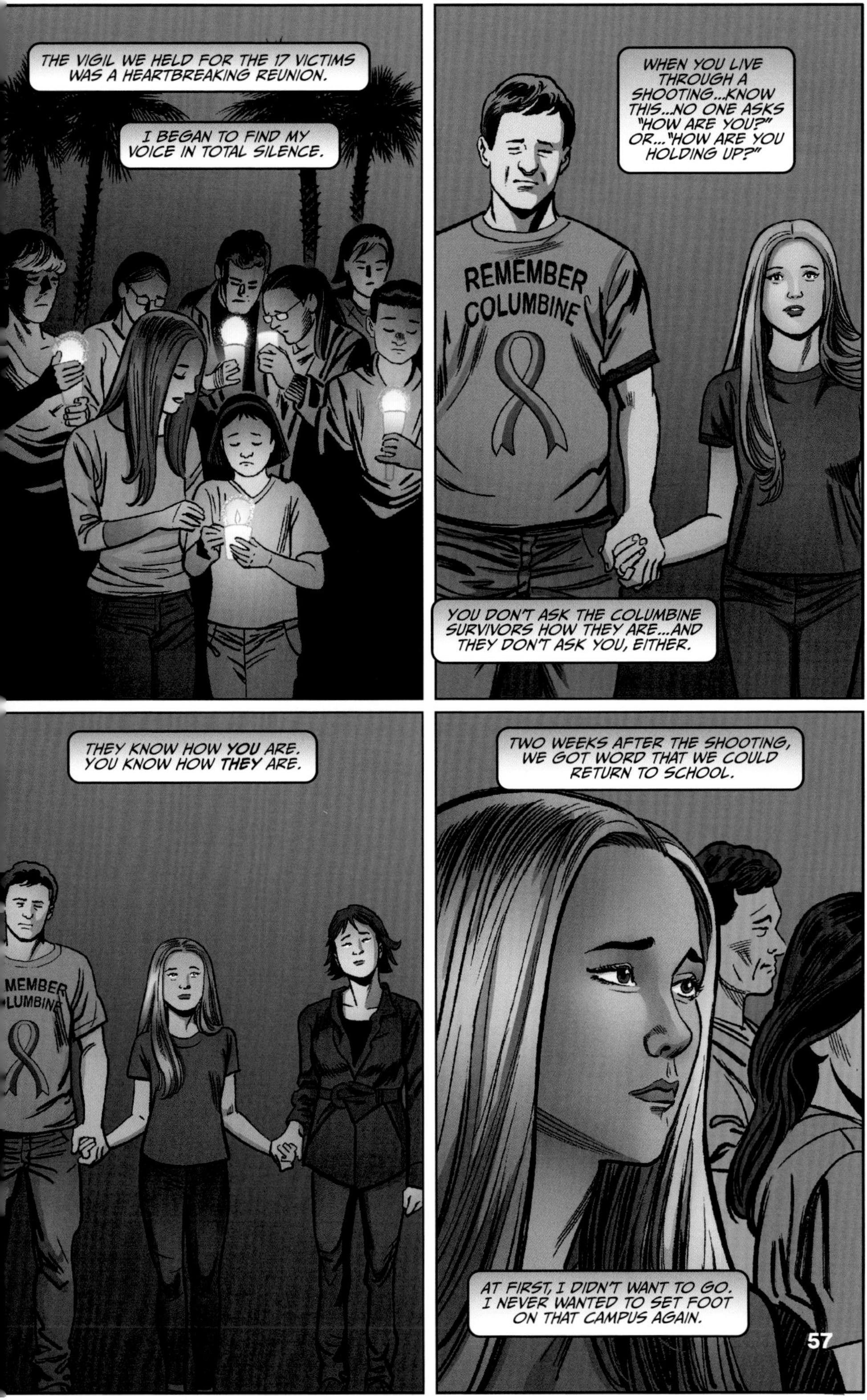
THE VIGIL WE HELD FOR THE 17 VICTIMS WAS A HEARTBREAKING REUNION.
I BEGAN TO FIND MY VOICE IN TOTAL SILENCE.
WHEN YOU LIVE THROUGH A SHOOTING...KNOW THIS...NO ONE ASKS "HOW ARE YOU?" OR..."HOW ARE YOU HOLDING UP?"
REMEMBER COLUMBINE
YOU DON'T ASK THE COLUMBINE SURVIVORS HOW THEY ARE...AND THEY DON'T ASK YOU, EITHER.
THEY KNOW HOW **YOU** ARE. YOU KNOW HOW **THEY** ARE.
MEMBER LUMBINE
TWO WEEKS AFTER THE SHOOTING, WE GOT WORD THAT WE COULD RETURN TO SCHOOL.
AT FIRST, I DIDN'T WANT TO GO. I NEVER WANTED TO SET FOOT ON THAT CAMPUS AGAIN.

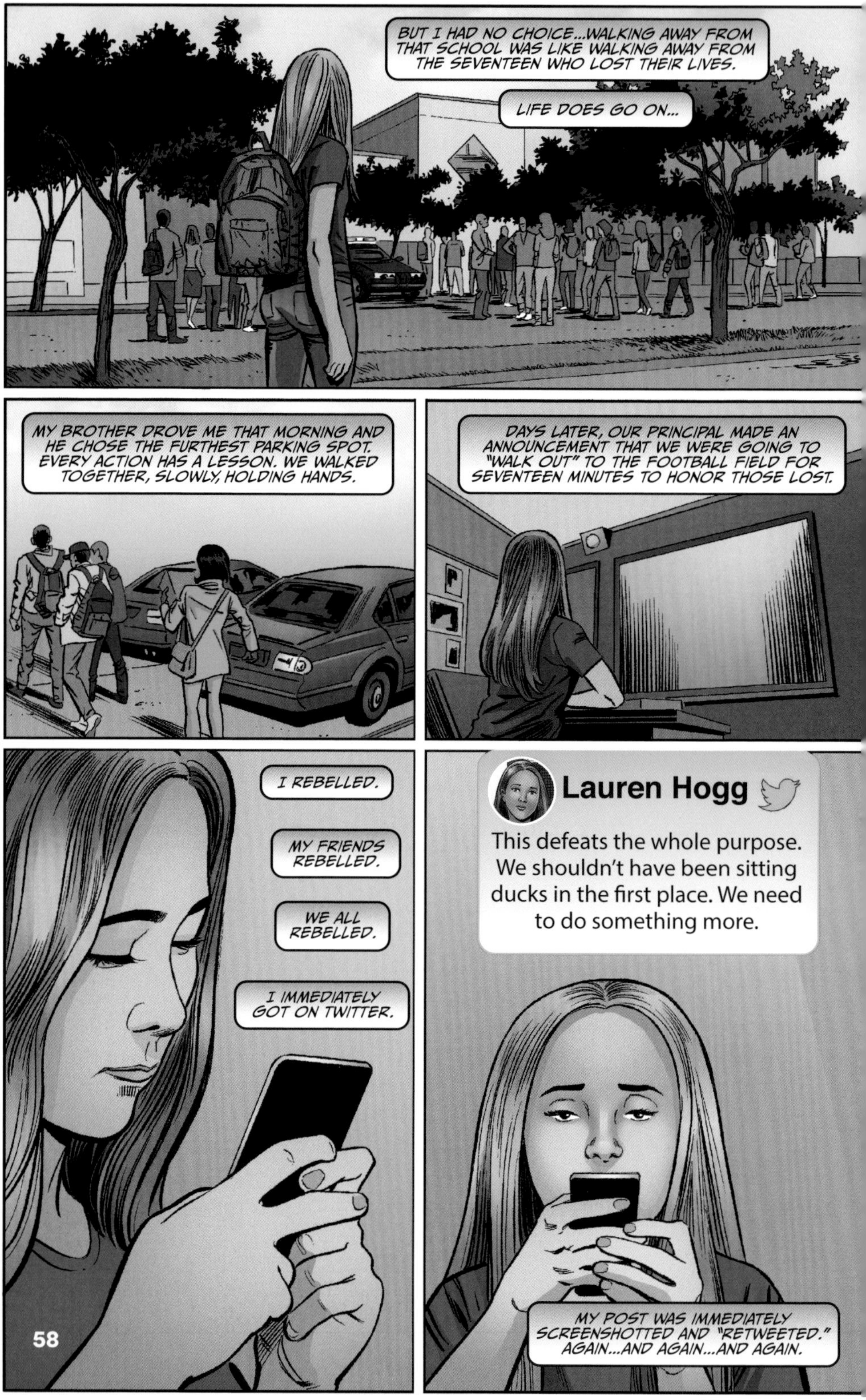
BUT I HAD NO CHOICE...WALKING AWAY FROM THAT SCHOOL WAS LIKE WALKING AWAY FROM THE SEVENTEEN WHO LOST THEIR LIVES.
LIFE DOES GO ON...
MY BROTHER DROVE ME THAT MORNING AND HE CHOSE THE FURTHEST PARKING SPOT. EVERY ACTION HAS A LESSON. WE WALKED TOGETHER, SLOWLY, HOLDING HANDS.
DAYS LATER, OUR PRINCIPAL MADE AN ANNOUNCEMENT THAT WE WERE GOING TO "WALK OUT" TO THE FOOTBALL FIELD FOR SEVENTEEN MINUTES TO HONOR THOSE LOST.
I REBELLED.
MY FRIENDS REBELLED.
WE ALL REBELLED.
I IMMEDIATELY GOT ON TWITTER.
Lauren Hogg
This defeats the whole purpose. We shouldn't have been sitting ducks in the first place. We need to do something more.
MY POST WAS IMMEDIATELY SCREENSHOTTED AND "RETWEETED." AGAIN...AND AGAIN...AND AGAIN.

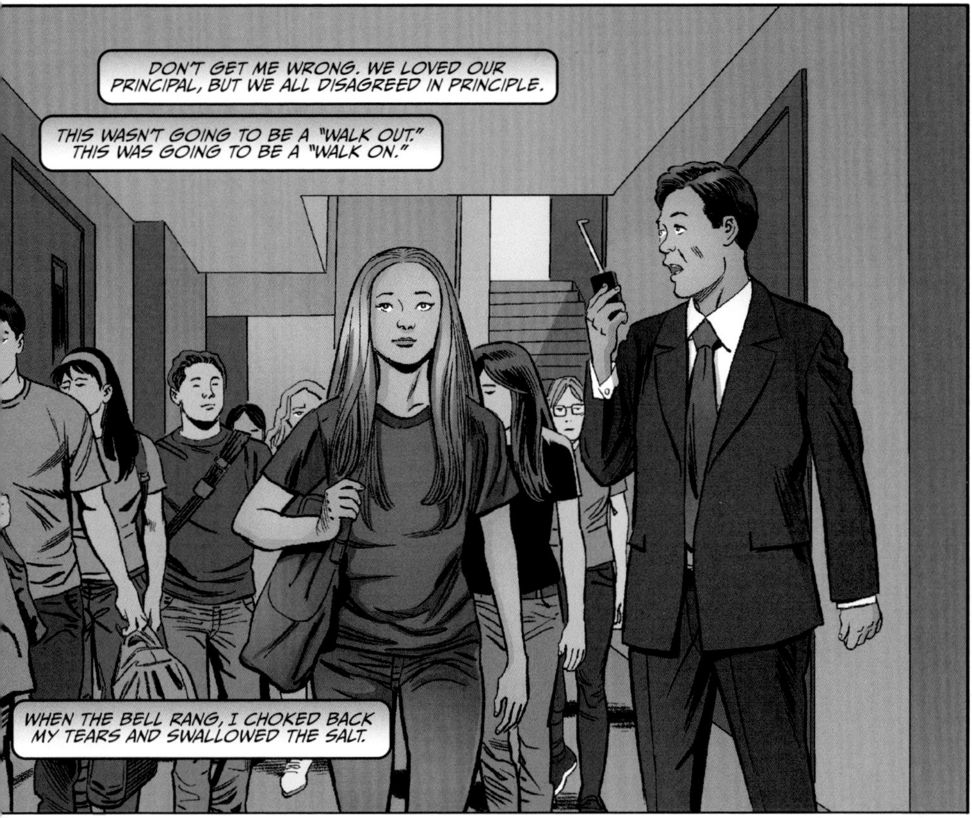
DON'T GET ME WRONG. WE LOVED OUR PRINCIPAL, BUT WE ALL DISAGREED IN PRINCIPLE.
THIS WASN'T GOING TO BE A "WALK OUT." THIS WAS GOING TO BE A "WALK ON."
WHEN THE BELL RANG, I CHOKED BACK MY TEARS AND SWALLOWED THE SALT.

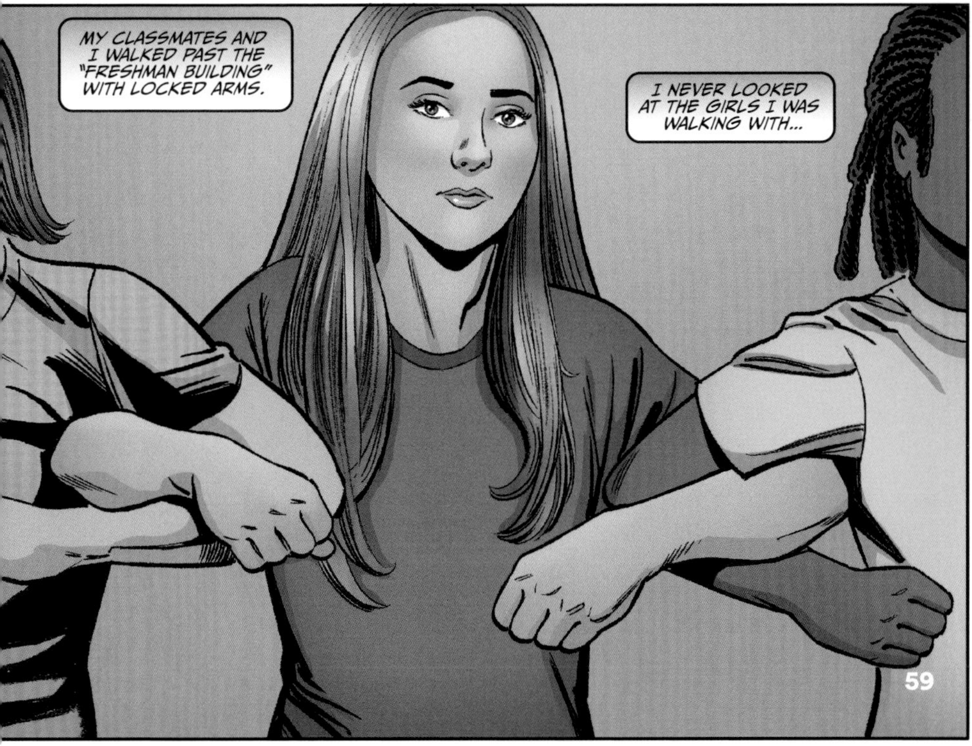
MY CLASSMATES AND I WALKED PAST THE "FRESHMAN BUILDING" WITH LOCKED ARMS.
I NEVER LOOKED AT THE GIRLS I WAS WALKING WITH...

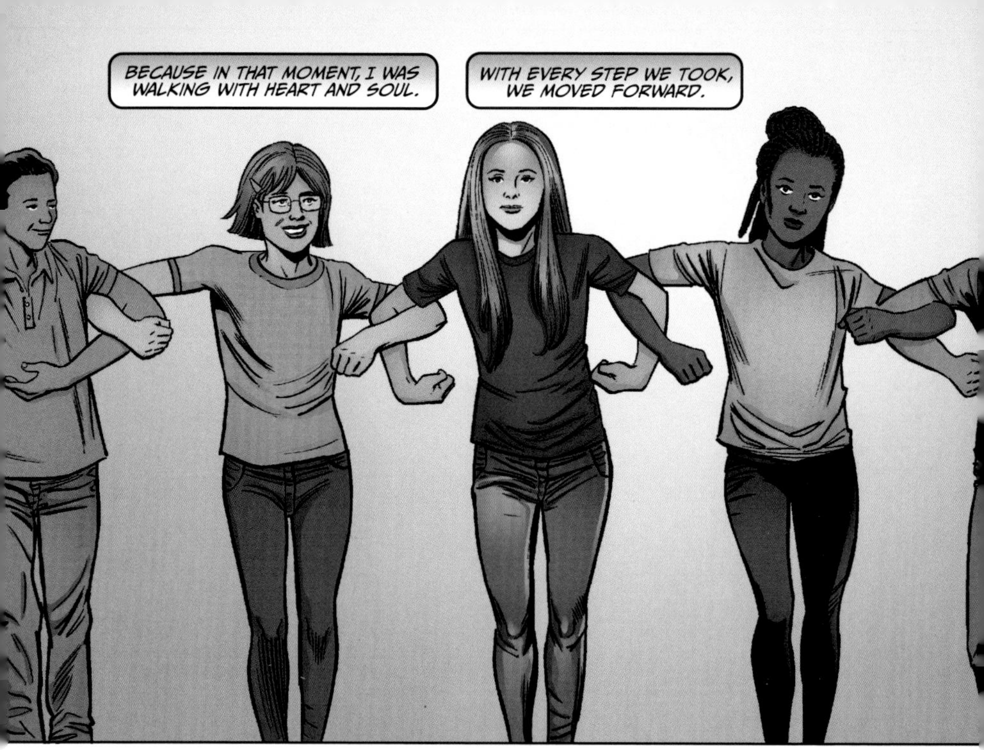
BECAUSE IN THAT MOMENT, I WAS WALKING WITH HEART AND SOUL.
WITH EVERY STEP WE TOOK, WE MOVED FORWARD.

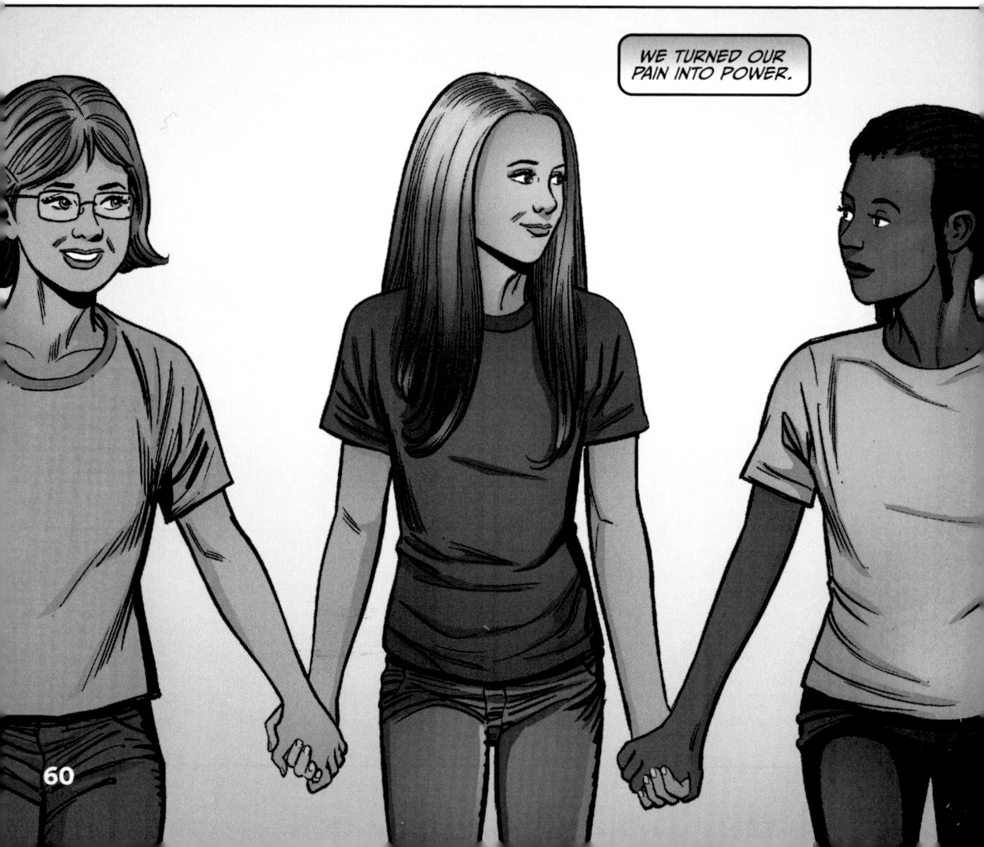
WE TURNED OUR PAIN INTO POWER.

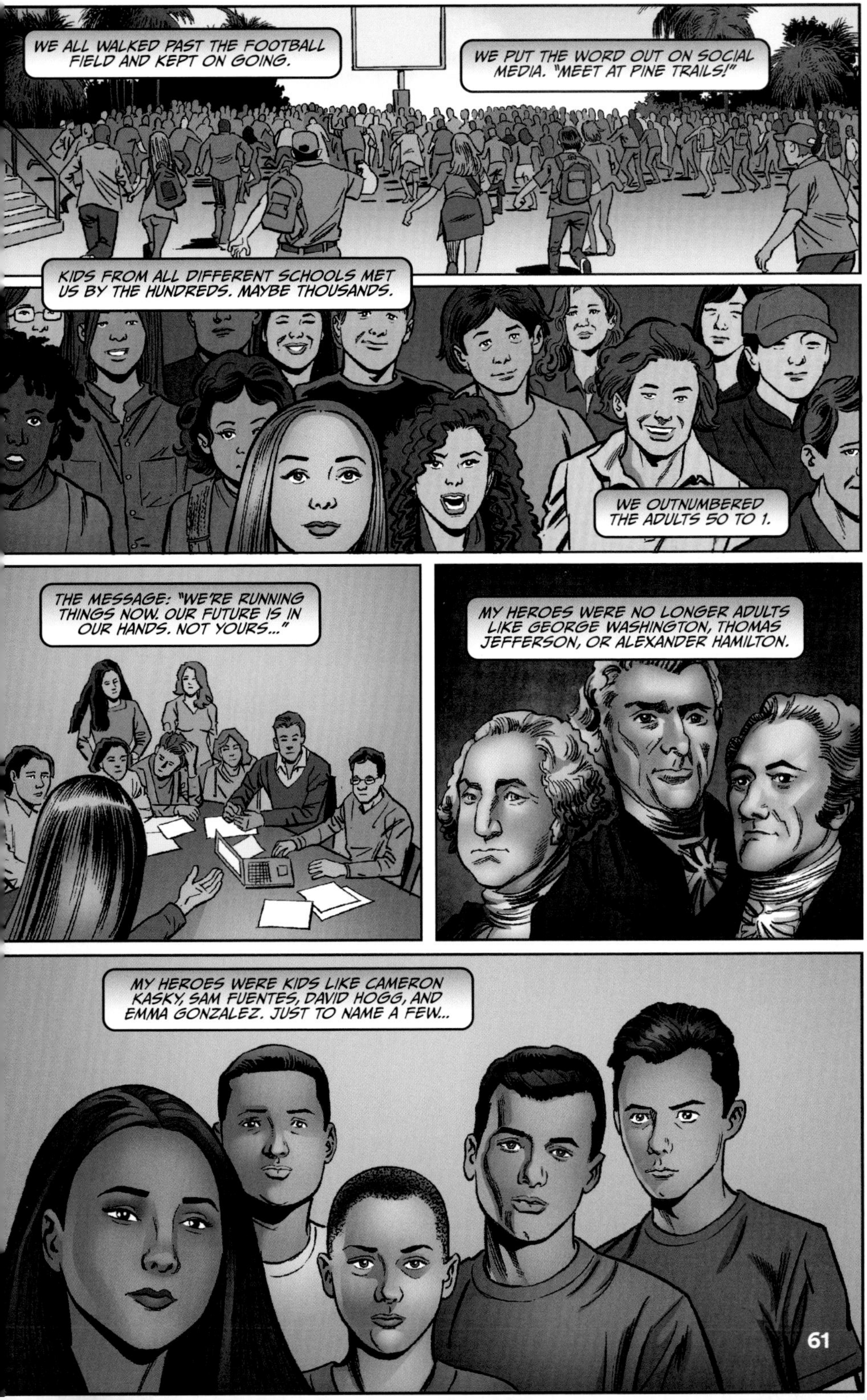
WE ALL WALKED PAST THE FOOTBALL FIELD AND KEPT ON GOING.
WE PUT THE WORD OUT ON SOCIAL MEDIA. "MEET AT PINE TRAILS!"
KIDS FROM ALL DIFFERENT SCHOOLS MET US BY THE HUNDREDS. MAYBE THOUSANDS.
WE OUTNUMBERED THE ADULTS 50 TO 1.
THE MESSAGE: "WE'RE RUNNING THINGS NOW. OUR FUTURE IS IN OUR HANDS. NOT YOURS..."
MY HEROES WERE NO LONGER ADULTS LIKE GEORGE WASHINGTON, THOMAS JEFFERSON, OR ALEXANDER HAMILTON.
MY HEROES WERE KIDS LIKE CAMERON KASKY, SAM FUENTES, DAVID HOGG, AND EMMA GONZALEZ. JUST TO NAME A FEW...

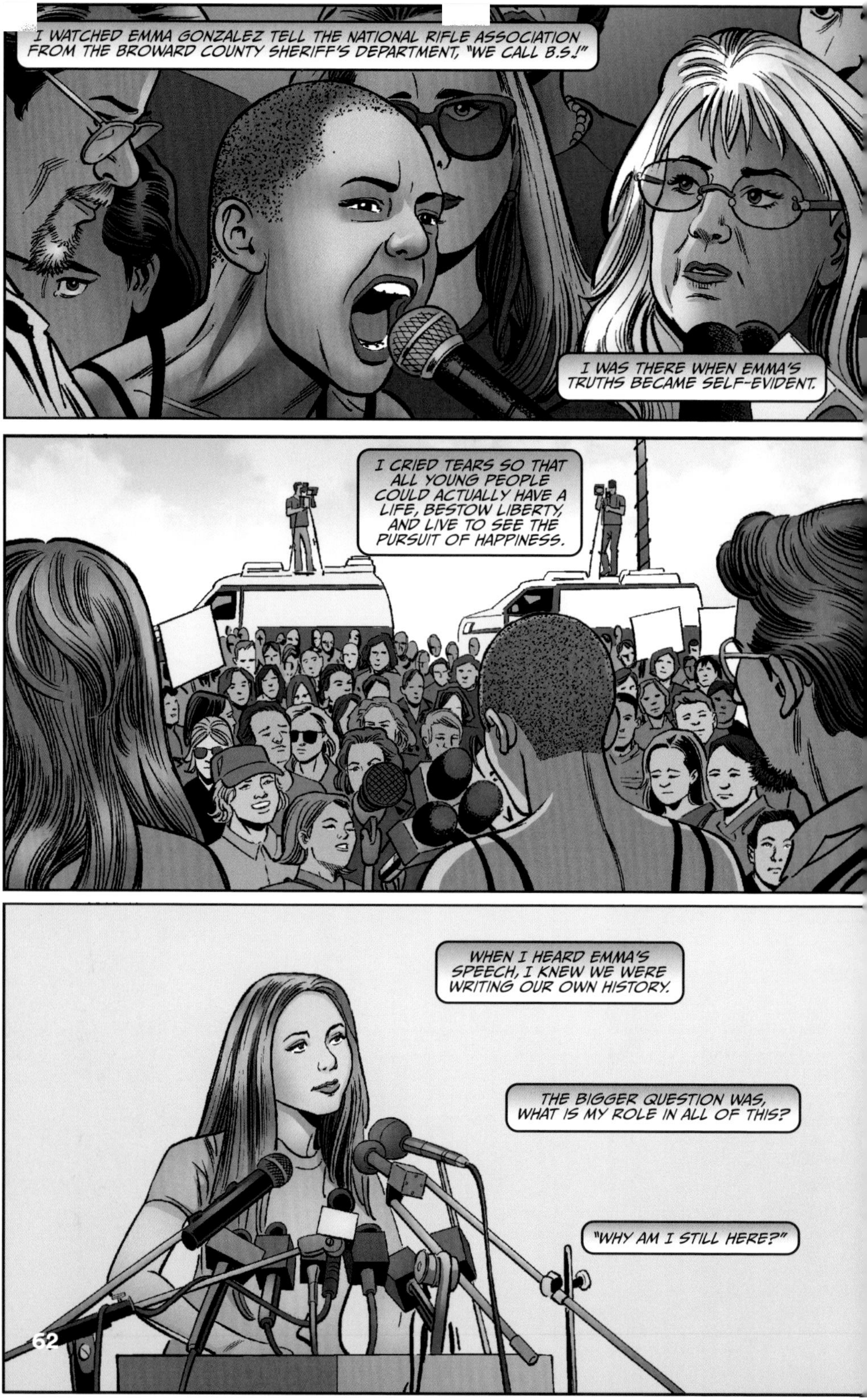
I WATCHED EMMA GONZALEZ TELL THE NATIONAL RIFLE ASSOCIATION FROM THE BROWARD COUNTY SHERIFF'S DEPARTMENT, "WE CALL B.S.!"
I WAS THERE WHEN EMMA'S TRUTHS BECAME SELF-EVIDENT.
I CRIED TEARS SO THAT ALL YOUNG PEOPLE COULD ACTUALLY HAVE A LIFE, BESTOW LIBERTY, AND LIVE TO SEE THE PURSUIT OF HAPPINESS.
WHEN I HEARD EMMA'S SPEECH, I KNEW WE WERE WRITING OUR OWN HISTORY.
THE BIGGER QUESTION WAS, WHAT IS MY ROLE IN ALL OF THIS?
"WHY AM I STILL HERE?"

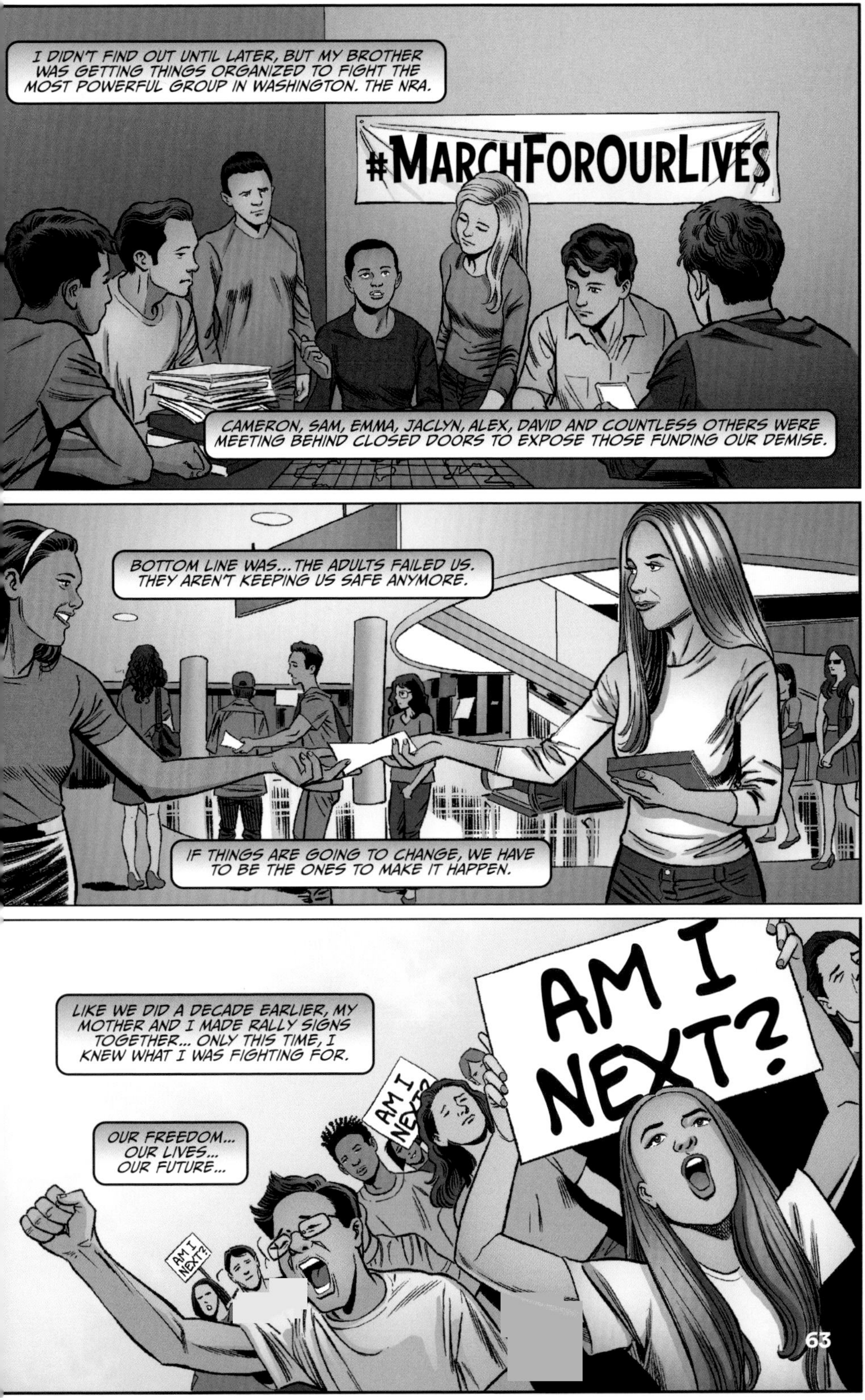
I DIDN'T FIND OUT UNTIL LATER, BUT MY BROTHER WAS GETTING THINGS ORGANIZED TO FIGHT THE MOST POWERFUL GROUP IN WASHINGTON. THE NRA.
#MARCHFOROURLIVES
CAMERON, SAM, EMMA, JACLYN, ALEX, DAVID AND COUNTLESS OTHERS WERE MEETING BEHIND CLOSED DOORS TO EXPOSE THOSE FUNDING OUR DEMISE.
BOTTOM LINE WAS... THE ADULTS FAILED US. THEY AREN'T KEEPING US SAFE ANYMORE.
IF THINGS ARE GOING TO CHANGE, WE HAVE TO BE THE ONES TO MAKE IT HAPPEN.
LIKE WE DID A DECADE EARLIER, MY MOTHER AND I MADE RALLY SIGNS TOGETHER... ONLY THIS TIME, I KNEW WHAT I WAS FIGHTING FOR.
AM I NEXT?
OUR FREEDOM... OUR LIVES... OUR FUTURE...
AM I NEXT?

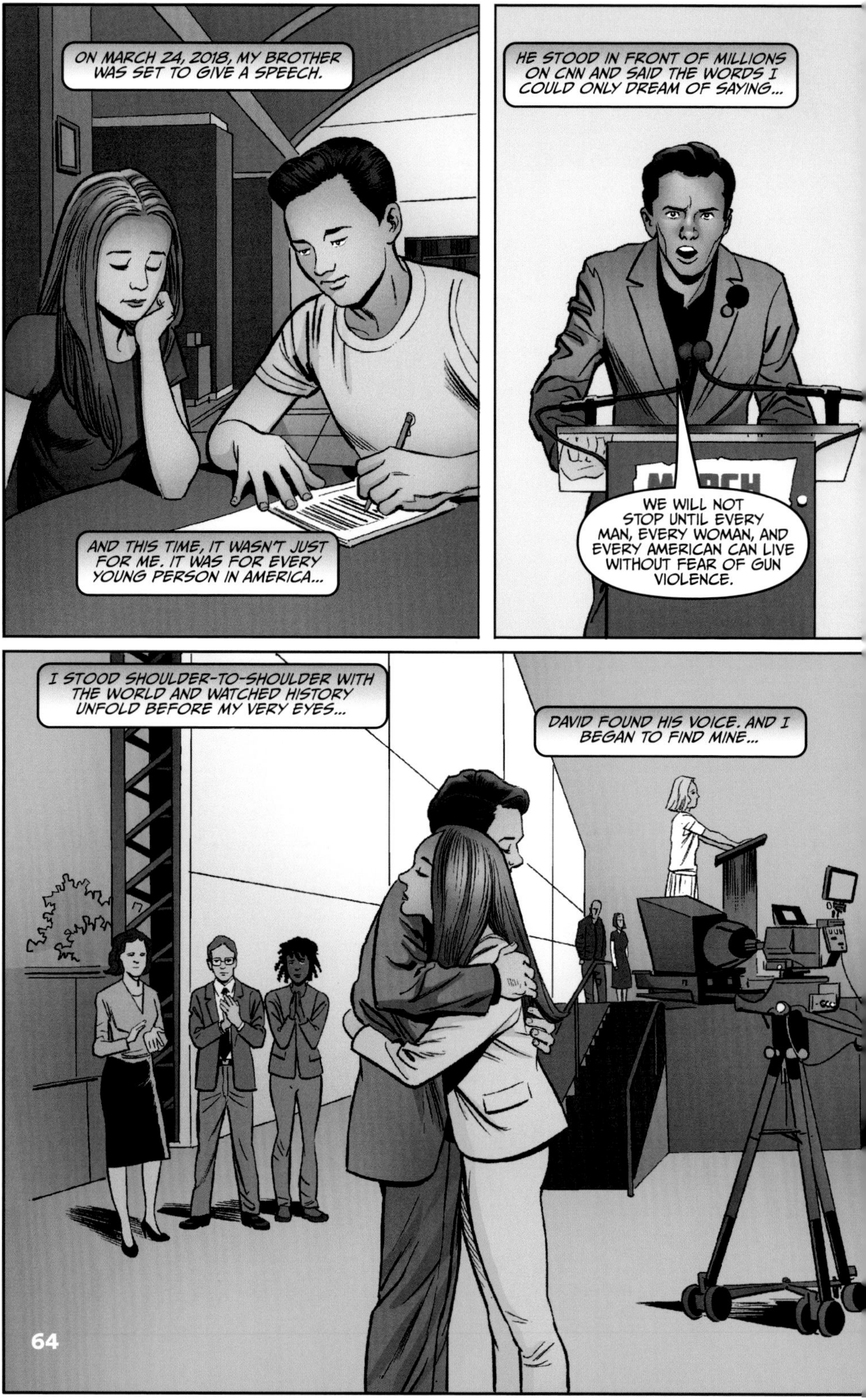
ON MARCH 24, 2018, MY BROTHER WAS SET TO GIVE A SPEECH.
AND THIS TIME, IT WASN'T JUST FOR ME. IT WAS FOR EVERY YOUNG PERSON IN AMERICA...
HE STOOD IN FRONT OF MILLIONS ON CNN AND SAID THE WORDS I COULD ONLY DREAM OF SAYING...
WE WILL NOT STOP UNTIL EVERY MAN, EVERY WOMAN, AND EVERY AMERICAN CAN LIVE WITHOUT FEAR OF GUN VIOLENCE.
I STOOD SHOULDER-TO-SHOULDER WITH THE WORLD AND WATCHED HISTORY UNFOLD BEFORE MY VERY EYES...
DAVID FOUND HIS VOICE. AND I BEGAN TO FIND MINE...

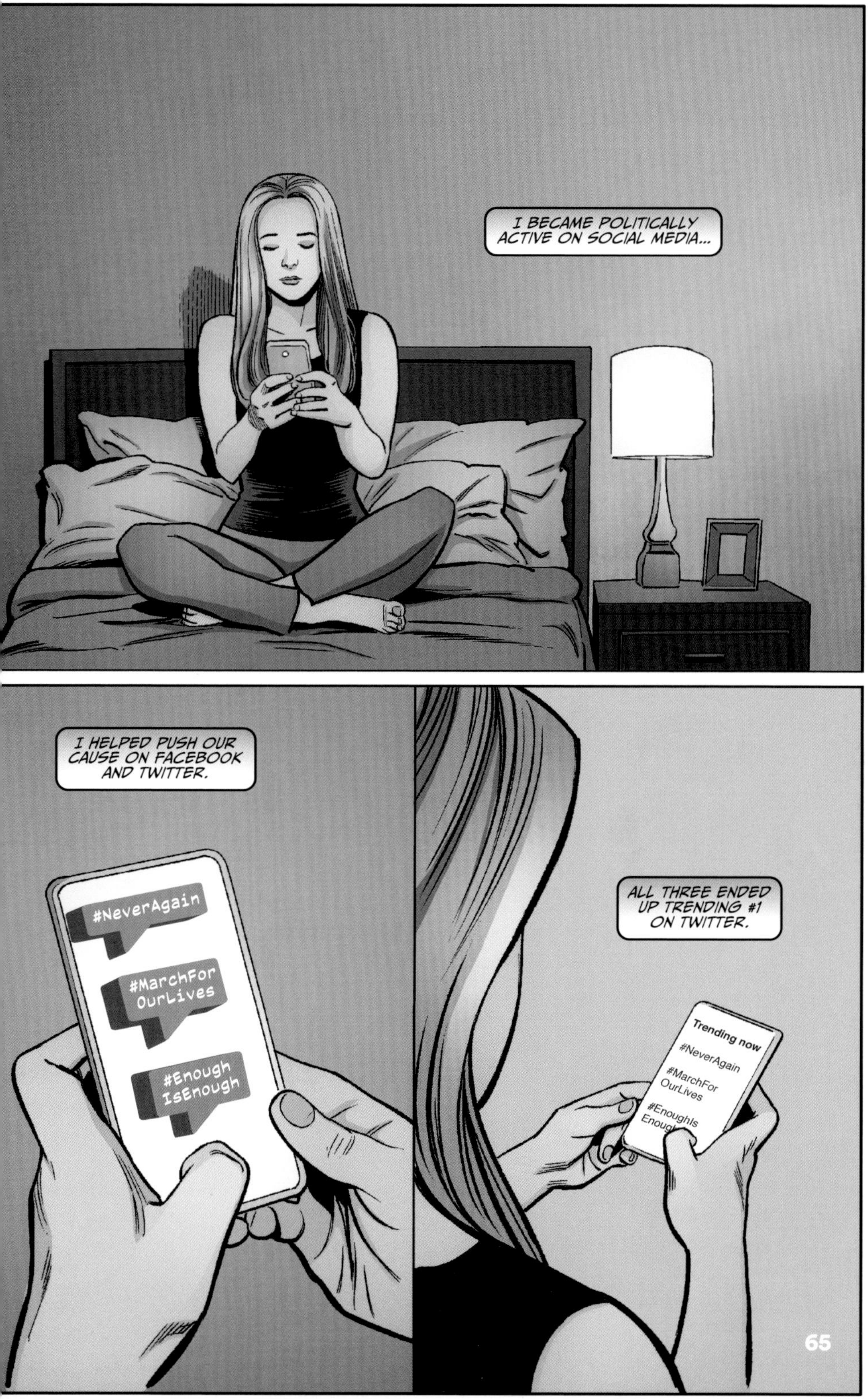
I BECAME POLITICALLY ACTIVE ON SOCIAL MEDIA...
I HELPED PUSH OUR CAUSE ON FACEBOOK AND TWITTER.
#NeverAgain
#MarchFor OurLives
#Enough IsEnough
ALL THREE ENDED UP TRENDING #1 ON TWITTER.
Trending now
#NeverAgain
#MarchFor OurLives
#EnoughIs

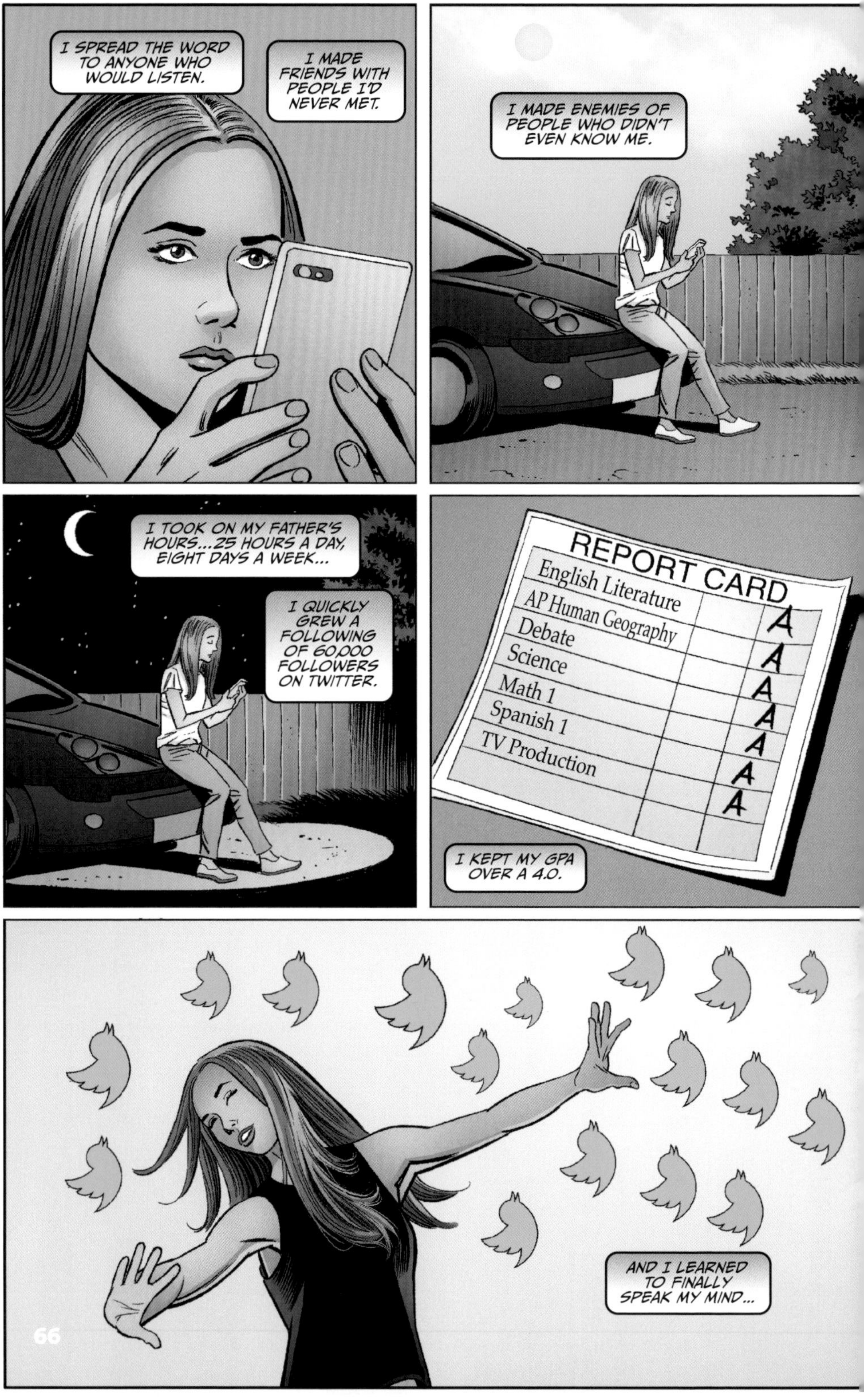
I SPREAD THE WORD TO ANYONE WHO WOULD LISTEN.
I MADE FRIENDS WITH PEOPLE I'D NEVER MET.
I MADE ENEMIES OF PEOPLE WHO DIDN'T EVEN KNOW ME.
I TOOK ON MY FATHER'S HOURS...25 HOURS A DAY, EIGHT DAYS A WEEK...
I QUICKLY GREW A FOLLOWING OF 60,000 FOLLOWERS ON TWITTER.
REPORT CARD
English Literature A
AP Human Geography A
Debate A
Science A
Math 1 A
Spanish 1 A
TV Production A
I KEPT MY GPA OVER A 4.0.
AND I LEARNED TO FINALLY SPEAK MY MIND...

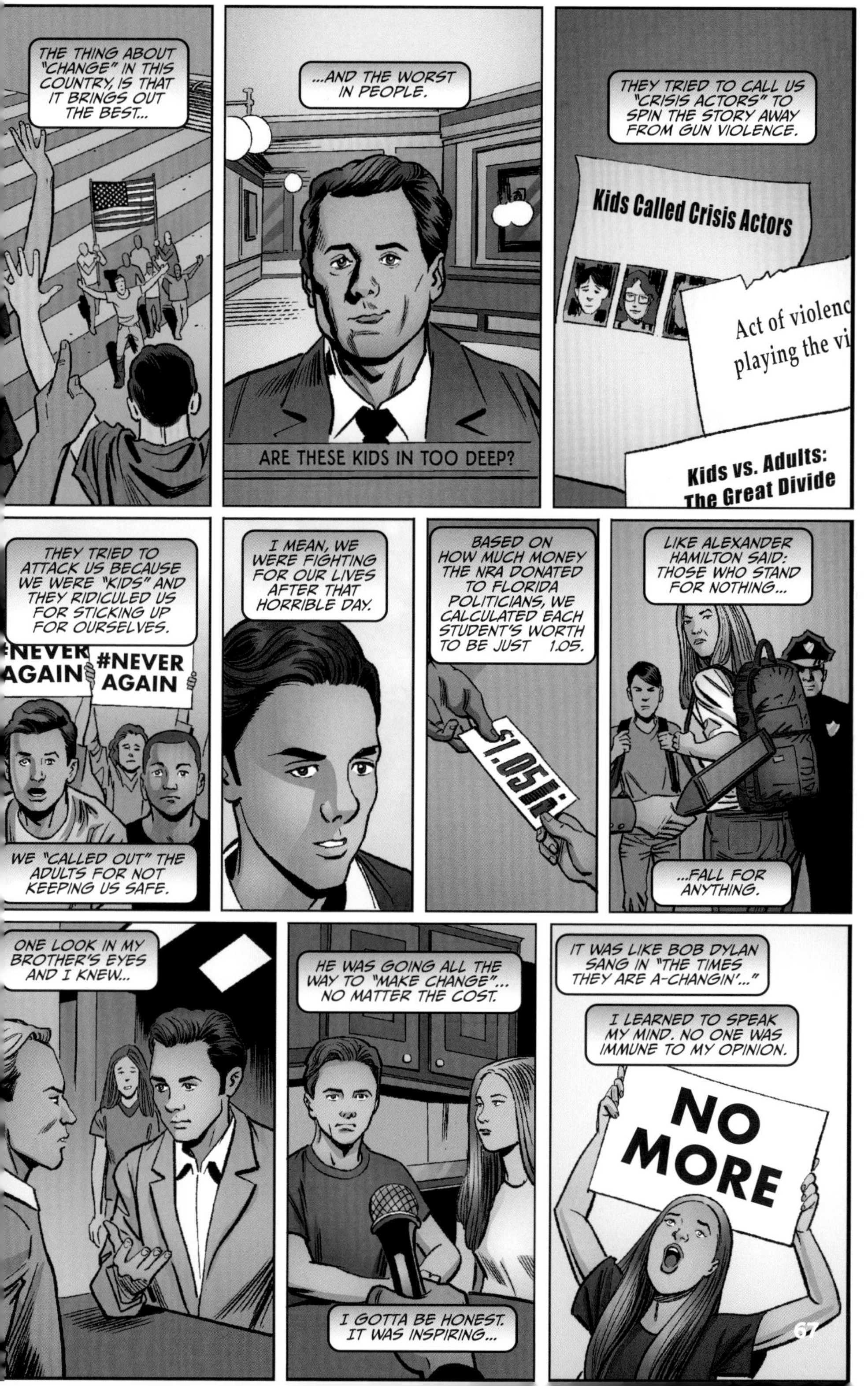

THE THING ABOUT "CHANGE" IN THIS COUNTRY, IS THAT IT BRINGS OUT THE BEST...
...AND THE WORST IN PEOPLE.
ARE THESE KIDS IN TOO DEEP?
THEY TRIED TO CALL US "CRISIS ACTORS" TO SPIN THE STORY AWAY FROM GUN VIOLENCE.
Kids Called Crisis Actors
Act of violenc
playing the vi
Kids vs. Adults: The Great Divide
THEY TRIED TO ATTACK US BECAUSE WE WERE "KIDS" AND THEY RIDICULED US FOR STICKING UP FOR OURSELVES.
#NEVER AGAIN
#NEVER AGAIN
WE "CALLED OUT" THE ADULTS FOR NOT KEEPING US SAFE.
I MEAN, WE WERE FIGHTING FOR OUR LIVES AFTER THAT HORRIBLE DAY.
BASED ON HOW MUCH MONEY THE NRA DONATED TO FLORIDA POLITICIANS, WE CALCULATED EACH STUDENT'S WORTH TO BE JUST 1.05.
$1.05
LIKE ALEXANDER HAMILTON SAID: THOSE WHO STAND FOR NOTHING...
...FALL FOR ANYTHING.
ONE LOOK IN MY BROTHER'S EYES AND I KNEW...
HE WAS GOING ALL THE WAY TO "MAKE CHANGE"... NO MATTER THE COST.
I GOTTA BE HONEST. IT WAS INSPIRING...
IT WAS LIKE BOB DYLAN SANG IN "THE TIMES THEY ARE A-CHANGIN'..."
I LEARNED TO SPEAK MY MIND. NO ONE WAS IMMUNE TO MY OPINION.
NO MORE

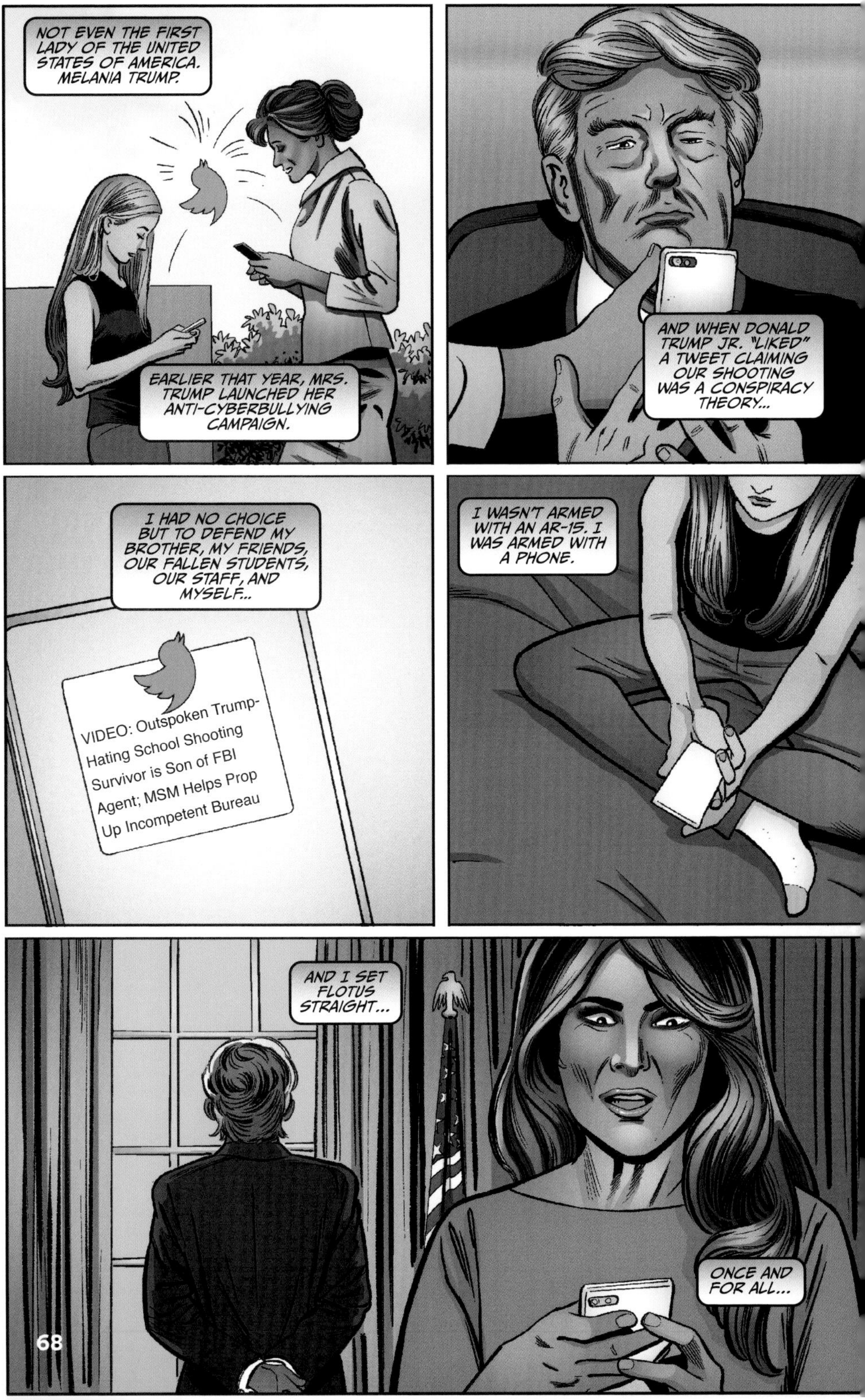
NOT EVEN THE FIRST LADY OF THE UNITED STATES OF AMERICA. MELANIA TRUMP.
EARLIER THAT YEAR, MRS. TRUMP LAUNCHED HER ANTI-CYBERBULLYING CAMPAIGN.
AND WHEN DONALD TRUMP JR. "LIKED" A TWEET CLAIMING OUR SHOOTING WAS A CONSPIRACY THEORY...
I HAD NO CHOICE BUT TO DEFEND MY BROTHER, MY FRIENDS, OUR FALLEN STUDENTS, OUR STAFF, AND MYSELF...
VIDEO: Outspoken Trump-Hating School Shooting Survivor is Son of FBI Agent; MSM Helps Prop Up Incompetent Bureau
I WASN'T ARMED WITH AN AR-15. I WAS ARMED WITH A PHONE.
AND I SET FLOTUS STRAIGHT...
ONCE AND FOR ALL...

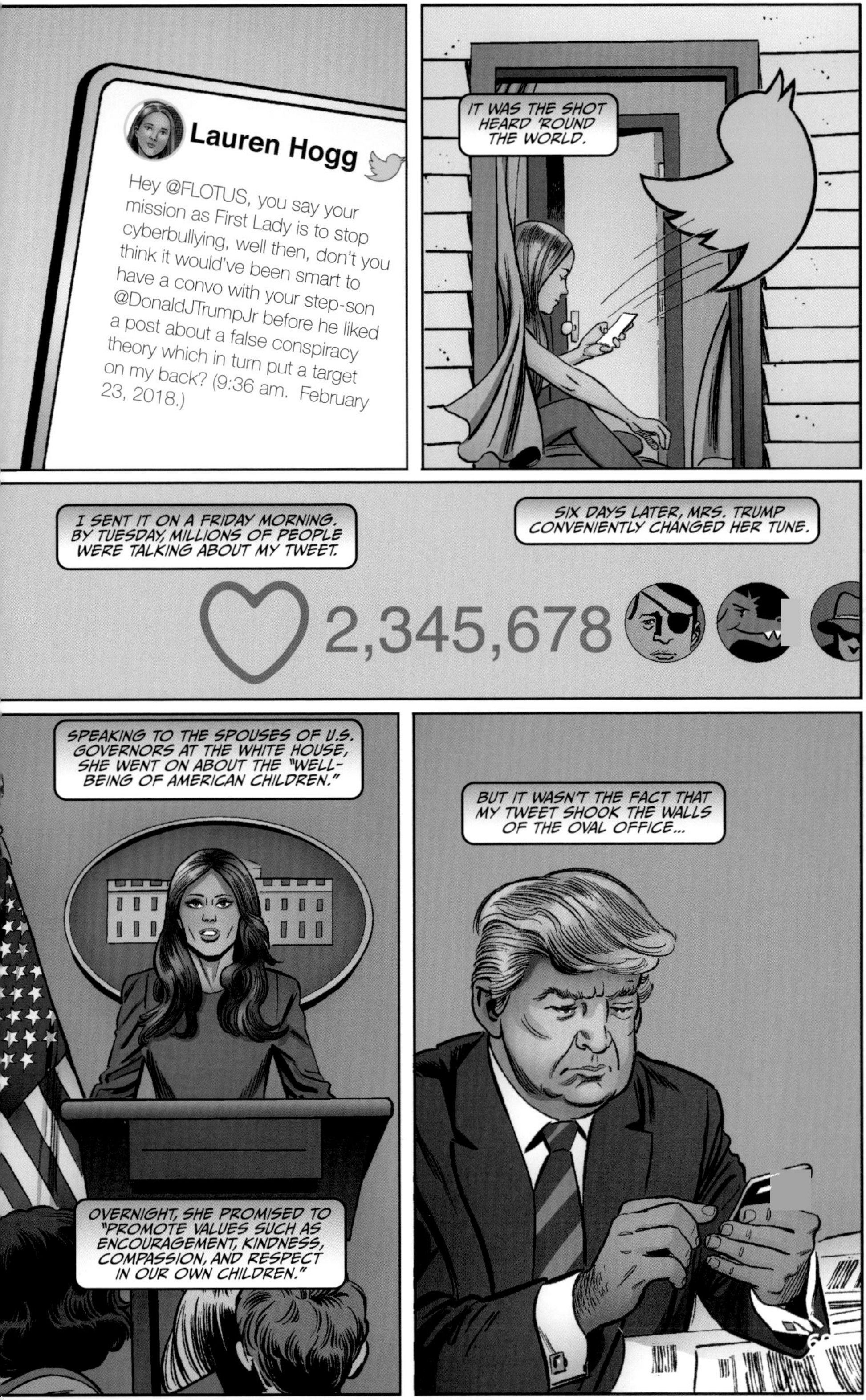
Lauren Hogg
Hey @FLOTUS, you say your mission as First Lady is to stop cyberbullying, well then, don't you think it would've been smart to have a convo with your step-son @DonaldJTrumpJr before he liked a post about a false conspiracy theory which in turn put a target on my back? (9:36 am. February 23, 2018.)
IT WAS THE SHOT HEARD 'ROUND THE WORLD.
I SENT IT ON A FRIDAY MORNING. BY TUESDAY, MILLIONS OF PEOPLE WERE TALKING ABOUT MY TWEET.
SIX DAYS LATER, MRS. TRUMP CONVENIENTLY CHANGED HER TUNE.
2,345,678
SPEAKING TO THE SPOUSES OF U.S. GOVERNORS AT THE WHITE HOUSE, SHE WENT ON ABOUT THE "WELL-BEING OF AMERICAN CHILDREN."
OVERNIGHT, SHE PROMISED TO "PROMOTE VALUES SUCH AS ENCOURAGEMENT, KINDNESS, COMPASSION, AND RESPECT IN OUR OWN CHILDREN."
BUT IT WASN'T THE FACT THAT MY TWEET SHOOK THE WALLS OF THE OVAL OFFICE...

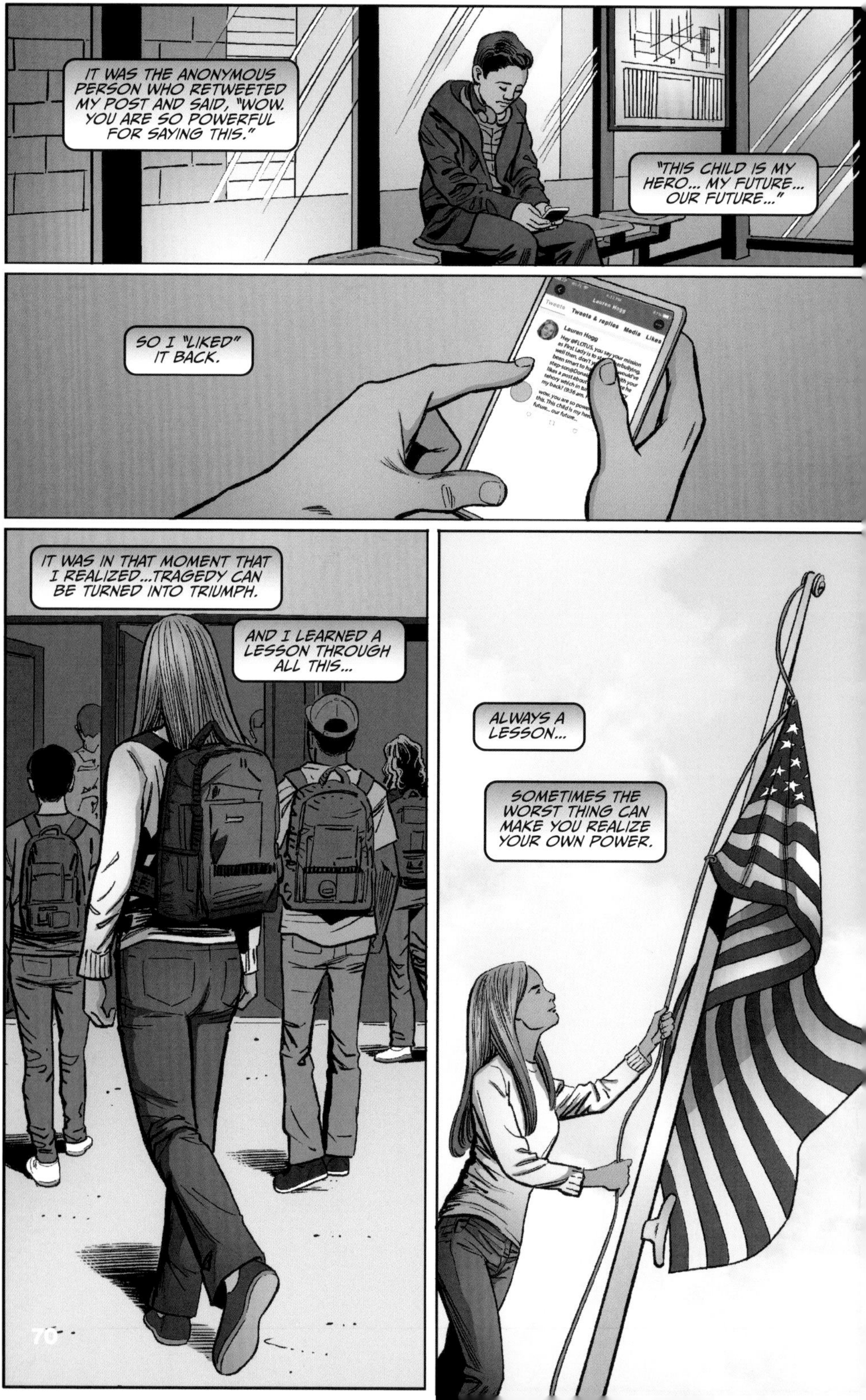
IT WAS THE ANONYMOUS PERSON WHO RETWEETED MY POST AND SAID, "WOW. YOU ARE SO POWERFUL FOR SAYING THIS."
"THIS CHILD IS MY HERO... MY FUTURE... OUR FUTURE..."
SO I "LIKED" IT BACK.
Lauren Hogg
Tweets & replies
Media
Likes
IT WAS IN THAT MOMENT THAT I REALIZED...TRAGEDY CAN BE TURNED INTO TRIUMPH.
AND I LEARNED A LESSON THROUGH ALL THIS...
ALWAYS A LESSON...
SOMETIMES THE WORST THING CAN MAKE YOU REALIZE YOUR OWN POWER.

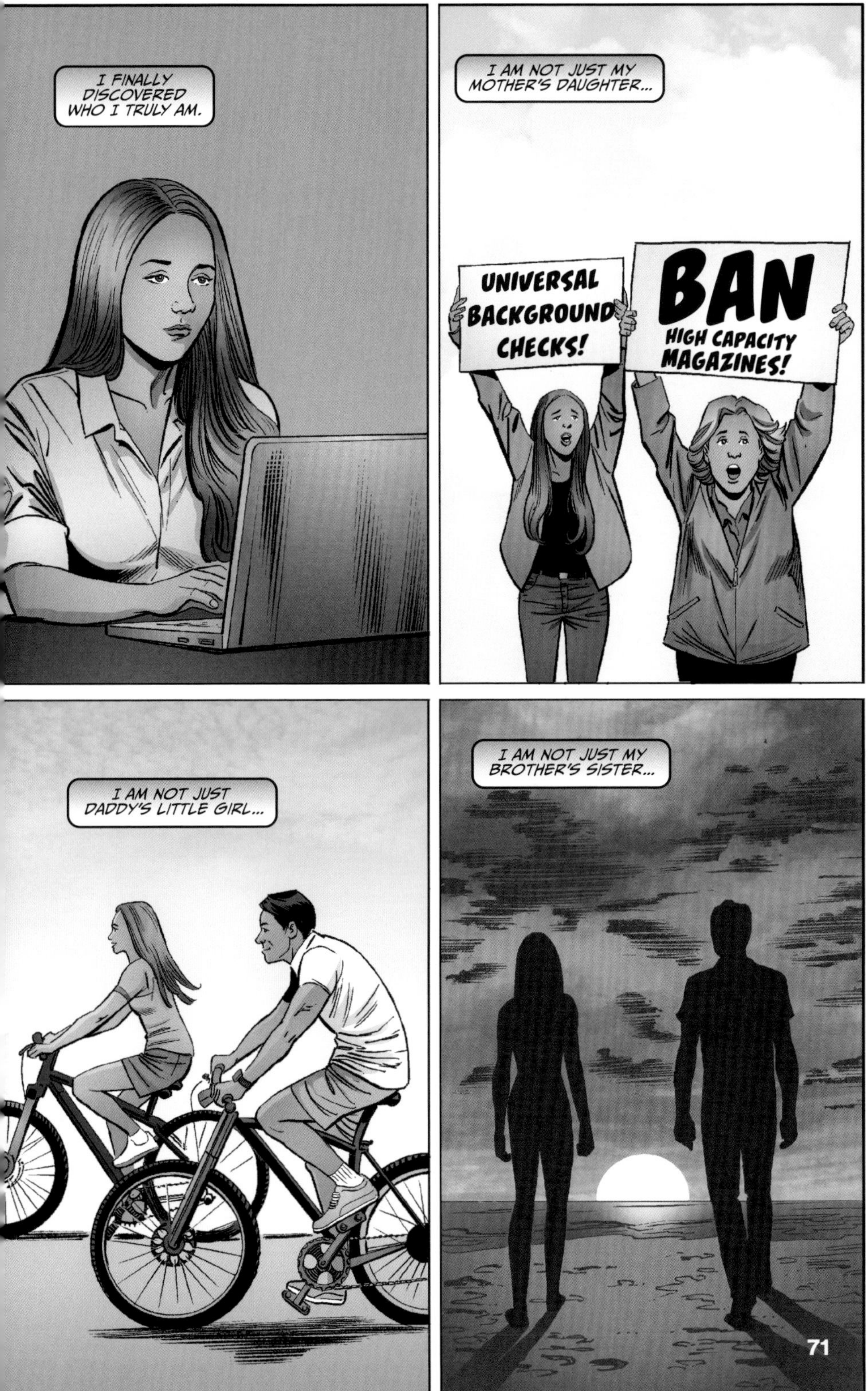
I FINALLY DISCOVERED WHO I TRULY AM.
I AM NOT JUST MY MOTHER'S DAUGHTER...
UNIVERSAL BACKGROUND CHECKS!
BAN HIGH CAPACITY MAGAZINES!
I AM NOT JUST DADDY'S LITTLE GIRL...
I AM NOT JUST MY BROTHER'S SISTER...

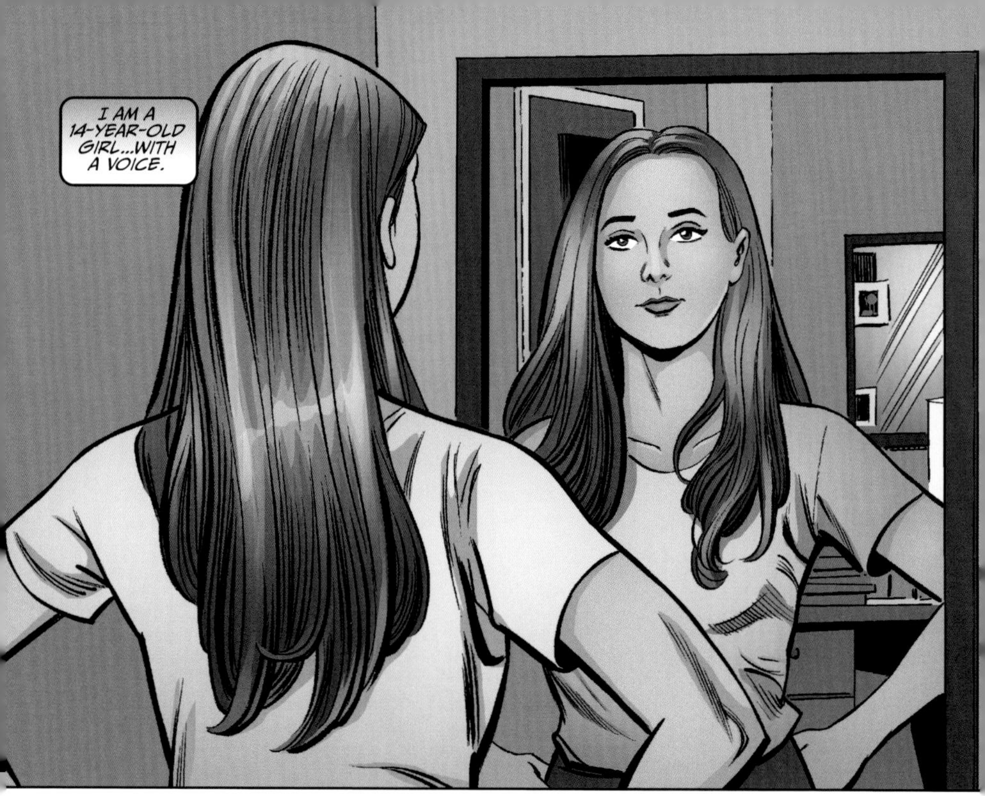
I AM A 14-YEAR-OLD GIRL...WITH A VOICE.

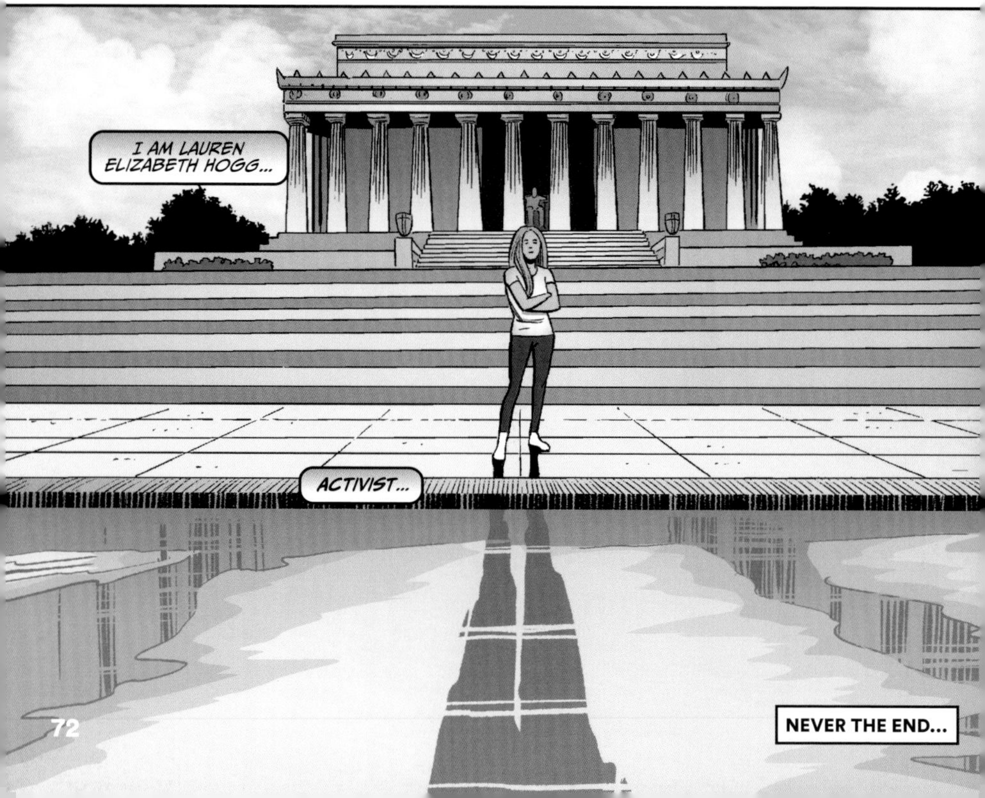
I AM LAUREN ELIZABETH HOGG...
ACTIVIST...
NEVER THE END...

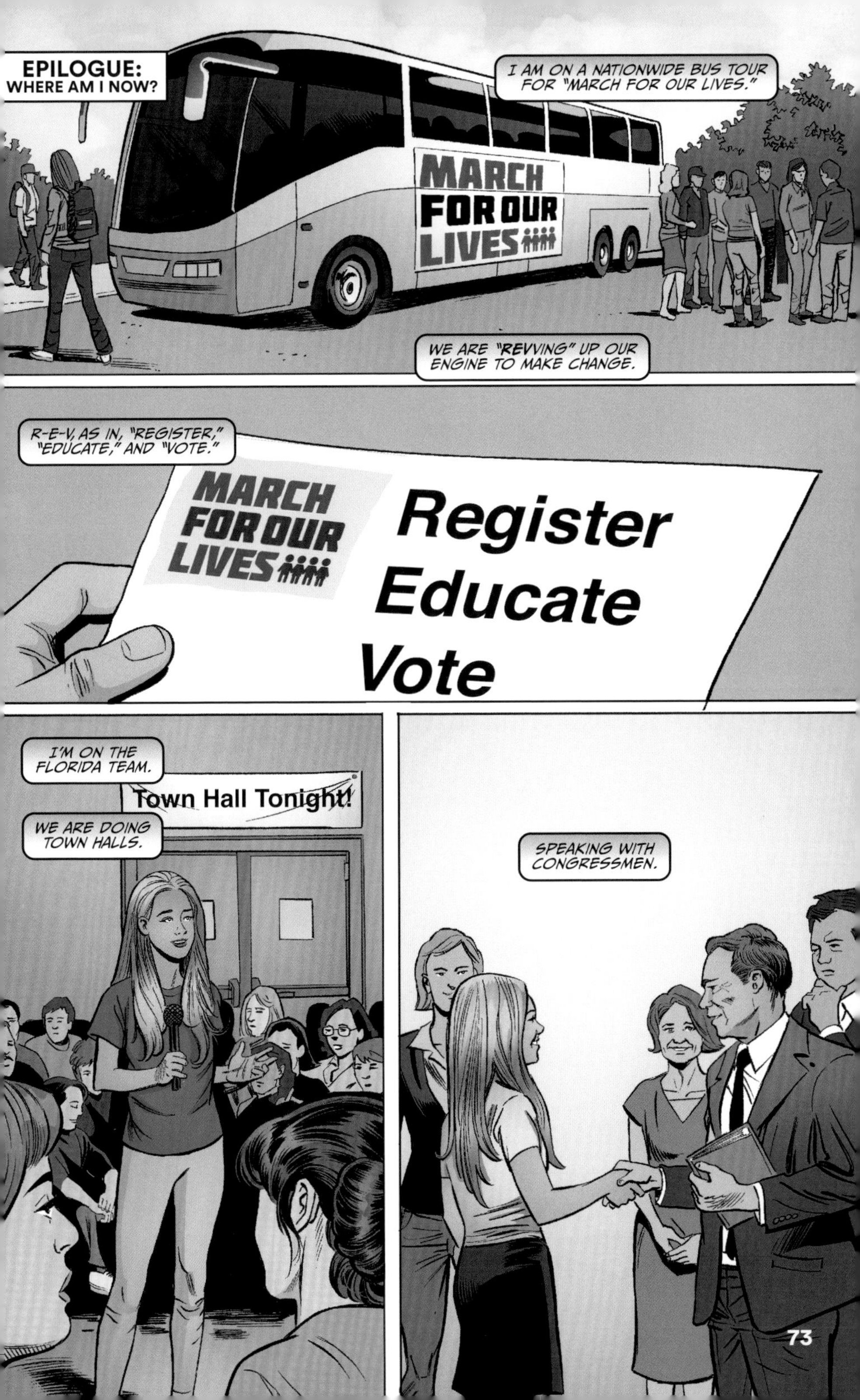
EPILOGUE:
WHERE AM I NOW?
I AM ON A NATIONWIDE BUS TOUR FOR "MARCH FOR OUR LIVES."
MARCH FOR OUR LIVES
WE ARE "REVVING" UP OUR ENGINE TO MAKE CHANGE.
R-E-V, AS IN, "REGISTER," "EDUCATE," AND "VOTE."
MARCH FOR OUR LIVES
Register
Educate
Vote
I'M ON THE FLORIDA TEAM.
Town Hall Tonight!
WE ARE DOING TOWN HALLS.
SPEAKING WITH CONGRESSMEN.

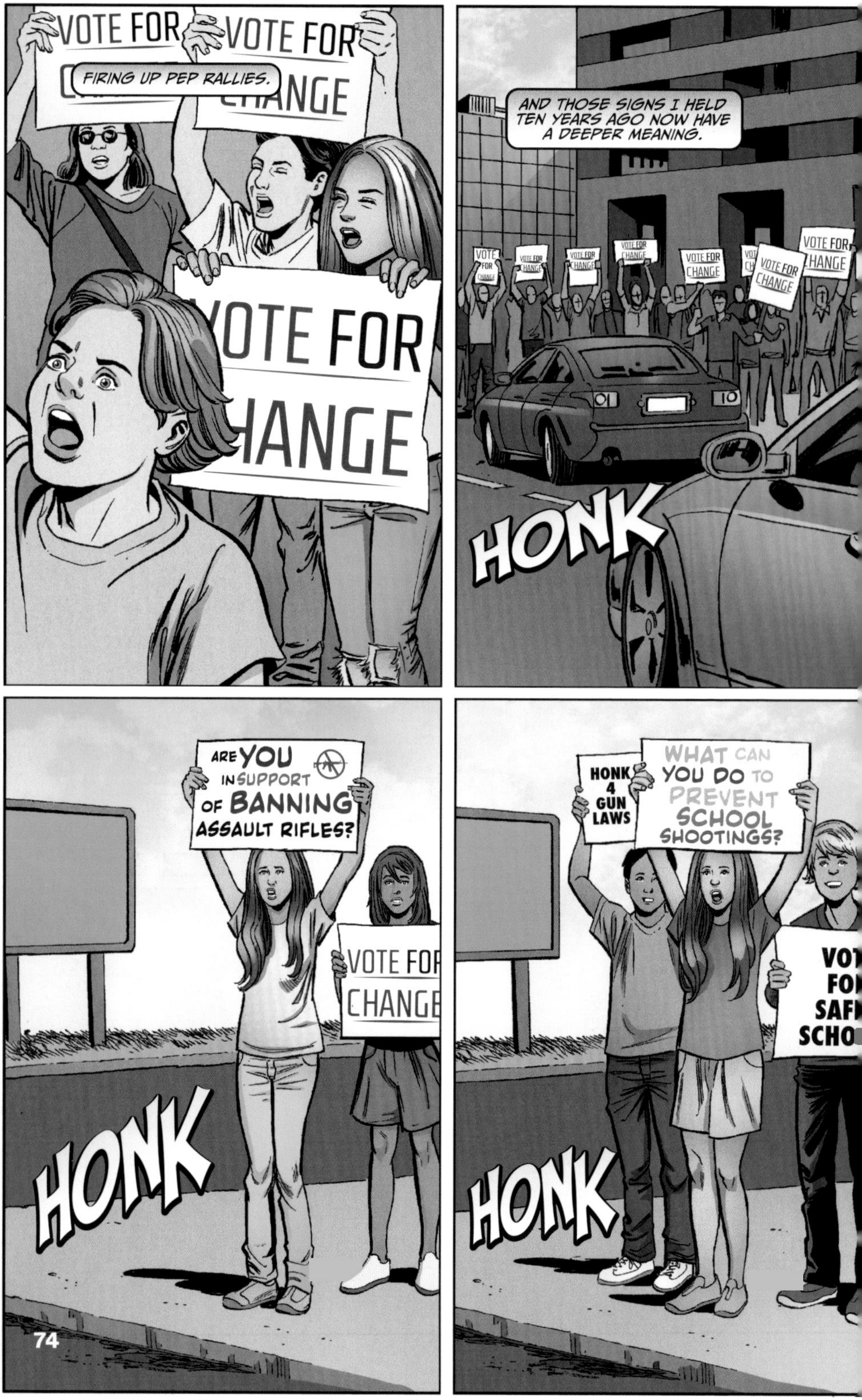

VOTE FOR
VOTE FOR
FIRING UP PEP RALLIES.
AND THOSE SIGNS I HELD TEN YEARS AGO NOW HAVE A DEEPER MEANING.
VOTE FOR CHANGE
HONK
ARE YOU IN SUPPORT OF BANNING ASSAULT RIFLES?
HONK
HONK 4 GUN LAWS
WHAT CAN YOU DO TO PREVENT SCHOOL SHOOTINGS?
HONK

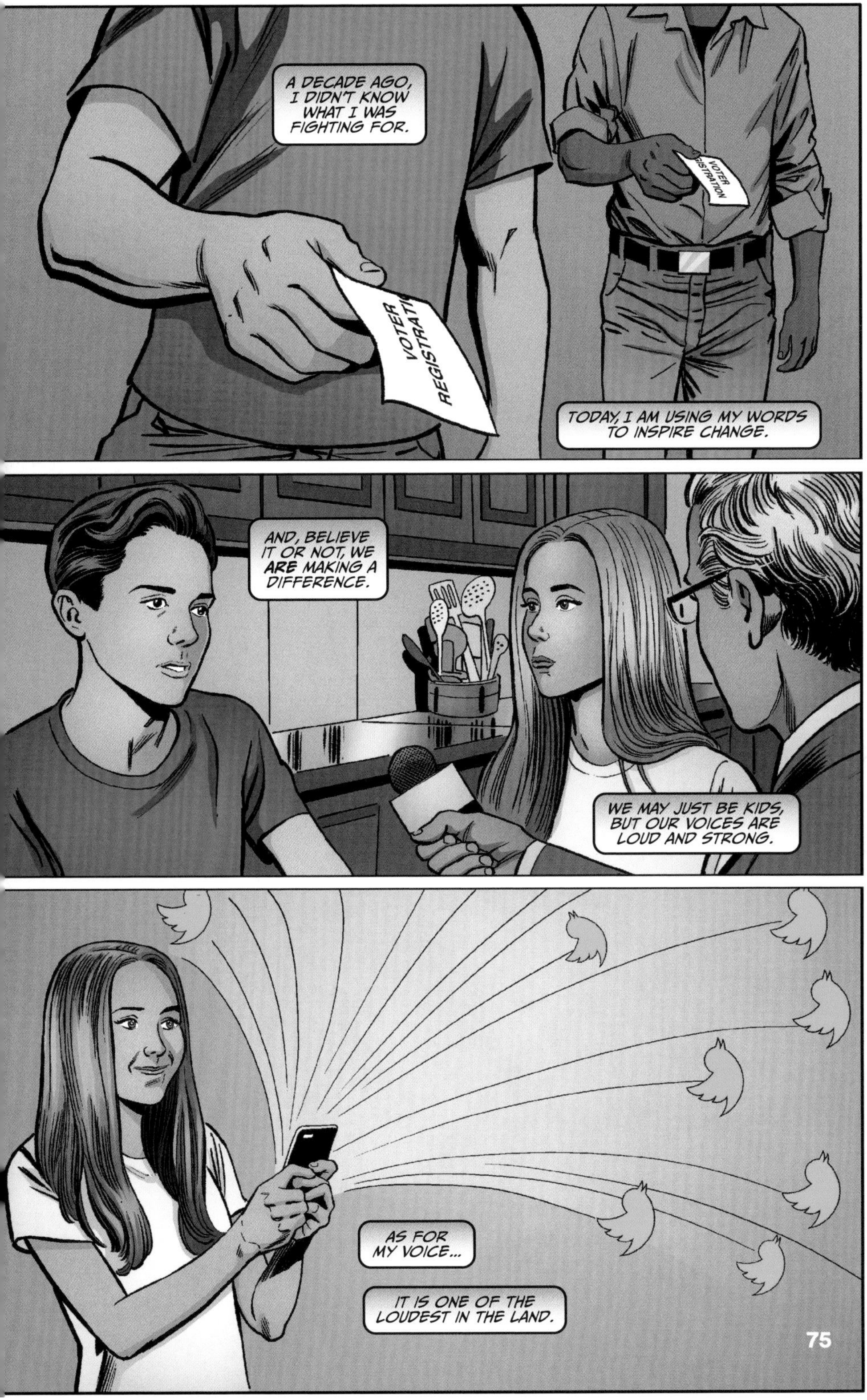
A DECADE AGO, I DIDN'T KNOW WHAT I WAS FIGHTING FOR.
VOTER REGISTRATION
VOTER REGISTRATION
TODAY, I AM USING MY WORDS TO INSPIRE CHANGE.
AND, BELIEVE IT OR NOT, WE **ARE** MAKING A DIFFERENCE.
WE MAY JUST BE KIDS, BUT OUR VOICES ARE LOUD AND STRONG.
AS FOR MY VOICE...
IT IS ONE OF THE LOUDEST IN THE LAND.

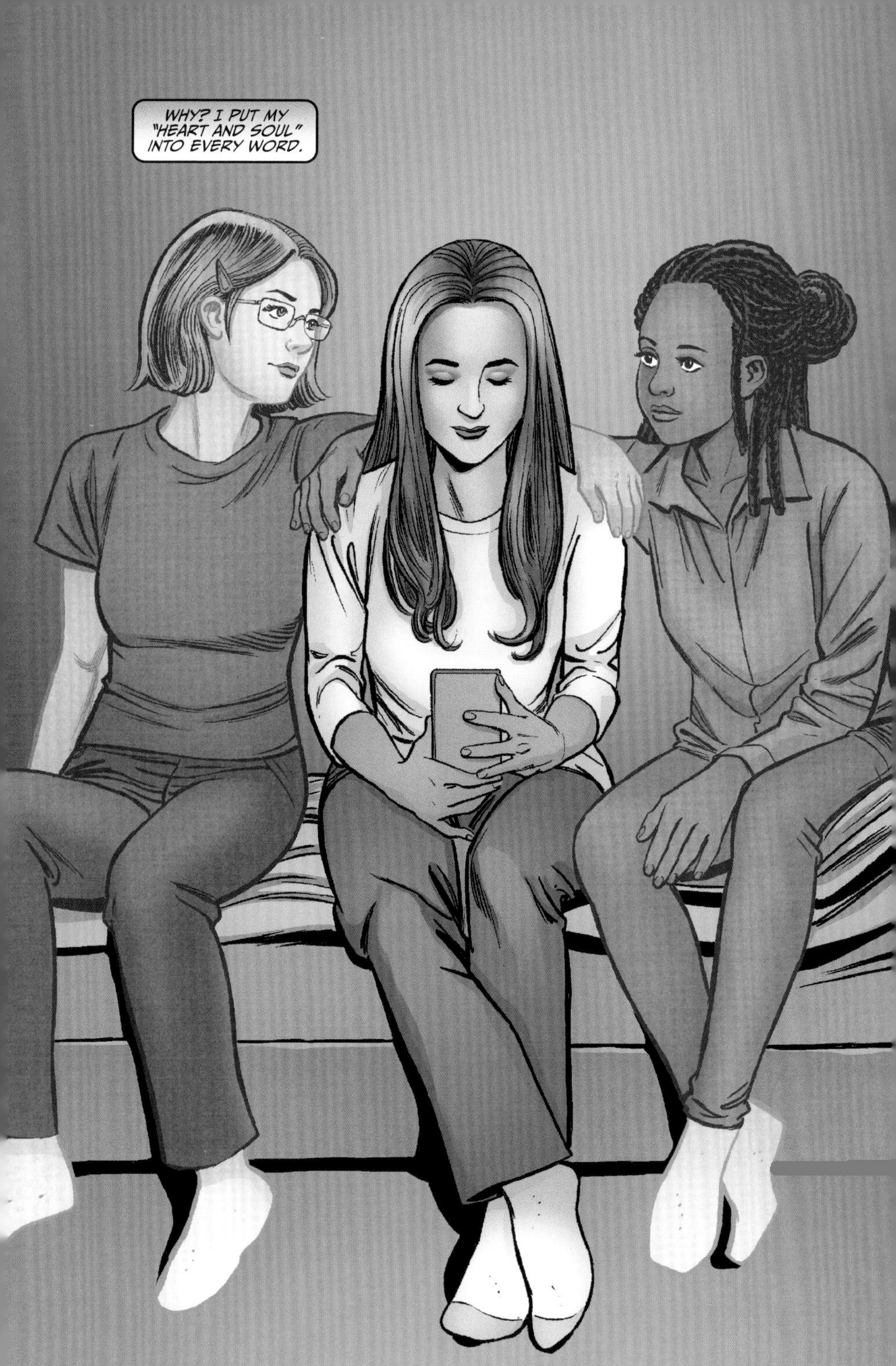
WHY? I PUT MY "HEART AND SOUL" INTO EVERY WORD.

ABOUT THE AUTHOR

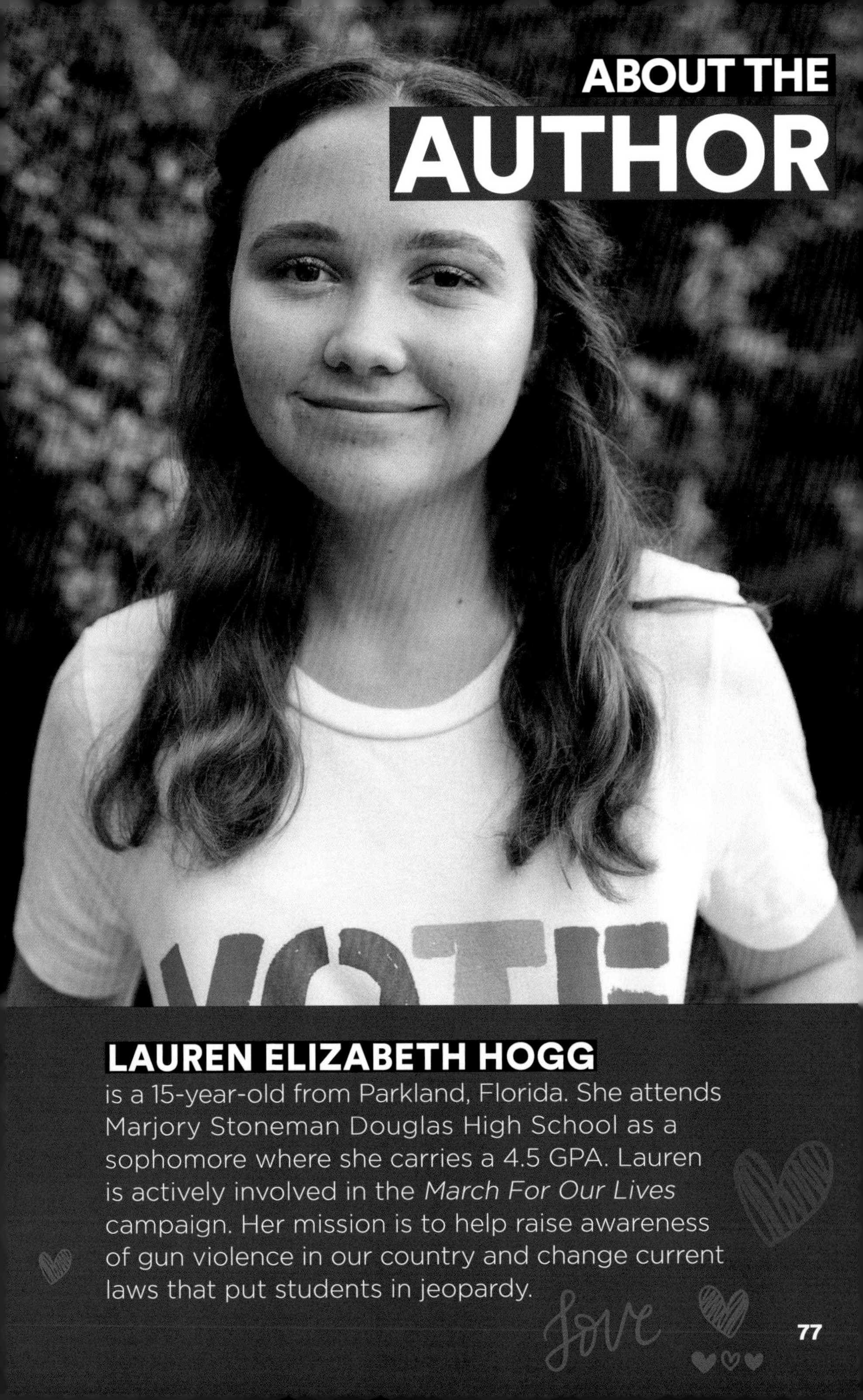

LAUREN ELIZABETH HOGG is a 15-year-old from Parkland, Florida. She attends Marjory Stoneman Douglas High School as a sophomore where she carries a 4.5 GPA. Lauren is actively involved in the *March For Our Lives* campaign. Her mission is to help raise awareness of gun violence in our country and change current laws that put students in jeopardy.

LAUREN...

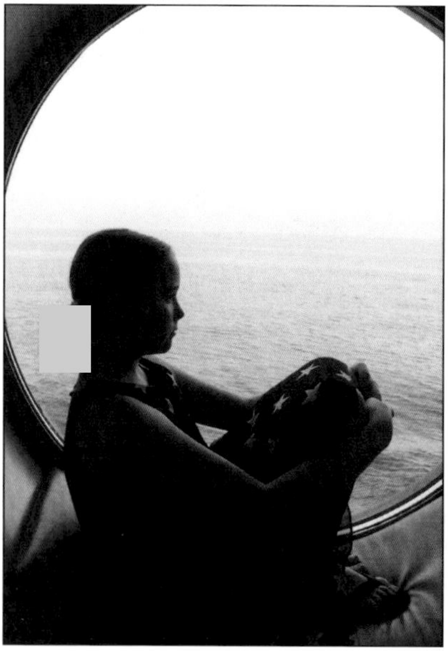

Disney Alaska cruise when I was in third grade.

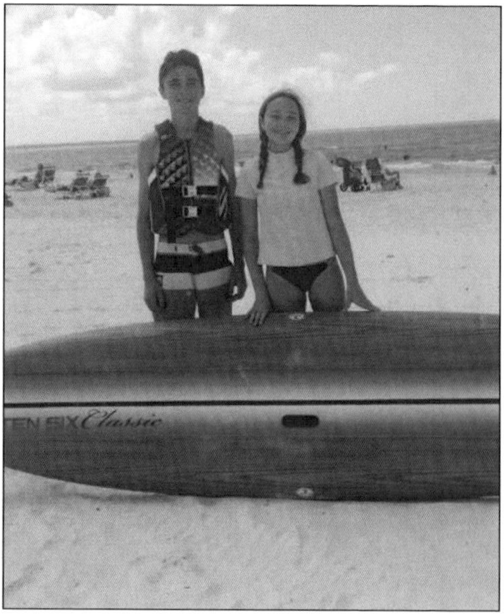
TEN SIX Classic

Fort Meyers Beach with my brother David.

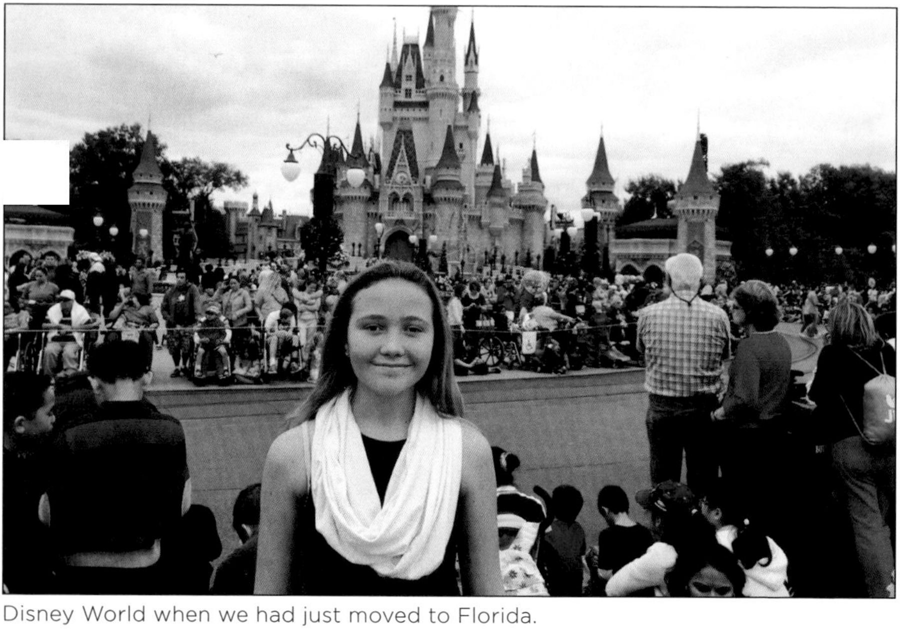

Disney World when we had just moved to Florida.

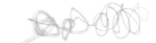

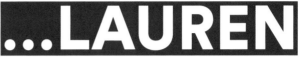

...LAUREN

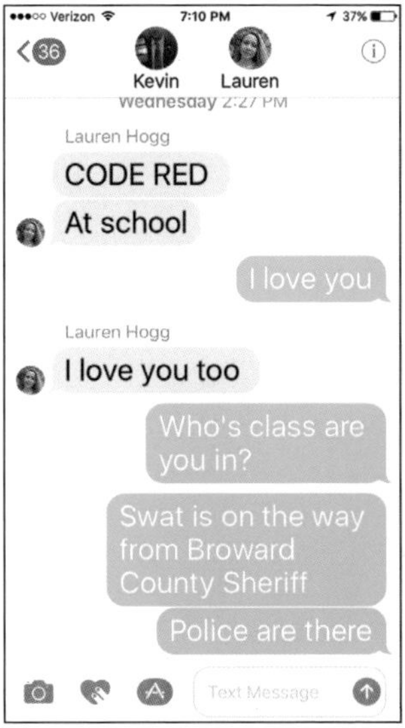

Verizon
7:10 PM
37%
36
Kevin
Lauren
Wednesday 2:27 PM
Lauren Hogg
CODE RED
At school
I love you
Lauren Hogg
I love you too
Who's class are you in?
Swat is on the way from Broward County Sheriff
Police are there
Text Message

The text I sent my parents.

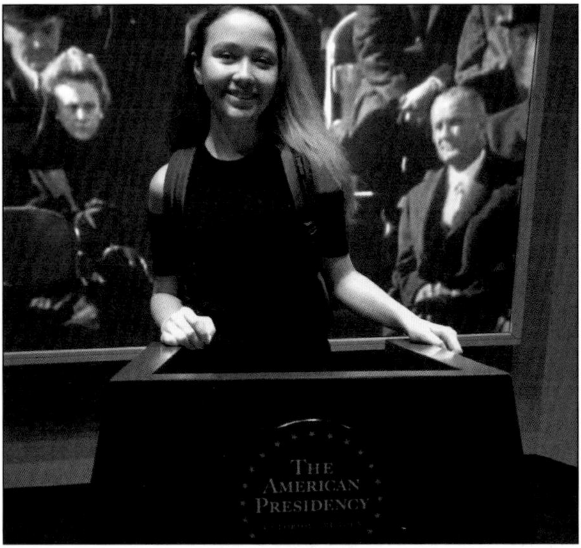

THE AMERICAN PRESIDENCY

Spring Break, Washington, DC, 2017.

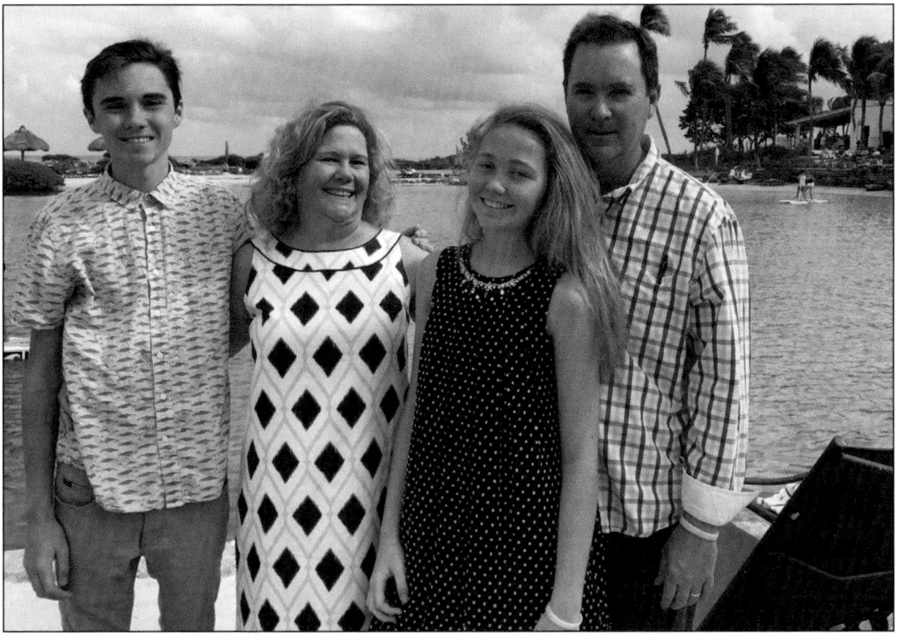

Florida Keys, Thanksgiving, 2016.

LAUREN...

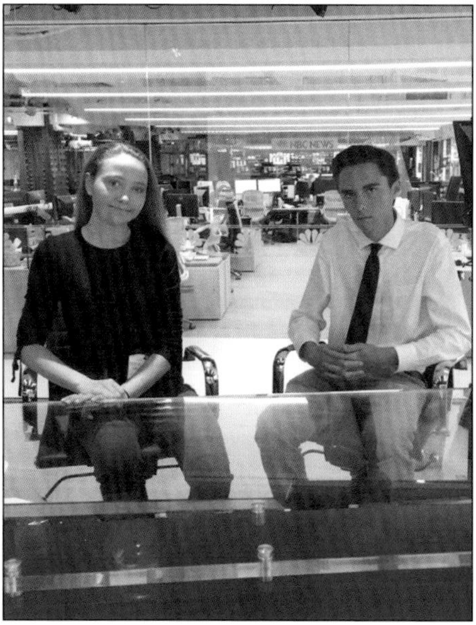

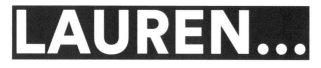

David and I at NBC News weeks after the shooting.

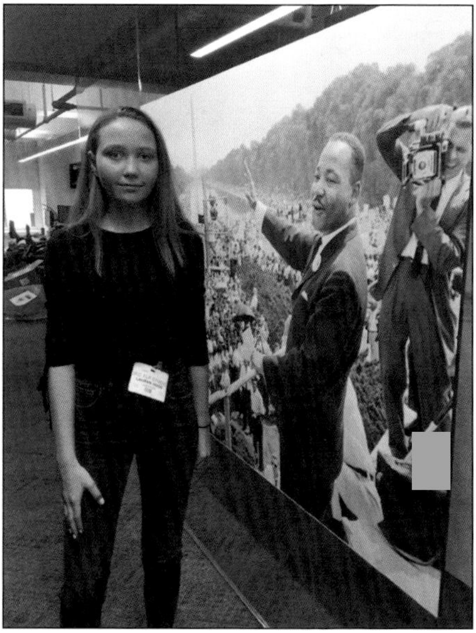

Picture my mom wanted at NBC because my brother and I are activists.

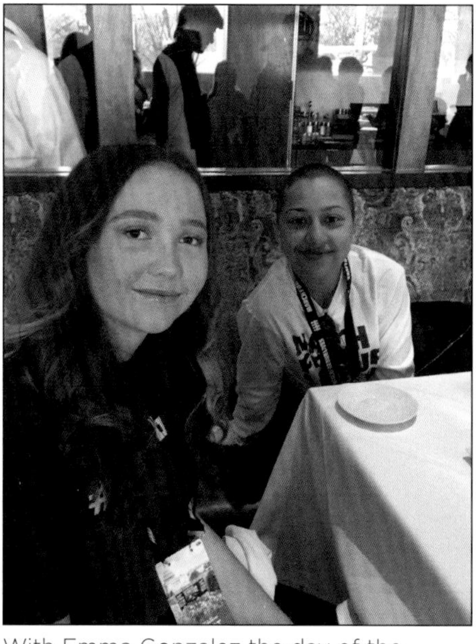

With Emma Gonzalez the day of the March for our Lives.

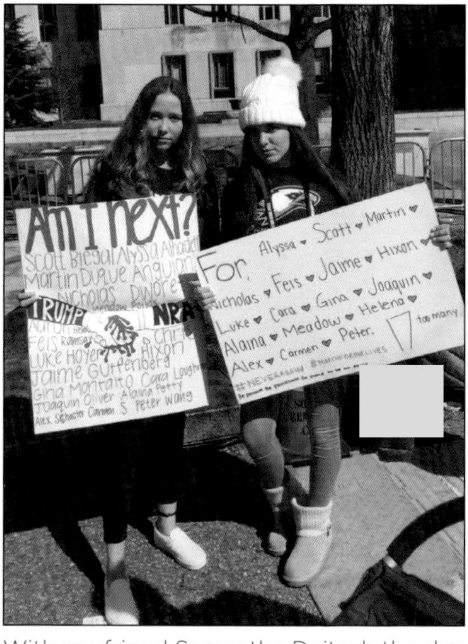
Am I next?
Scott Biegal Alyssa
Martin Duque
Nicholas
TRUMP
NRA
Feis
Luke Hoyer
Hixon
Jaime Guttenberg
Gina Montalto Cara
Alaina Petty
Joaquin Oliver
Peter Wang
Alex Schachter Carmen
For, Alyssa ♥ Scott ♥ Martin ♥
Nicholas ♥ Feis ♥ Jaime ♥ Hixon ♥
Luke ♥ Cara ♥ Gina ♥ Joaquin ♥
Alaina ♥ Meadow ♥ Helena ♥
Alex ♥ Carmen ♥ Peter.
17
too many.

With my friend Samantha Deitsch the day of the March for our Lives.

TAKE 5!

FIVE PARENT TAKE-AWAYS ABOUT ACTIVISM

REBECCA BOLDRICK HOGG

Rebecca Boldrick Hogg, M.A. Ed., has been a public school teacher for 30 years, and has taught in four school districts in California and Florida. She is the mother of Marjory Stoneman Douglas shooting survivors and activists David and Lauren Hogg.

THERE IS NO BLUEPRINT FOR WHAT TO DO AFTER A SCHOOL SHOOTING.

IF YOUR CHILDREN ARE CONCERNED ABOUT SCHOOL SHOOTINGS IN THEIR SCHOOL, LISTEN TO THEM.

Give space to your child and listen when they feel like talking. Do not ask them questions about the event, just give them words of reassurance. Allow them to spend time with friends who have experienced the same traumatic event. There is power in shared healing. There is no easy way to go around the pain. You must go through the pain, feel the hurt of loss.

IF YOUR CHILD IS A SURVIVOR OF A SCHOOL SHOOTING, GET HELP.

Get your kids professional help immediately after a traumatic event. Don't wait for them to be in crisis, because it will happen. Support your child. The mental health professional they are seeing may recommend medication to help with anxiety or depression. We learned from Columbine that survivors all suffer collateral damage, such as relationship and addiction issues.

PROTECT YOUR CHILD FROM MEDIA COVERAGE.

Avoid media and social media exposure after a traumatic event. It may cause further post-traumatic stress to watch the event played out over and over. Get out of the house and away from your screens in the days following a shooting.

ROUTINE IS IMPORTANT AFTER THE INCIDENT.

Keep the routine at home as normal as possible. Children especially find comfort in routine. Make sure your child is eating, sleeping, and exercising. As soon as possible have your child go back to school.

PREPARE YOUR CHILD TO TAKE ACTION IN THE EVENT OF A SHOOTING.

Make sure your children are always aware of their surroundings. Shootings are happening at schools, movie theaters, concerts, malls, etc. Train them what to do if they are in a situation with a shooter: run, hide, fight. If you can, run. If you can't run, hide. If you can't run, or hide, you need to fight.

THE STORY
DOESN'T
END HERE...

VISIT
ZUIKERPRESS.COM

... to learn more about Lauren's story, see behind-the-scenes videos of Lauren and her family,

Our **WEBSITE** is another resource to help our readers deal with the issues that they face every day. Log on to find advice from experts, links to helpful organizations and literature, and more real-life experiences from young people just like you.

Spotlighting young writers with heartfelt stories that enlighten and inspire.

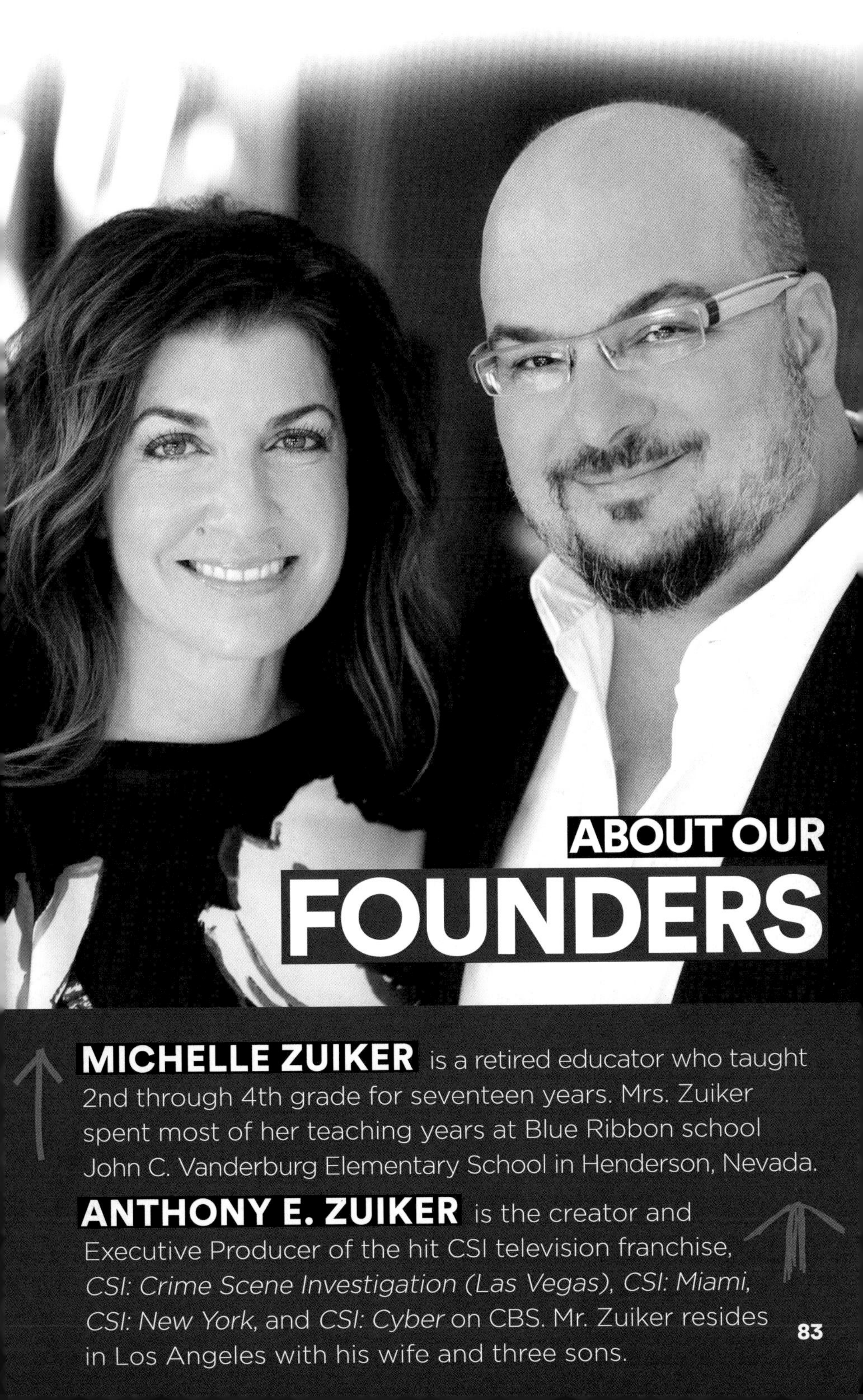

ABOUT OUR FOUNDERS

MICHELLE ZUIKER is a retired educator who taught 2nd through 4th grade for seventeen years. Mrs. Zuiker spent most of her teaching years at Blue Ribbon school John C. Vanderburg Elementary School in Henderson, Nevada.

ANTHONY E. ZUIKER is the creator and Executive Producer of the hit CSI television franchise, *CSI: Crime Scene Investigation (Las Vegas)*, *CSI: Miami*, *CSI: New York*, and *CSI: Cyber* on CBS. Mr. Zuiker resides in Los Angeles with his wife and three sons.

ABOUT OUR
ILLUSTRATORS & EDITOR...

DON HUDSON— ILLUSTRATOR

Don Hudson has been a professional artist in Los Angeles for twenty years. He's had the opportunity to work in comics, animation, advertising and even Broadway!

If you want to know more about Don, go to **www.dchudson.blogspot.com**.

MONICA KUBINA— COLORIST

Monica Kubina is a digital artist and comic book colorist. She has worked with a number of publishers throughout her career, including DC Comics, Marvel, Warner Bros., Dark Horse Comics and IDW Publishing. She has colored hundreds of issues of some of the most popular comic books such as the *Justice League*, the *X-Men*, *Spider-Man*, *SpongeBob*, *Star Wars* and currently the DC *Super Hero Girls*. You can see some of her work on **www.monicakubina.com** and follow her updates on twitter.com/monicakubina.

JOSE MARZAN JR- INKER

Jose Marzan Jr. is a 35-year veteran of the comic book industry, working for DC Comics, Marvel Comics, Crossgen, and Disney Comics. Some titles from his long list of credits include *Dr. Strange*, *The Silver Surfer*, *GI Joe*, *Marvel Comics Presents*, *Roger Rabbit*, *Time Masters*, *The Justice League of America*, *The Flash*, *Action Comics featuring Superman*, *The Adventures of Superman*, *Jack of Fables*, and *The House of Mystery*.

In 2008, Marzan completed a five-year run on Vertigo Comics' Y: The Last Man, having the distinction of being the sole inker on the title over its five-year, 60-issue run. Jose Marzan Jr. received two 2008 Will Eisner Comic Industry Awards.

For more information, check out **JoseMarzan.com**.

ROB TOKAR-EDITOR

Rob Tokar got his start as an intern at Marvel Comics and eventually worked his way up to senior editor. He had the honor of working directly for Stan Lee for two years. After Marvel, Rob gained additional experience as a freelance editor, writer, and artist before joining TokyoPop's editorial staff for five years, with two years as editor-in-chief. Additional editorial credits include Disney Publishing Worldwide and working on Disney properties for Joe Books. Rob is also the co-founder of Tokartoons, which creates animation for education and presentations.

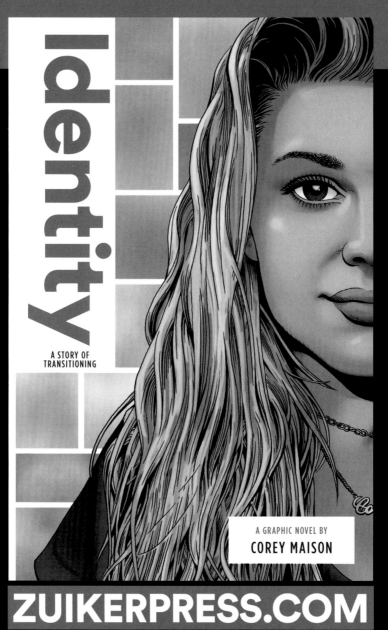

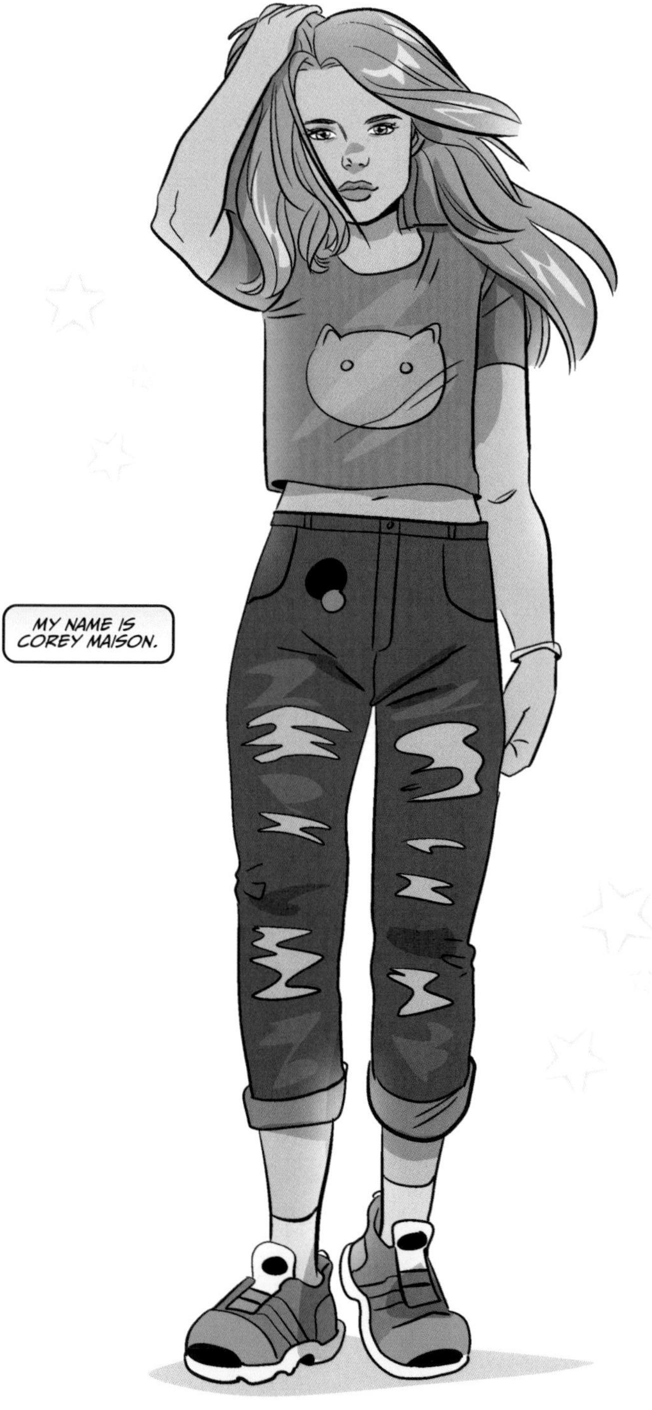
MY NAME IS COREY MAISON.

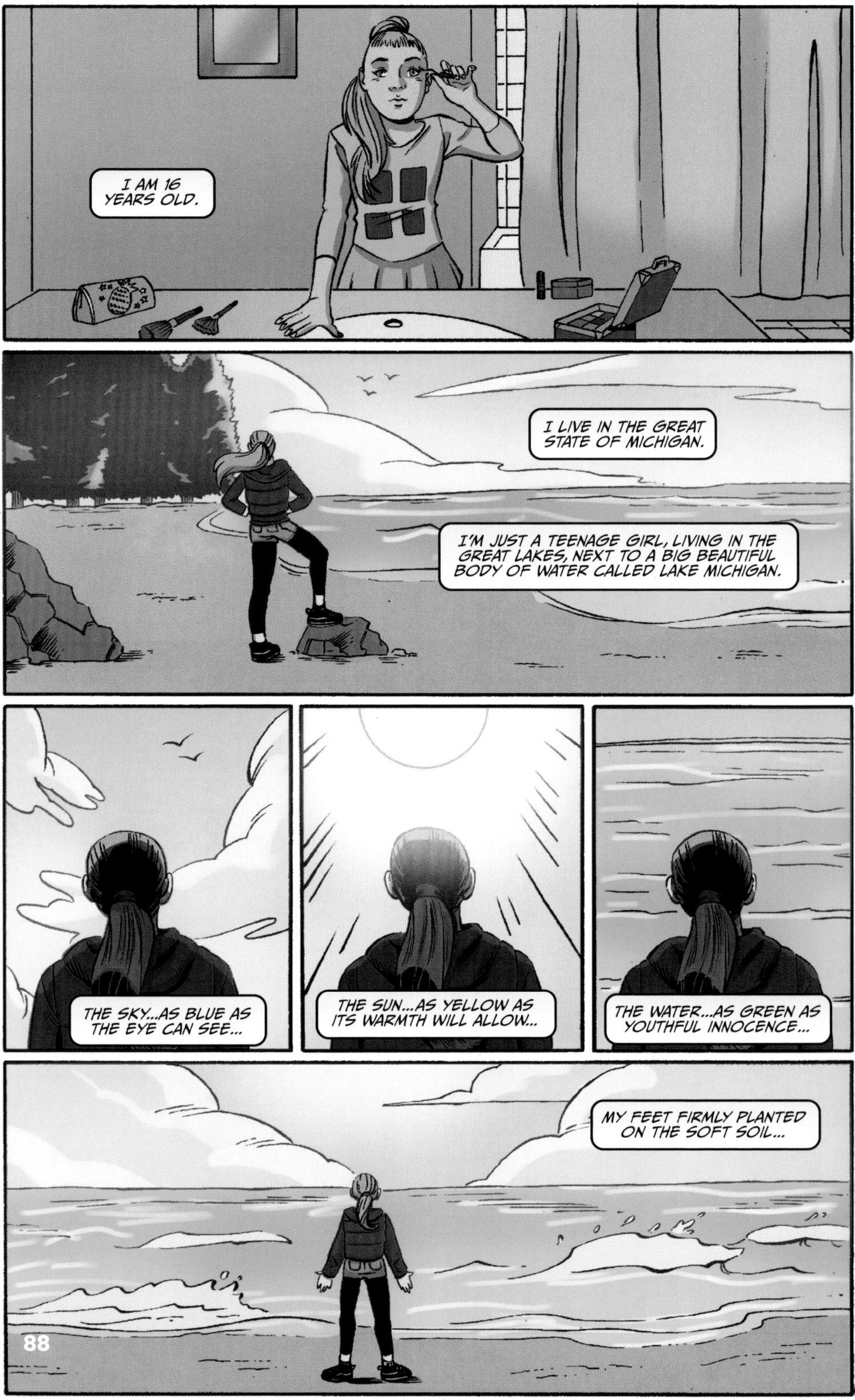
I AM 16 YEARS OLD.
I LIVE IN THE GREAT STATE OF MICHIGAN.
I'M JUST A TEENAGE GIRL, LIVING IN THE GREAT LAKES, NEXT TO A BIG BEAUTIFUL BODY OF WATER CALLED LAKE MICHIGAN.
THE SKY...AS BLUE AS THE EYE CAN SEE...
THE SUN...AS YELLOW AS ITS WARMTH WILL ALLOW...
THE WATER...AS GREEN AS YOUTHFUL INNOCENCE...
MY FEET FIRMLY PLANTED ON THE SOFT SOIL...

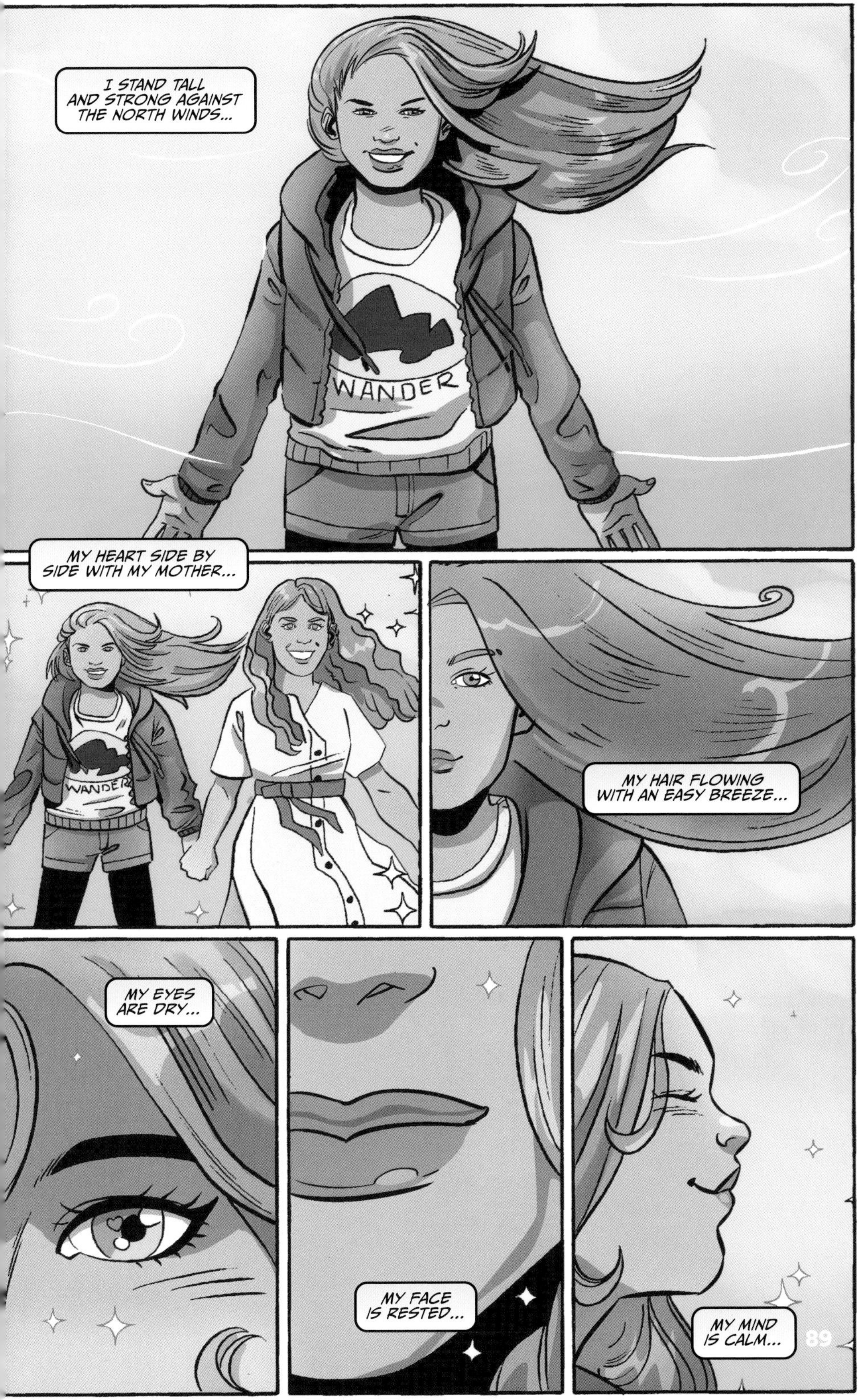
I STAND TALL AND STRONG AGAINST THE NORTH WINDS...
MY HEART SIDE BY SIDE WITH MY MOTHER...
WANDER
MY HAIR FLOWING WITH AN EASY BREEZE...
MY EYES ARE DRY...
MY FACE IS RESTED...
MY MIND IS CALM...

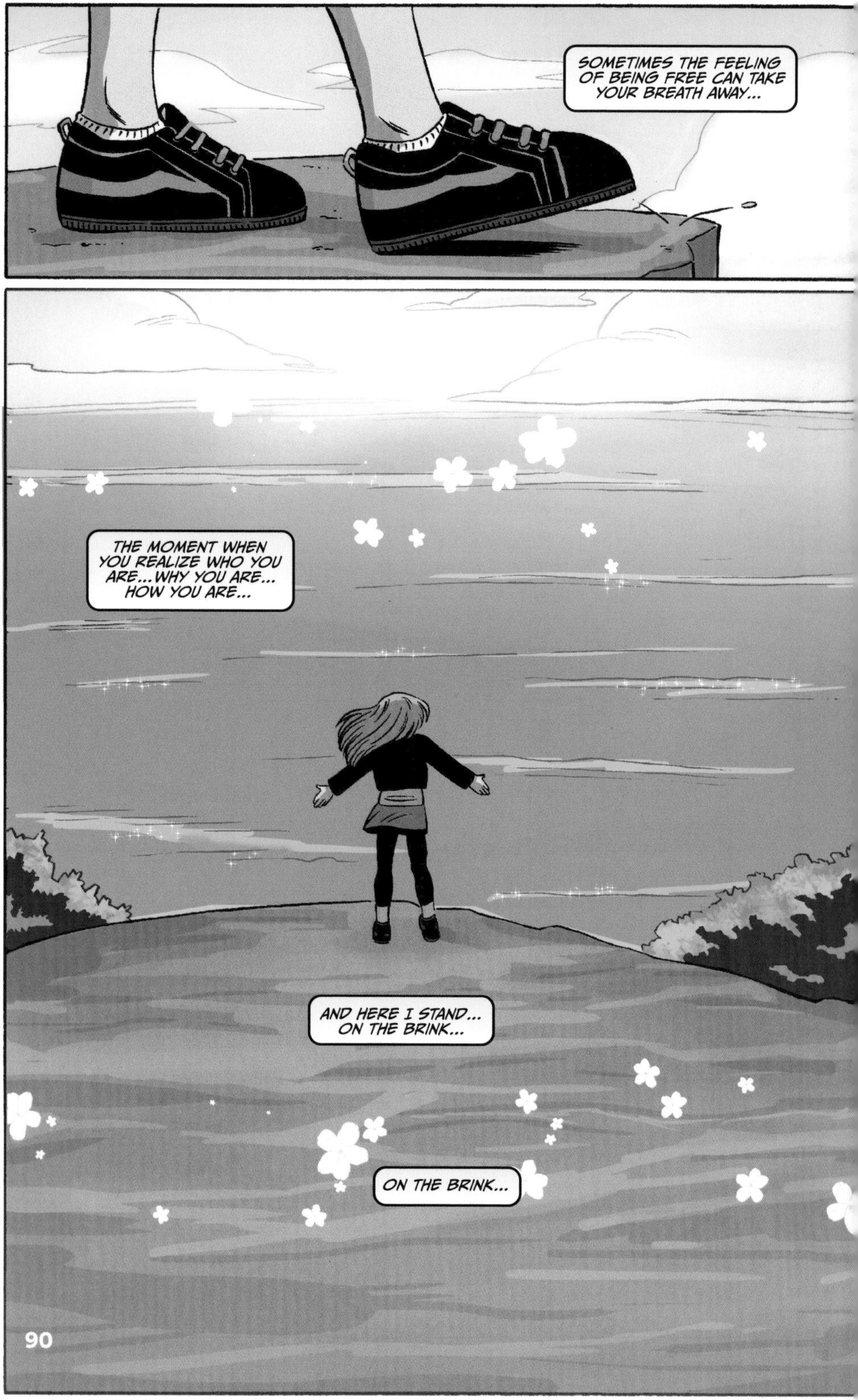
SOMETIMES THE FEELING OF BEING FREE CAN TAKE YOUR BREATH AWAY...
THE MOMENT WHEN YOU REALIZE WHO YOU ARE...WHY YOU ARE... HOW YOU ARE...
AND HERE I STAND... ON THE BRINK...
ON THE BRINK...

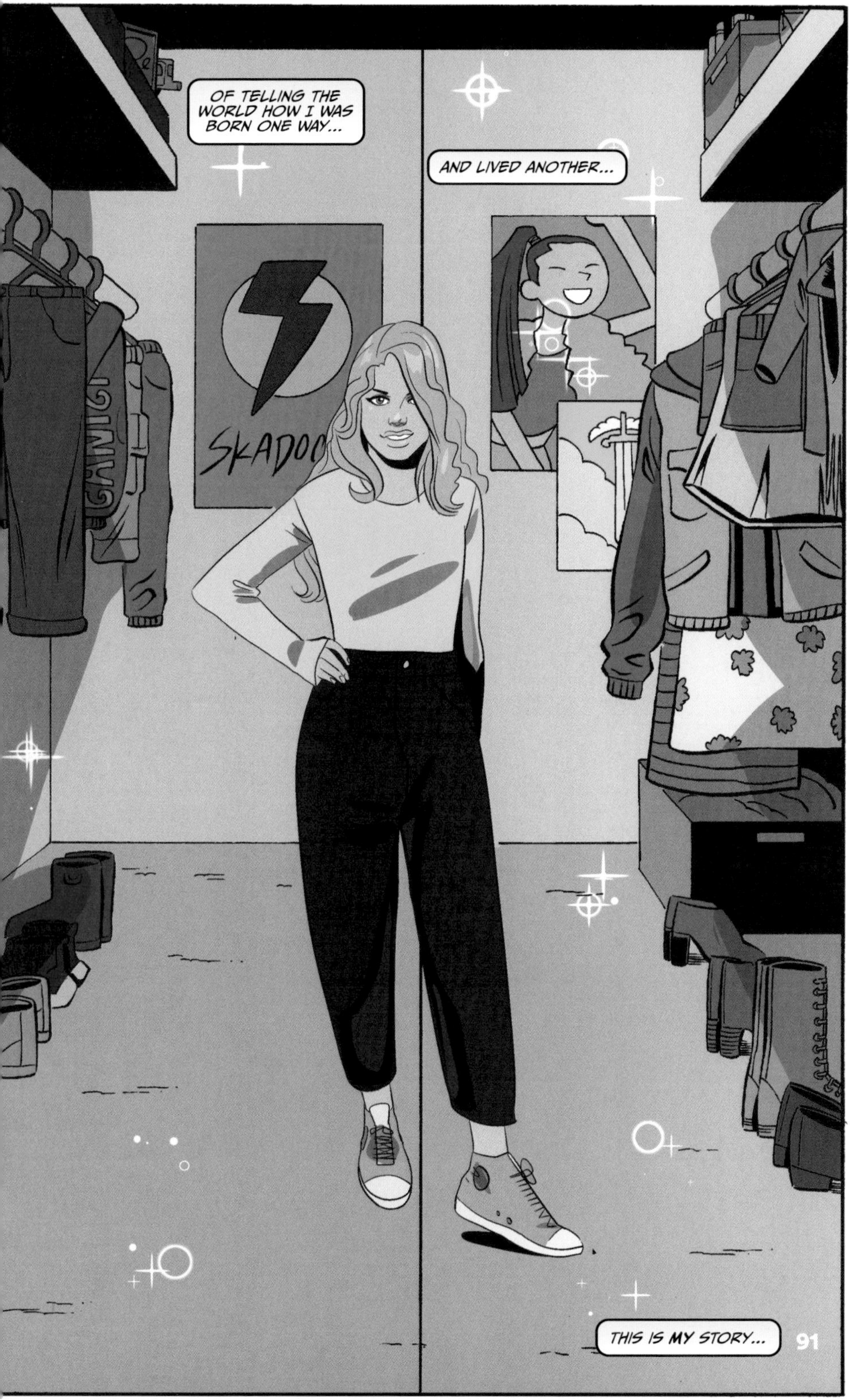
OF TELLING THE WORLD HOW I WAS BORN ONE WAY...
AND LIVED ANOTHER...
SKADOO
THIS IS MY STORY...

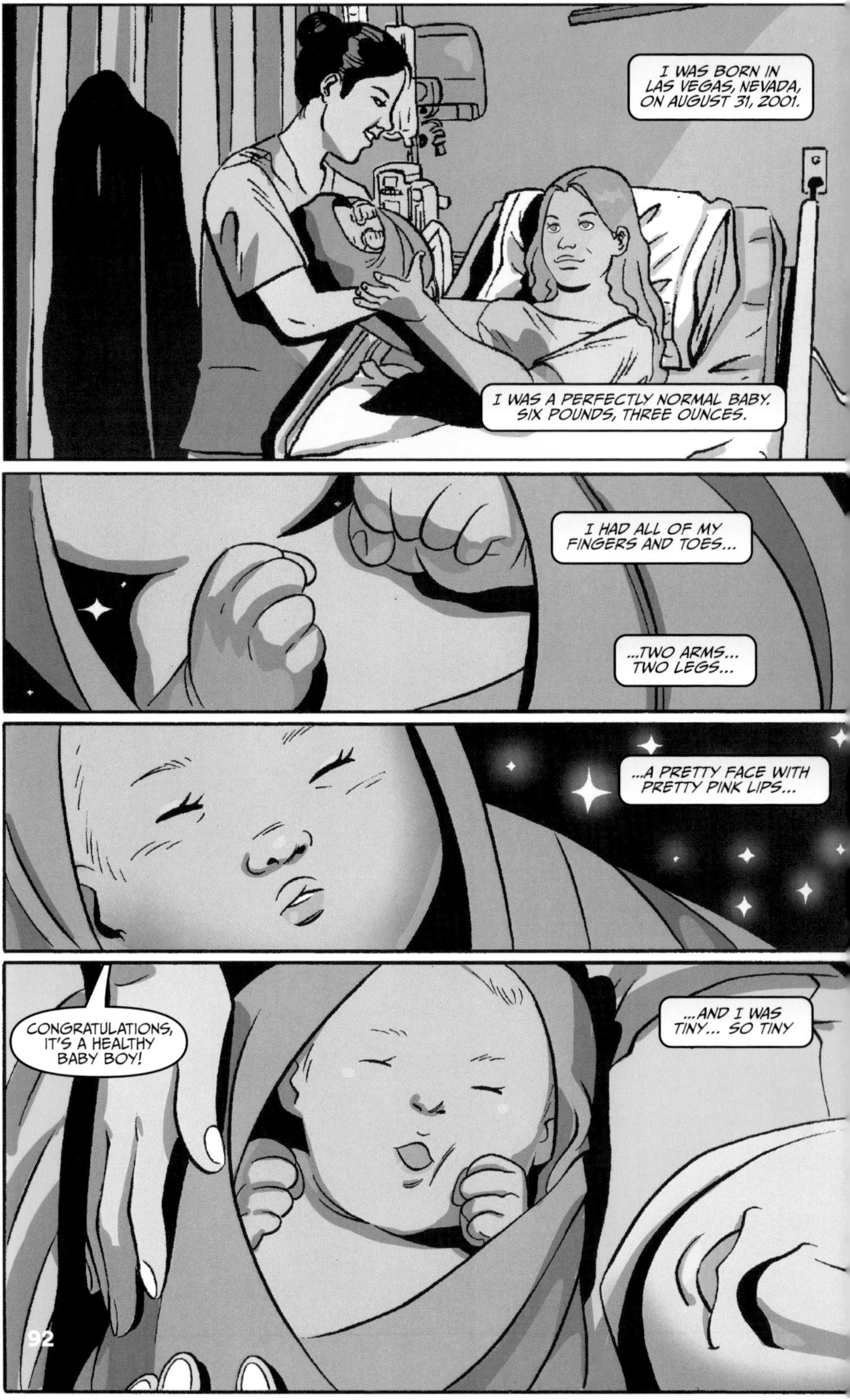
I WAS BORN IN LAS VEGAS, NEVADA, ON AUGUST 31, 2001.
I WAS A PERFECTLY NORMAL BABY. SIX POUNDS, THREE OUNCES.
I HAD ALL OF MY FINGERS AND TOES...
...TWO ARMS... TWO LEGS...
...A PRETTY FACE WITH PRETTY PINK LIPS...
CONGRATULATIONS, IT'S A HEALTHY BABY BOY!
...AND I WAS TINY... SO TINY

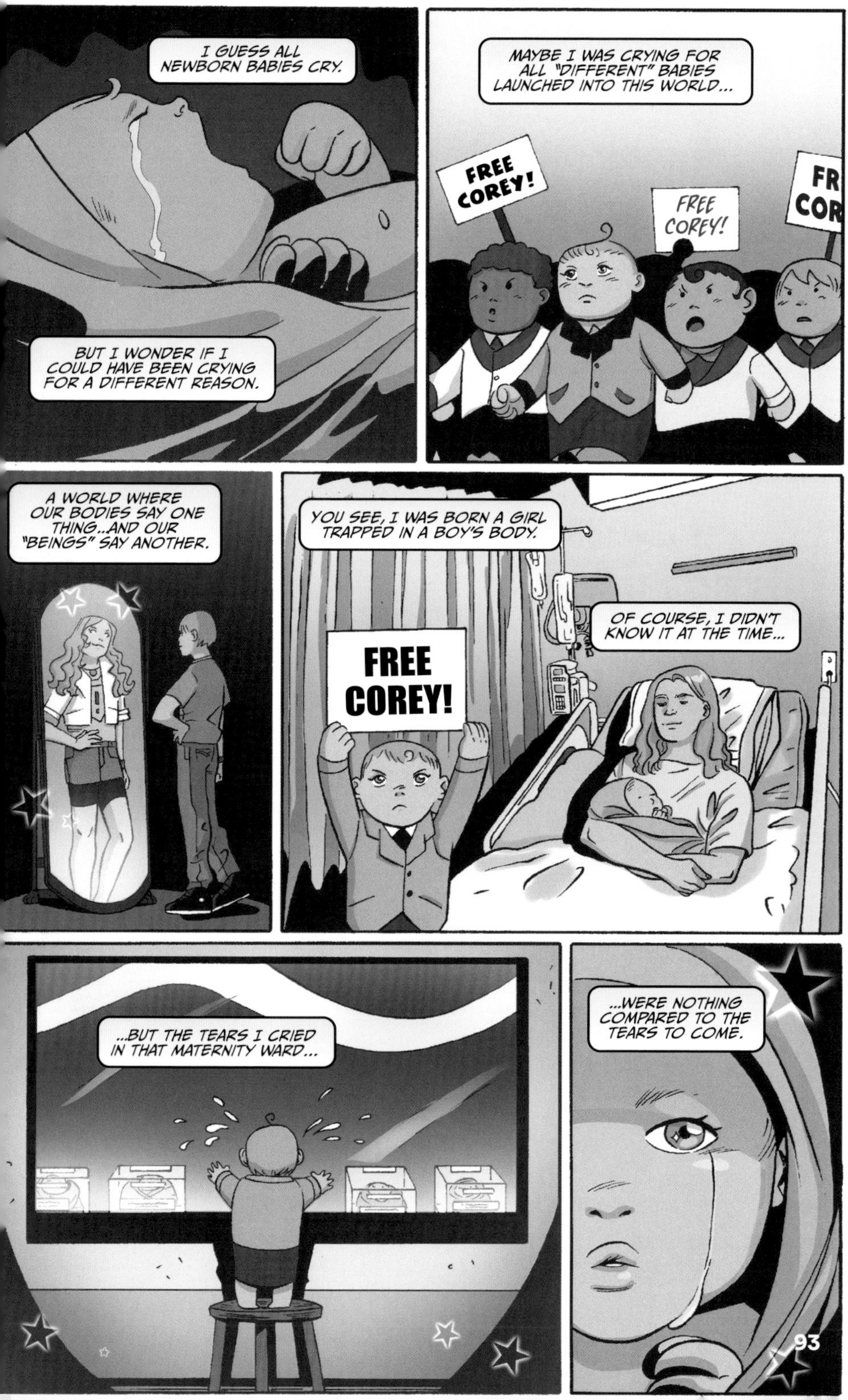
I GUESS ALL NEWBORN BABIES CRY.
BUT I WONDER IF I COULD HAVE BEEN CRYING FOR A DIFFERENT REASON.
MAYBE I WAS CRYING FOR ALL "DIFFERENT" BABIES LAUNCHED INTO THIS WORLD...
FREE COREY!
FREE COREY!
A WORLD WHERE OUR BODIES SAY ONE THING...AND OUR "BEINGS" SAY ANOTHER.
YOU SEE, I WAS BORN A GIRL TRAPPED IN A BOY'S BODY.
FREE COREY!
OF COURSE, I DIDN'T KNOW IT AT THE TIME...
...BUT THE TEARS I CRIED IN THAT MATERNITY WARD...
...WERE NOTHING COMPARED TO THE TEARS TO COME.

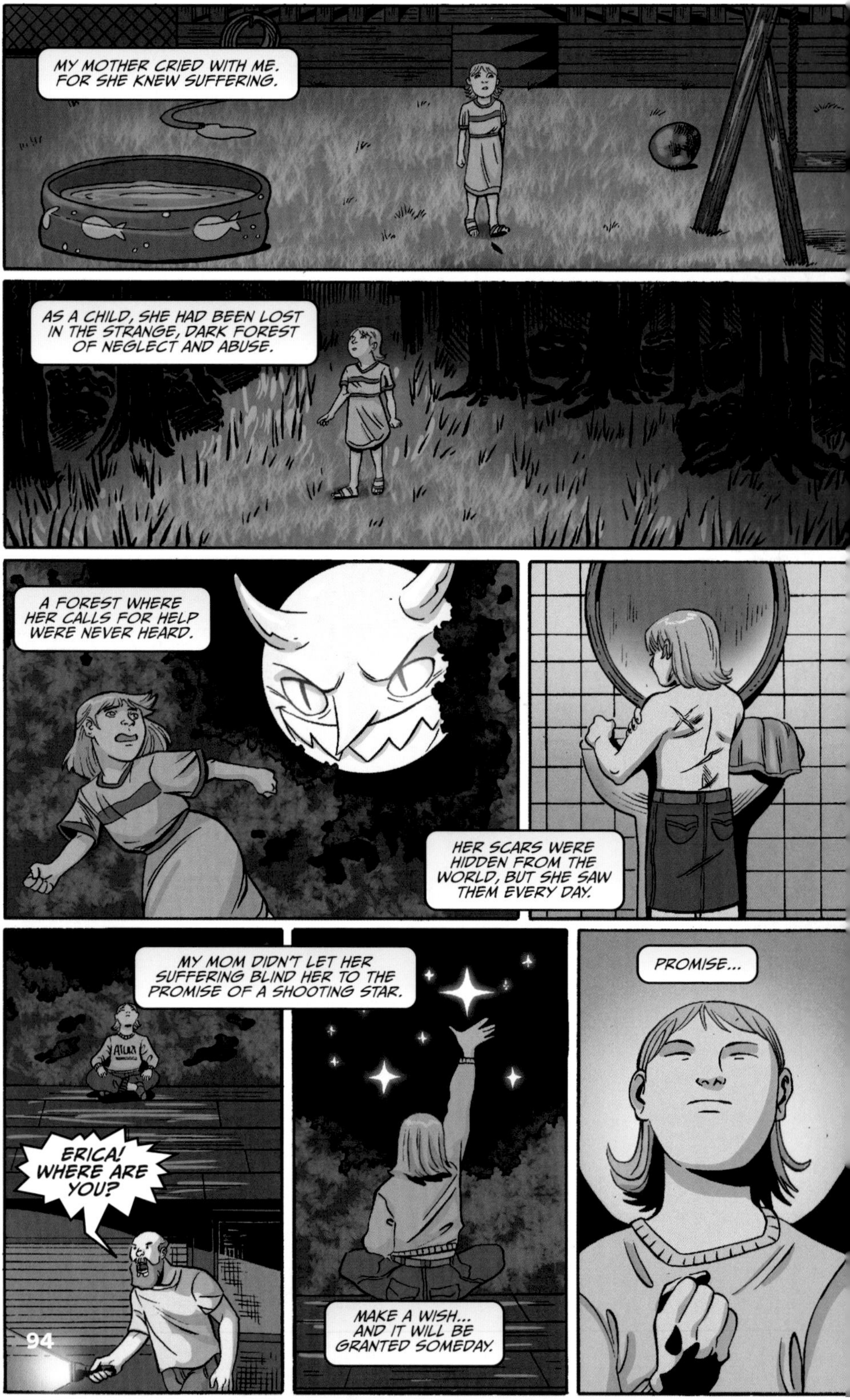
MY MOTHER CRIED WITH ME. FOR SHE KNEW SUFFERING.
AS A CHILD, SHE HAD BEEN LOST IN THE STRANGE, DARK FOREST OF NEGLECT AND ABUSE.
A FOREST WHERE HER CALLS FOR HELP WERE NEVER HEARD.
HER SCARS WERE HIDDEN FROM THE WORLD, BUT SHE SAW THEM EVERY DAY.
MY MOM DIDN'T LET HER SUFFERING BLIND HER TO THE PROMISE OF A SHOOTING STAR.
ERICA! WHERE ARE YOU?
MAKE A WISH... AND IT WILL BE GRANTED SOMEDAY.
PROMISE...

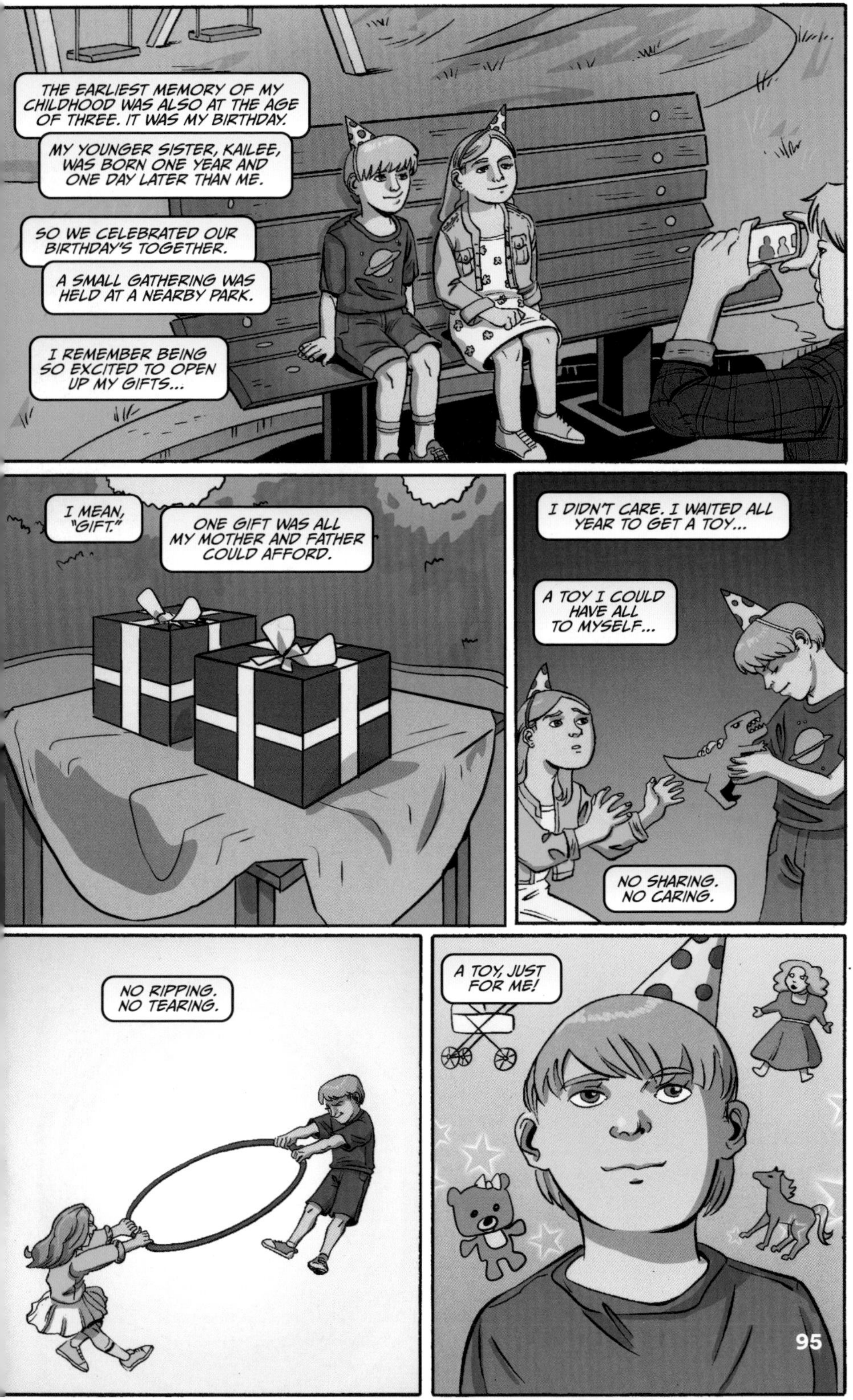
THE EARLIEST MEMORY OF MY CHILDHOOD WAS ALSO AT THE AGE OF THREE. IT WAS MY BIRTHDAY.
MY YOUNGER SISTER, KAILEE, WAS BORN ONE YEAR AND ONE DAY LATER THAN ME.
SO WE CELEBRATED OUR BIRTHDAY'S TOGETHER.
A SMALL GATHERING WAS HELD AT A NEARBY PARK.
I REMEMBER BEING SO EXCITED TO OPEN UP MY GIFTS...
I MEAN, "GIFT."
ONE GIFT WAS ALL MY MOTHER AND FATHER COULD AFFORD.
I DIDN'T CARE. I WAITED ALL YEAR TO GET A TOY...
A TOY I COULD HAVE ALL TO MYSELF...
NO SHARING. NO CARING.
NO RIPPING. NO TEARING.
A TOY, JUST FOR ME!

NEW FOR FALL 2019

ACTIVIST: A STORY OF THE MARJORY STONEMAN DOUGLAS SHOOTING

IDENTITY: A STORY OF TRANSITIONING

COMING SPRING 2020

BROTHER: A STORY OF AUTISM

GOODBYE: A STORY OF SUICIDE